THE POLITICS OF INTERNATIONAL CRIMINAL JUSTICE

To anyone setting out to explore the entanglement of international criminal justice with the interests of States, Germany is a particularly curious, exemplary case. Although a liberal democracy since 1949, its political position has altered radically in the last 60 years. Starting from a position of harsh scepticism in the years following the Nuremberg Trials, and opening up to the rationales of international criminal justice only slowly – and then mainly in the context of domestic trials against functionaries of the former East German regime after 1990 – Germany is today one of the most active supporters of the International Criminal Court. The climax of this is its campaigning to make the ICC independent of the UN Security Council – a debate in which Germany took a position in stark contrast to the United States. This book offers new insight into the debates leading up to such policy shifts. Drawing on government documents and interviews with policymakers, it enriches a broader debate on the politics of international criminal justice which has to date often been focused primarily on the United States.

Volume 41 in the series Studies in International Law

Studies in International Law

Recent titles in this series

International Law and Dispute Settlement: New Problems and Techniques
Edited by Duncan French, Matthew Saul and Nigel White

The Democratic Legitimacy of International Law
Steven Wheatley

Reflections on the UN Declaration on the Rights of Indigenous Peoples
Edited by Stephen Allen and Alexandra Xanthaki

Contracting with Sovereignty: State Contracts and International Arbitration
Ivar Alvik

Multi-Sourced Equivalent Norms in International Law
Edited by Yuval Shany and Tomer Broude

The Distinction and Relationship between *Jus ad Bellum* **and** *Jus in Bello*
Keiichiro Okimoto

International Humanitarian Law and Terrorism
Andrea Bianchi and Yasmin Naqvi

The Militarisation of Peacekeeping in the Twenty-First Century
James Sloan

Accounting for Hunger: The Right to Food in the Era of Globalisation
Edited by Olivier De Schutter and Kaitlin Y Cordes

Promises of States under International Law
Christian Eckart

Multilevel Regulation of Military and Security Contractors: The Interplay between International, European and Domestic Norms
Edited by Christine Bakker and Mirko Sossai

Europe and Extraterritorial Asylum
Maarten den Heijer

The Practice of International and National Courts and the (De) Fragmentation of International Law
Edited by Ole Kristian Fauchald and André Nollkaemper

For the complete list of titles in this series, see
'Studies in International Law' link at
www.hartpub.co.uk/books/series.asp

The Politics of International Criminal Justice

German Perspectives from Nuremberg to The Hague

Ronen Steinke

·HART·
PUBLISHING

OXFORD AND PORTLAND, OREGON
2012

Published in the United Kingdom by Hart Publishing Ltd
16C Worcester Place, Oxford, OX1 2JW
Telephone: +44 (0)1865 517530
Fax: +44 (0)1865 510710
E-mail: mail@hartpub.co.uk

Website: http://www.hartpub.co.uk
Published in North America (US and Canada) by
Hart Publishing
c/o International Specialized Book Services
920 NE 58th Avenue, Suite 300
Portland, OR 97213-3786
USA
Tel: +1 503 287 3093 or toll-free: (1) 800 944 6190
Fax: +1 503 280 8832
E-mail: orders@isbs.com
Website: http://www.isbs.com

British Library Cataloguing in Publication Data
Data Available

ISBN: 978-1-84946-313-3

Typeset by Hope Services, Abingdon
Printed and bound in Great Britain by
Lightning Source UK Ltd

For Dr Sorel Shaim

Acknowledgements

A number of key participants and intimate observers of Germany's politics of international criminal justice agreed to share their insights with me in connection with this project, and I thank them greatly for this. I have listed their names under 'Sources' in the Introduction. I am deeply indebted to Professor *Rainer Keller* of Hamburg University, who made several invaluable comments and suggestions to the manuscript. More thanks are due to Professor *Stefan Oeter,* who discussed democracy and legitimacy in international relations with me; to *Philip von der Meden,* who sparred with me on many of the penological questions raised in chapter one; and to *Michael Moineau* for his meticulous criticism of the final draft. Finally, I am grateful to the Heinrich Böll Foundation, whose support made this book possible.

Ronen Steinke, October 2011, Munich

Table of Contents

Introduction

WHAT CAN STATE actors expect from courts of international criminal justice and what thus motivates them to support some of these courts with resources, while they ignore or even oppose other, similar ones? The entanglement of international criminal justice with interests of particular State actors has sparked great academic attention recently, especially since the fierce political debates surrounding the creation of the International Criminal Court (ICC). Much theory has already been generated, based primarily on the example of the United States. Most assuredly, this has led to some excellent analyses of the power politics behind US opposition to an independent ICC. Remarkably however, the power political interests associated with the political position *in opposition* to that of the United States – that is, Europe's advocacy of an entirely independent ICC – has remained almost a blind spot in analyses. This is where, it is hoped, this book will offer new insights.

One important motive for pursuing this line of enquiry, with a view particularly on Germany, is to allow for a fresh look at the still heated debates surrounding the ICC. Germany played a key role in pulling Europe towards the ultimately prevailing argument for an independent ICC in the 1990s, going against the initial reluctance of France and the United Kingdom, which, like the United States, preferred to envision the ICC as a court under the control of the UN Security Council. This places Germany in an interesting, exemplary position to anyone setting out to explore the politics at the heart of this entire debate. Germany today stands as an example for the European position in the debate on the ICC, which can be labelled cosmopolitan because it rests on the idea that international criminal justice should serve only humankind and not States (this is in contrast to the United States' sovereigntist position).[1] The political dispute between proponents and critics of the ICC's independence on either side of the Atlantic has often been portrayed as a clash between the particular interests of a Great Power – the United States – on the one side and the idealism of a democratic, post-Westphalian project on the other side. But are we really witnessing a struggle of brute power politics versus liberal values? Or which role, if any, do considerations of power political interest play in defining the policies at *both* ends of this spectrum?

[1] See, eg Jason G Ralph, *Defending the Society of States* (Oxford, Oxford University Press, 2007).

The example of Germany is particularly interesting not only because of Germany's exemplary position at one end of this spectrum, but also because of the particular way in which Germany came to its current position. Germany's politics of international criminal justice display a history of radical shifts. For many years, West Germany actually harboured what was perhaps the most rigorous criticism of international criminal law per se throughout western democracies. This is examined in detail in chapter two. In the early days of Germany's post-war democracy, German legal scholars and policymakers widely denied the legal validity of the Nuremberg Trials. These attempts to delegitimise Nuremberg were, for the most part, openly driven by self-interest, as has been analysed by numerous fine authors. It would take the better part of half a century for Germany's legal community to reconsider their position. Only in 1989, with Germany facing the crimes of the fallen communist regime in East Germany, would the mainstream of German policymakers and scholars officially accept the legal rationales established at Nuremberg (particularly regarding the principle of *nullum crimen sine lege*), thereby allowing German courts to put the crimes of communism on trial. Only from this point in time did Germany redefine its stance. And only after which in the 1990s did Germany become a supporter of the nascent system of international criminal justice at the level of the UN in general and of an independent ICC in particular.

Such a series of fundamental shifts in policy obviously raises the question what drove them?

Liberal theories in the study of international relations could view Germany as a prime example for the (belated) triumph of liberal rule-of-law ideals over the jealous protection of self-interest. In the perspective of liberal theories, 'The values and practices of domestic political life are apt to be preferred in international politics.'[2] In this vein, Samuel Huntington has sought to analyse much of American foreign policy as an attempt to transpose domestic successes – in particular, the security provided by the rule of law and contract – to the international level.[3] For Immanuel Kant, the classic liberal, such a transposition even presented the path to perpetual peace: Kant emphatically recommended a republican constitution for the international order.[4] Consequently, Jürgen Habermas, one of Kant's most eminent followers, analyses the recent political efforts towards the creation of an international criminal judiciary as welcome steps in exactly this direction (while Habermas asserts that this project is currently promoted primarily by Europe as the other half of the West, the United States,

[2] David H Lumsdaine, *Moral Vision in International Politics* (Princeton, Princeton University Press, 1993) 22.

[3] Samuel P Huntington, *The Soldier and the State* (Cambridge, Massachusetts, Belknap Press, 2002).

[4] Immanuel Kant, *Perpetual Peace* (first published in 1795)

has somewhat lost its commitment).[5] Adding to this, Gary Bass has argued that liberal democracies are presently more inclined to help build international criminal justice because they value the ideals of this judicial system more than illiberal States do.[6]

Perhaps unsurprisingly, this theoretical explanation is supported and promoted as an explanation for Germany's recent politics of international criminal justice by German policymakers themselves. Professor Claus Kreß, who has been a personal protagonist of Germany's politics of international criminal justice since the late 1990s, suggests that Germany 'made its peace with Nuremberg'[7] after the end of the Cold War to pursue a new, values-inspired approach to international criminal law, promoting the rule of law on the international level. Hans-Peter Kaul, perhaps the most important political mind behind Germany's advocacy of an independent ICC in the late 1990s, reinforces this idealist explanation by pointing to Germany's own atrocious history. Kaul argues that German guilt for unparalleled international crimes in the twentieth century inspired policymakers in the 1990s with a feeling of 'historical duty' towards the project of establishing a system of international criminal justice.[8]

Neoliberal institutionalism theorists have illustrated that the promotion of liberal ideals might not actually be as purely idealistic as it occasionally presents itself. This is because the interests of transnational economic actors (not only States) are best served by the integration and, ideally, the political and legal homogeneity of larger regions. Transnational norms reduce transaction costs. Thus, transnational actors benefit from them.[9] In this perspective, international tribunals, like all institutions that enforce a set of rules that transcend national borders, can be seen as political integrators: they serve to make different political systems more homogenous.[10] Yet, if this perspective is only seldom adopted with respect to international criminal justice, it is because the legal and political homogeneity promoted here is, or course, primarily in respect of the most basic guarantees of humanitarian law. Admittedly, there is the hope that international criminal tribunals will reduce the frequency and scope of

[5] Jürgen Habermas, *The Divided West* (Cambridge, Polity, 2006) 113–93.

[6] Gary J Bass, *Stay the Hand of Vengeance* (Princeton, Princeton University Press, 2000).

[7] Claus Kreß, 'Versailles – Nürnberg – Den Haag: Deutschland und das Völkerstrafrecht' (2006) 61 *JuristenZeitung* 986.

[8] Kaul interview (6 August 2009, The Hague)

[9] Robert O Keohane, *International Institutions and State Power* (Boulder, Westview Press, 1989) 3. See also Christian Reus-Smit, 'The Politics of International Law' in Christian Reus-Smit (ed), *The Politics of International Law* (Cambridge, Cambridge University Press, 2009) 18–21.

[10] Mark A Drumbl, 'Policy Through Complementarity: The Atrocity Trial as Justice' in Carsten Stahn and Mohamed El Zeidy (eds), *The International Criminal Court and Complementarity: From Theory to Practice* (Cambridge, Cambridge University Press, 2011) argues that the complementarity regime of the ICC coerces diverse States into subscribing to Western-style liberal criminal trials even where alternative, non-punitive mechanisms for dealing with crimes may hold a long tradition.

atrocities. All State actors can hope to gain from this.[11] However, in terms of the level on which international criminal tribunals take effect, theories about integrators such as the World Bank or the World Trade Organisation can nonetheless not easily be transposed.

Both of the aforementioned theoretical approaches – liberal theories and neoliberal institutionalism theories – explain State support for international criminal justice with the underlying support for certain international *norms*. This is different with the third line of theories.

Realist theories in the study of international relations work with the assumption that State actors – who, as a group, find no sovereign above themselves to enforce any rules and are therefore in a natural state of dangerous anarchy[12] – permanently competing with one another. Since altruistic idealism in international politics is a 'luxury that states can ill afford',[13] their policy choices with respect to international lawmaking will always reflect their pursuit of relative gain over other State actors. If particular State actors choose to devote their resources to distant international organisations – such as an international court – or to relinquish part of their sovereignty to international treaties, then this can only be explained by their expectation of some gain over others.[14] To John Mearsheimer, for instance, 'institutions are basically a reflection of the distribution of power in the world' and they 'are based on the self-interested calculations of the great powers'.[15] Specifically in the field of international criminal justice, this means that States will support particular tribunals insofar as they expect to gain from them, while they then oppose other tribunals that are not deemed advantageous despite the fact that all of these tribunals enforce the exact same abstract norms. As Frédéric Mégret nicely summarises, 'The conventional explanation from a realist perspective since Nuremberg, put simply, is that states create international criminal tribunals to legitimize their goals and because they think or know they can control them.'[16]

This realist perspective is often used to explain why the United States support the UN ad hoc tribunals for the former Yugoslavia and Rwanda (neither of which target US nationals), while they oppose the ICC (which could, in theory, target US nationals). By contrast, Germany's shift towards the 'cosmopolitan position', as described above, appears particularly puz-

[11] Benjamin N Schiff, *Building the International Criminal Court* (Cambridge, Cambridge University Press, 2008) 4–9.

[12] Hedley Bull, *The Anarchical Society* (Houndmills, Palgrave, 2007).

[13] Bass, *Stay the Hand* (n 6) 17.

[14] See for instance John A Vasquez, *The Power of Power Politics* (Cambridge, Cambridge University Press, 1998). For a lively discussion, see Jeffrey W Legro and Andrew Moravcsik, 'Is Anybody Still a Realist?' (1999) 24 *International Security*.

[15] John J Mearsheimer, 'The False Promise of International Institutions' (1994) 19 *International Security* 7.

[16] Frédéric Mégret, 'The Politics of International Criminal Justice' (2002) 13 *European Journal of International Law* 1267.

zling from this realist perspective. While Germany assuredly made an effort in the 1990s to gain additional international influence through a permanent seat on the UN Security Council, Germany also argued against that political body maintaining any control over international criminal justice. When it came to debating the creation of the ICC, Germany was a strong voice within a group of States which advocated freeing the court of any such political control. That would minimise the influence of all States, including Germany itself. How could this improve Germany's position in relation to its competitors? Does realist theory – at least in this particular case – thus stand entirely corrected? Did the pursuit of political interests, which had previously been so closely connected to the entire subject within Germany, simply end in the 1990s, perhaps due to a new, more idealist generation taking the political stage in Germany, as several German protagonists of this development in the 1990s suggest? Or had the shape of their rational interests merely changed and with it the preferable strategy for the pursuit of these interests? These questions are the focus of this book.

The book begins by first gaining clarity with respect to the central term of political interest (chapter one) and then proceeds in the next four chapters (chapter two through chapter five) to chronologically examine (from 1949 to present day) the role that such interests played in shaping Germany's politics of international criminal justice.

Chronological accounts of the politics of international criminal justice often begin in Versailles or Leipzig, ie at the end of the First World War. By contrast, I have chosen to begin my analysis in 1949 with the founding of the same democratic West German State that still exists today. This is due to the particular focus of my enquiry. My aim is to analyse the various shifts in Germany's politics of international criminal justice over time. For this, it is helpful to refer to one and the same continuous political framework. To observe the fact that political debates can take a sharp turn when the participants in these debates are exchanged is not as remarkable – or as intriguing – as to observe such changes of paradigm within one and the same political context. For this reason, my analysis also does not focus on the debate in East Germany, which was politically split from the rest of the country from 1949 to 1989. Instead, it begins with the early days of the West German democracy and it follows policymakers and the legal community from there into the Germany of today. Along the way, I obviously pay more attention to certain episodes than to others, namely: Germany's reactions to Nuremberg as an important starting point in shaping Germany's particular perspective on the subject; the debate within Germany over the East German trials and with it the first change of (legal) paradigm in the early 1990s; and the subsequent support and active promotion of the International Criminal Tribunal for the former Yugoslavia (ICTY) and ICC by Germany. By contrast, Germany's involvement in other tribunals – such as the UN tribunal for Rwanda, the Cambodian Extraordinary Chambers in the Courts of Cambodia (ECCC), or the Special Tribunal for Lebanon where a German national even briefly served as Chief Prosecutor – did not mark important milestones in Germany's overall politics of international criminal justice; therefore, they are not central to my particular inquiry.

SOURCES

In addition to literature available in the public domain, I was able to obtain copies of files from the archive of the German Ministry of Foreign Affairs, documenting the Ministry's communications throughout the 1990s regarding the ICC. These documents are available through the German Freedom of Information Act (*Informationsfreiheitsgesetz*). Although they offer a fascinating first-hand source, it should be noted for accuracy that there is no way of verifying how comprehensive the copies are that one receives. The Ministry of Foreign Affairs preselects documents before sharing them.

More importantly, I am grateful to a number of key participants and intimate observers of Germany's politics of international criminal justice, who kindly agreed to be interviewed in connection with this project. These discussions were insightful, thought-provoking and highly enjoyable. Any errors, of course, remain my own.

- Kai Ambos was a member of Germany's delegation to Rome and is presently Professor of International Criminal Law at the University of Göttingen (interviewed on 15 September 2009 in The Hague).
- Hans-Jörg Behrens was a member of Germany's delegation to PrepCom and Rome and is presently Deputy Head of the International Law Department at the German Ministry of Justice (interviewed on 15 April 2010 by telephone).
- Serge Brammertz was formerly Deputy Prosecutor of the ICC and presently the ICTY Prosecutor (interviewed on 14 October 2009 in The Hague).
- Josef Brink is presently Head of the Division for International Relations and Rule of Law Dialogue at the German Ministry of Justice (interviewed on 6 July 2009 in Berlin).
- Eberhard Desch is the Head of the Division of International Law at the Germany Ministry of Justice and was a member of Germany's delegation to Kampala (interviewed on 22 September 2010 by telephone).
- Hans-Peter Kaul was formerly Head of the International Law Department at the German Ministry of Foreign Affairs, as well as the Head of the German delegation at Rome and is presently judge and

Second Vice President at the ICC (interviewed on 6 August 2009 in The Hague).

- Claus Kreß was a member of Germany's delegations to Rome and Kampala and is presently Professor of International Criminal Law at the University of Cologne (interviewed on 6 September 2010 by telephone).
- Christian Tomuschat was formerly a member of the UN's International Law Commission and an adviser to the German Ministry of Foreign Affairs and is presently Professor emeritus of International Law at the Humboldt University in Berlin (interviewed on 27 October 2009 by telephone).
- Peter Wilkitzki was formerly Head of the Criminal Law Department at the German Ministry of Justice (interviewed on 24 April 2010 by telephone).
- Andreas Zimmermann was a member of Germany's delegations to PrepCom and Rome and is presently Professor of International Law at the University of Potsdam (interviewed on 18 August 2010 by telephone).

1

The Politics of 'Historical Truth': An Outline

WHAT CAN STATE actors expect from courts of international criminal justice? The more traditional penological goals, which are associated with criminal justice in the domestic realm, are less realistic in the international context. As Robert Sloane rightly notes, 'Justifications for punishment common to national systems of criminal law cannot be be transplanted unreflectively to the distinct legal, moral and institutional context of [international criminal law]'.[1] Systemic crimes, which international criminal justice deals with, are typically committed repeatedly over a long period of time, on a large scale and by numerous perpetrators; yet not all, and not even most cases, can realistically be prosecuted in the international forum. For purely practical reasons,[2] only a tiny fraction of cases from one conflict situation can be introduced into the international forum.[3] The system's promise of deterrence is, therefore, weak.[4] Additionally, since international criminal law, by definition,[5] targets persons who acted in conformity with the rules of their particular system for as long as it was in place, rehabilitative goals – at least in a conventional sense – would appear somewhat misplaced

[1] Robert D Sloane, 'The Expressive Capacity of International Punishment: The Limits of the National Law Analogy and the Potential of International Criminal Law' (2007) 43 *Stanford Journal of International Law* 40.

[2] Compare eg the former President of the International Criminal Tribunal for the former Yugoslavia, Theodor Meron, *The Humanization of International Law* (Leiden, Martinus Nijhoff, 2006) 141, illustrating the 'more mundane institutional and procedural problems' of atrocity trials: 'Often, the crimes charged, connected to entire military campaigns, occurred over the course of months or years, across many locations, and involved many defendants. The Milošević case offers one illustration. It is not typical, but it is not as far from the norm as one might think. Milošević is actually only one of four defendants who were originally indicted together. With 66 counts, hundreds of witnesses, tens of thousands of pages of documents – most of which must be translated from Serbo-Croatian into French and English, the Tribunal's working languages – trials are extremely complex.'

[3] This is highlighted by Payam Akhavan, 'Justice in The Hague, Peace in the former Yugoslavia? A Commentary on the United Nations War Crimes Tribunal' (1998) 20 *Human Rights Quarterly* 774–77; also Luc Côté, 'Reflections on the Exercise of Prosecutorial Discretion in International Criminal Law' (2005) 3 *Journal of International Criminal Justice* 165.

[4] Sloane, 'Expressive Capacity of International Punishment' (n 1) 71–75.

[5] Compare Kai Ambos, *Der Allgemeine Teil des Völkerstrafrechts* (Berlin, Duncker & Humblot, 2002) 50.

here.[6] Finally, retribution remains painfully incomplete when the overwhelming majority of mid-level perpetrators will, inevitably, not be processed in the international forum at all.

As a result, many commentators point instead to the more communicative, educative function of international criminal justice: the expressive value of its judgements.[7] This goal has been described as the 'least controversial' function of international criminal tribunals[8] and this is true in the sense that most commentators would probably agree that it *can* work. Yet, what exactly is it that these trials express?

In this first chapter, I argue that the authoritative confirmation of a certain narrative of 'historical truth' is central to this system's effects and that, for a number of reasons, this narration can never simply result out of a neutral act of deduction but instead always depends on a series of sensitive policy choices to be made by the court of international criminal justice. The chances of making such choices with any claim to quasi-mathematical objectivity are regrettably slim where 'historical truth' and proportions of guilt are concerned. Political actors on all sides of a conflict will then typically hope for a tribunal to sway in their direction.

1. 'HISTORICAL TRUTH' AS A GOAL AND A PROBLEM

Two basic messages which every court of international criminal justice expresses through its trials are distinguishable.[9] While the first is more commonly emphasised by idealist proponents of international criminal justice, the second should prove more interesting to power political stakeholders (and thus to our enquiry).

Combatting Impunity: Where All Trials are Similar

First, atrocity trials are hoped to express a symbolic protest against a 'culture of impunity',[10] which domestic penal systems (which are better

[6] Frank Neubacher, Kriminologische Grundlagen einer internationalen Strafgerichtsbarkeit (Tübingen, Mohr Siebeck, 2005) 423.

[7] See, eg Sloane, 'Expressive Capacity of International Punishment' (n 1) 70; Mark A Drumbl, 'The Expressive Value of Prosecuting and Punishing Terrorists: Hamdan, the Geneva Conventions, and International Law' (2007) 75 *George Washington Law Review* 1182, 1195.

[8] Gary J Bass, *Stay the Hand of Vengeance* (Princeton, Princeton University Press, 2000) 302. Assuredly, it is not usually the first to be named among the numerous ambitious goals associated which international criminal justice. Compare eg Sloane, 'Expressive Capacity of International Punishment' (n 1) 45, who notes that these 'include combating impunity, individuating guilt, promoting accountability, contributing to the reestablishment of international peace and security, deterring future atrocities, achieving retribution, creating an accurate historical record, and fostering both national and international reconciliation.'

[9] See also Drumbl, 'The Expressive Value of Prosecuting and Punishing Terrorists' (n 7) 1182, 1195.

[10] See, eg Akhavan, 'Justice in The Hague' (n 3) 743, 748.

equipped to try large numbers of cases) are then hoped to respond to. Such proceedings are hoped to restore (or to create for the first time) confidence in the basic norms of international humanitarian law. Commenting on the International Criminal Tribunal for the former Yugoslavia's (ICTY) early proceedings in 1997, then New York law professor Theodor Meron noted, 'Without the establishment of the tribunal and the example of the Tadić trial, the *perception* that even the most egregious violations of international humanitarian law can be committed with impunity would have been confirmed' (emphasis added).[11] To Meron, the strong international interest in this trial was based on its enabling the international community 'authoritatively to disavow that conduct, to indicate symbolically its refusal to acquiesce in the crimes'.[12]

In even clearer terms, Payam Akhavan, working at the time as Legal Advisor at the ICTY Office of the Prosecutor, noted in 1998, 'The punishment of particular individuals . . . becomes an instrument through which respect for the rule of law is instilled into the public consciousness.'[13]

This, however, is what all trials express, quite regardless of which crimes and perpetrators they target. A generic interest in symbolically reinforcing international humanitarian law – the set of norms to which international criminal law per se gives teeth – can hardly explain why State actors would support one trial but not another or support one tribunal but not another.

Establishing 'Historical Truth': Where Each Trial is Different

Second, tribunals also reconstruct historical events in a particular way. They generate a narrative on 'historical truth'. Compared with domestic trials, 'International trials have a better chance of becoming the kinds of "popular trials" that define a debate' on one particular historical complex, as Mark Drumbl notes. The particular value of these trials lies in their serving 'as intergenerational "signposts" in history'.[14] In this respect, naturally, every trial expresses a different message of its own.

This presents us with a paradox. On the one hand, this second element to expressive trials (their clarification of 'historical truth') is no less soundly idealist than the first element (the reinforcement of international humanitarian law in general). To reveal the 'truth' is, of course, a noble goal and it will often even be the most a tribunal can do for surviving vic-

[11] Theodor Meron, *War Crimes Law Comes of Age* (Oxford, Oxford University Press, 1998) 283. The passage is a reprint of a 1997 article.

[12] Sloane, 'Expressive Capacity of International Punishment' (n 1) 71.

[13] Akhavan, 'Justice in The Hague' (n 3) 749.

[14] Mark A Drumbl, *Atrocity, Punishment, and International Law* (Cambridge, Cambridge University Press, 2007) 175.

tims. Commentators have pointed to the phenomenon of revisionist denial with which victims will often be faced in post-conflict scenarios,[15] noting that the official confirmation of 'truth' may help to defend the injured against such additional insult.[16] The authoritative confirmation of 'historical truth' was therefore openly presented as a central component of the newly-created UN tribunals' ideology at the beginning of the 1990s.[17] '[I]t is only the truth that can cleanse the ethnic and religious hatreds and begin the healing process', stated Madeleine Albright, then US Ambassador to the UN, during the Security Council deliberations that led to the establishment of the ICTY in 1993.[18] In what was perhaps the clearest expression of this idea, the UN even allowed the ICTY to hold courtroom hearings where the accused remains at large, which means that these proceedings are solely for the purpose of creating a historical record in what is almost a trial in absentia, albeit without a sentence.[19] In hindsight, some scepticism is surely in place as to how much the ICTY's 'truth-telling' has effectively contributed to pacifying the former Yugoslavia.[20] At least for some of the victims, though, it has doubtlessly had meaning.

On the other hand, any dedication to establishing the 'historical truth' of a conflict obviously raises the question of whose 'truth'. After a conflict, the 'truth' of what has transpired, of which party bears which part of historical responsibility and of who has victimised whom is usually a controversial matter. After all, this is the very reason why the tribunal's task of establishing a historical record is important in the first place. And the harder it is to see through a chaos of misinformation and denial, the larger the victims' need for an authoritative clarification becomes.

[15] See, eg Gerhard Werle, 'Menschenrechtsschutz durch Völkerstrafrecht' (1997) 109 *Zeitschrift für die gesamte Strafrechtswissenschaft* 822.

[16] Frank Neubacher, 'Strafzwecke und Völkerstrafrecht' (2006) 59 *Neue Juristische Wochenschrift* 969.

[17] Akhavan, 'Justice in The Hague' (n 3) 765–66.

[18] UN Doc S/PV.3217 (25 May 1993).

[19] Compare Rule 61 of the ICTY Rules of Procedure and Evidence. Available at www.icty.org. A series of Rule 61 hearings was held in 1996 particularly to shed light on the massacre in Srebrenica, inter alia as a case against Radovan Karadžić and Ratko Mladić (IT-95-05/18). For a vivid account, see Pierre Hazan, *Justice in a Time of War* (Station, Texas A&M University Press, 2004) 76–89. After taking over as ICTY Prosecutor in 1996, Louise Arbour stopped this practice. See ibid 96.

[20] It has been noted that the local media have seldom taken an interest in communicating the findings of the ICTY accurately. Carla Del Ponte, *Madame Prosecutor* (New York, Other Press, 2009) 333, for instance, complains that '[t]he prosecution of the Bosnian Croat leadership . . . would garner little attention beyond doses of disinformation administered through Croatia's press.' Moreover, the interest of local political actors in reconciliation is, of course, not automatically fuelled by such 'truth'. See also Sloane, 'Expressive Capacity of International Punishment' (n 1) 84.

Whose 'Truth'?

Different narratives on 'truth' not only clash within the conflict region itself, but since many conflicts that enter the focus of international criminal justice will, at some stage, have led international actors to decide for a particular course of reaction (even if this consists of inaction) which is in need of moral justification, the struggle for interpretative authority on 'historical truth' can easily have more interested parties than the original conflict did and 'can become a political contest over historical truth or political responsibility'[21] elsewhere as well. Ultimately, the politically interesting question at a court of international criminal justice is whose views decide. Each side naturally has an interest in an authoritative confirmation of its own historical narrative.

While a society's views of 'truth' will, of course, be shaped to a certain extent by political interests (just as political interests are, in turn, shaped by a particular view of 'truth'), different perspectives can be held in entirely good faith. For this reason, it would be simplistic to suggest that the political ambition of State actors to promote their own historical narrative is necessarily an expression of brute power politics and a negation of judicial ideals. Rather, it may indeed be a genuine wish to show solidarity with those whom one perceives to be the 'true' victims of a conflict.

And this is the paradox: while State actors will typically have a *self*-interest in defending their own narrative of 'truth', the pursuit of this interest only gives reason for embarrassment insofar as that narrative of 'truth' is not held in good faith. That aside, the protection of 'truth' from distortion is nothing which even the most liberal of democracies would need to hide. The pursuit of this interest can be entirely idealistic.

2. EXTREME SELECTIVITY AND SLICES OF TRUTH

How do courts of international criminal justice generate the aforementioned historical narrative which is so central to the social and political impact of these tribunals? Criminal courts, even at the most basic domestic level, are always tasked with generating an understandable account of a crime out of disparate and sometimes contradictory sources of information in a process that is impossible without some *selection* of facts.[22] This is

[21] Gerry J Simpson, 'Politics, Sovereignty, Remembrance' in Dominic McGoldrick, Peter Rowe and Eric Donelly (eds), *The Permanent International Criminal Court: Legal and Policy Issues* (Oxford, Hart Publishing, 2004) 49.

[22] Nina Burkhardt, '"Die Stiefel ausgezogen…": Täterbilder und die Sicht auf Deutschland in belgischen und niederländischen Radio- und Presseberichten über den Nürnberger Hauptprozess' in Helia-Verena Daubach (ed), *Leipzig – Nürnberg – Den Haag: Neue Fragestellungen und Forschungen zum Verhältnis von Menschenrechtsverbrechen justizieller Säuberung und Völkerstrafrecht* (Düsseldorf, Justizministerium des Landes NRW, 2008) 146.

true in a much wider sense at the international level however. Unlike at domestic courts, the 'truth' which courts of international criminal justice are tasked with illuminating is necessarily spread out over hundreds if not thousands of criminal cases. It is the 'big picture' which they hope to illuminate. Hence, it is not just one trial which produces an authoritative narrative of 'truth'. Rather, it is the entire tribunal with its many trials which produces one overarching narrative. For this overarching narrative, the selection between cases – not merely between facts within one case – becomes central.

The Need to Select between Cases

International criminal justice is forced to be selective to a degree unimaginable in domestic criminal law. Whereas 'domestic prosecution is never really seriously called upon to be selective in the prosecution of serious crimes', as the former ICTY/ International Criminal Tribunal for Rwanda (ICTR) Prosecutor Louise Arbour notes, the prosecutor at an international tribunal 'has to be highly selective before committing resources to investigate and prosecute'.[23] To Arbour, this power to select between targets even represents the 'main distinction between domestic enforcement of criminal law, and the international context'.[24]

To illustrate: with the entire horrors of World War II laid out before them, the Prosecutors of the International Military Tribunal (IMT) at Nuremberg were able to indict only a total of 199 persons in 1 major and 12 subsequent war crimes trials.[25] After operating for the better part of two decades, the Office of the Prosecutor at the ICTY has indicted only a total of 161 persons for crimes that implicated tens of thousands on the Balkans. At the ICTY's sister tribunal, the ICTR, only 90 persons have been indicted for the 1994 genocide, which, according to an estimate by Gérard Prunier, was perpetrated by a total of 80,000 to 100,000 murderers.[26]

Arbour's successor, Carla Del Ponte, stated to the UN Security Council in 2001 that even though she had already narrowed her focus down to

[23] Louise Arbour, 'Progress and Challenges in International Criminal Justice' (1997) 21 *Fordham International Law Journal* 531. See also Allison M Danner, 'Enhancing the Legitimacy and Accountability of Prosecutorial Discretion at the International Criminal Court' (2003) 97 *American Journal of International Law* 520–22.

[24] Quoted in Morten Bergsmo, 'The Jurisdictional Regime of the International Criminal Court (Part II, Articles 11–19)' (1998) 6 *European Journal of Crime, Criminal Law, and Criminal Justice* 355.

[25] Michael Stolleis, 'Der Historiker als Richter – der Richter als Historiker' in Norbert Frei, Dirk van Laak and Michael Stolleis (eds), *Geschichte vor Gericht: Historiker, Richter und die Suche nach Gerechtigkeit* (Munich, Beck, 2000) 173.

[26] Gérard Prunier, *The Rwanda Crisis* (New York, Columbia University Press, 1995) 342.

top-level offenders, she still found herself forced to select from 'many thousands of significant targets'.[27]

The Difference between International and Domestic Selectivitiy

Undoubtedly, cases also have to be selected at the domestic level.[28] Although regulatory models in this respect are diverse[29] – the German system, for instance, notionally requires the mandatory prosecution of all offences (*Legalitätsprinzip*). Kai Ambos rightly analyses that the various legal models all allow for a concentration of resources on the few most 'important' cases: 'Even if a strict mandatory prosecution is called for, there are mechanisms of factual discretion since no criminal justice system has nowadays the capacity to prosecute all offences no matter how serious they are.'[30]

However, there is still a great difference between the *effects* of selectivity at the domestic level and at the international level. At the domestic level, each individual case of theft or fraud, for instance, is primarily an individual story and the 'truth' of such a story is not distorted if another individual story is left untold. (For instance, nobody would expect a domestic court to produce a representative picture of the entire 'truth' of thefts.) By contrast, at an international tribunal, each trial is part of one overall historical account; the selection of a tiny fraction of cases from a conflict will inevitably focus the audience on one particular version of that larger 'truth'.

The 'historical truth' of an entire conflict situation, which tribunals are ultimately tasked with illuminating, consists of more than just the sum of particular, isolated crimes, however accurately these may be judged in their particular trials. In addition, and perhaps in essence, it is the relationship between these crimes and the proportions in which they stand to one another and to other political occurrences that defines the broader historical narrative on an entire conflict situation. Even where 'all sides' to a conflict have committed crimes, the question at a tribunal is which portion of the international community's attention is due to one party and which to the other. Akhavan rightly notes that '[D]omestic criminal justice

[27] Address by Carla Del Ponte, Prosecutor of the ICTY, to the UN Security Council (27 November 2001) ICTY Press Release GR/P.I.S./642–e.

[28] This parallel is examined by Robert Cryer, *Prosecuting International Crimes* (Cambridge, Cambridge University Press, 2005) 192.

[29] ibid 201.

[30] Kai Ambos, 'Comparative Summary of the National Reports' in Louise Arbour and others (eds), *The Prosecutor of a Permanent International Criminal Court: International Workshop in Co-operation with the Office of the Prosecutor of the International Criminal Tribunals (ICTY and ICTR), Freiburg im Breisgau, May 1998* (Freiburg im Breisgau, Edition iuscrim, 2000) 525.

systems', which also have to select between cases, 'do not provide a useful model in this regard'.[31]

3. THE NEED FOR REPRESENTATIVE CASE SELECTIONS

Given the responsibility of tribunals to reflect – or, at the very least, not to distort – the 'historical truth' of the entire conflict situation to which they are assigned, there is arguably a normative consequence: cases here must be selected *representatively*. This is a challenge that does not exist at the domestic level.

The Expressive Impact of Case Selections

Illustrative examples for the narrative impact made by case selections at the international level can be seen both at the ICTY and ICTR. While post-conflict governments would advocate one particular narrative of 'truth', the selection of cases by the tribunals would often wilfully promote a different one. After Carla Del Ponte, as Prosecutor of the ICTR, explained her intention to target not only Hutu *génocidaires* responsible for the 1994 genocide against the Tutsi minority in Rwanda but also a number of Tutsi rebels allegedly responsible for several massacres in vengeance,[32] Rwanda's Tutsi-dominated post-genocide government was reportedly outraged, claiming that Del Ponte was distorting history by subscribing to 'negationist theories of "equal guilt"' between Hutu *génocidaires* and the Tutsi rebels who had ended the genocide.[33] As Del Ponte notes in her memoir, 'Opening an investigation of the [Tutsi rebel force] RPF would strike a raw nerve in Kigali, because President Kagame and the other Tutsi leaders had staked so much of their claim to political legitimacy' upon their victim status and their defeat of the *génocidaires* in 1994.[34] Kagame reportedly protested to Del Ponte: 'If you investigate, people will believe there were two genocides.'[35] Obviously, the 13 cases of Tutsi atrocities which Del Ponte sought to investigate would not have marginalised the hundreds of Hutu *génocidaire* atrocities which were also under investigation at the same time. However, Kagame's statement does nicely illustrate how individual proceedings here are 'inevitably symbolic' in the sense described by Gary Bass: '[A] few war criminals stand for a much larger

[31] Akhavan, 'Justice in The Hague' (n 3) 775.

[32] Del Ponte, *Madame Prosecutor* (n 20) 179.

[33] Martin Ngoga, the Rwandan government representative to the ICTR, quoted in 'UN Prosecutor Rallies UK Support to Investigate Rwandan Army', *Hirondelle News Agency*, 29 November 2002.

[34] ibid 183.

[35] ibid 225.

group of guilty individuals.'[36] To place a person in the dock in this particular judicial system with its symbolic trials means to symbolically place a (political or military) group in the dock, at least in the eyes of observers.

In another example, a Serbian nationalist NGO complained in 2003 of the ICTY's primary focus on Serbs as being unfair to 'historical truth':

> 45 indictments have been brought in against the Serbs, 12 against the Croats, 5 against the Muslims, one against the Albanians, and none against the Americans and their NATO allies. Among those sentenced were 13 Serbs, 4 Croats and 3 Muslims. Three Croats and two Muslims were acquitted.[37]

To this Serbian NGO, which goes on to downplay the dominant role of Serb perpetrators in the multiparty conflict, 'these statistics alone speak of bias and the political character of the Tribunal'.[38] Similarly, Serbia's government in the 1990s repeatedly claimed that all parties to the conflict had simply committed an equal share of atrocities and that the ICTY's selection of cases thus distorted the true proportions.[39] On one occasion, a former high-level member of the ICTY Office of the Prosecutor, Paul Stuebner, engaged in a direct discussion about these proportions in the dock with the leader of the Bosnian Serbs in 1996:

> Karadžić said that the tribunal was 'partial' . . . that too few non-Serbs had been indicted. I told him that in my sense the Serb forces were responsible for 80 percent of the atrocities of this war, and even 90 percent before Operation Storm launched by the Croats. And that the accusations of the tribunal reflected these differences in the responsibility for criminal acts.[40]

On the other hand, political groups on the Croatian side, who like to cite a CIA report, according to which Serb forces committed 90 per cent of the war crimes,[41] argued that the ICTY's selection policy was actually *too* evenhanded.[42]

The disagreement here is on historical facts and not on law. All sides accept – and even advocate – the normative principle that a selection of cases should be representative of 'historical truth'. Judging by such political debates, the need for 'upholding [a tribunal's] neutrality by achieving proportionality in indictments', as Victor Peskin describes it,[43] is widely accepted.

[36] Bass, *Stay the Hand* (n 8) 300.
[37] Vladimir Kršljanin, pamphlet of *Sloboda/Freedom Association, Belgrade*, May 2003. Available at www.icdsm.org/more/future.htm.
[38] ibid.
[39] See Victor Peskin, *International Justice in Rwanda and the Balkans* (Cambridge, Cambridge University Press, 2008) 33–34.
[40] Hazan, *Justice in a Time of War* (n 19) 107.
[41] Roger Cohen, 'CIA Report Finds Serbs Guilty of Majority of Bosnia War Crimes', *New York Times*, 9 March 1995.
[42] See Peskin, *International Justice in Rwanda and the Balkans* (n 39) 115.
[43] ibid 33.

A Responsibility to Paint the 'Truth' through Case Selections?

Tribunal audiences are quick to translate a small selection of cases into a miniature model of the entire conflict, with the proportions in the dock representing the proportions in 'historical truth'. Moreover, as illustrated in the aforementioned examples, audiences are quick to ask whether this selection is fair based on their own views of 'historical truth'. Prosecutors, who operate in this highly expressive system and aim to bring the 'historical truth' of a conflict to light, cannot ignore these communicative mechanisms.

An experienced practitioner, Luc Côté notes:

> [I]t has become an open secret that international Prosecutors, in selecting a potential indictee, may take into account criteria related to their belonging to or affiliation with a certain group in order to present in court more balanced cases involving all parties to the conflict that committed serious violations of [international humanitarian law].[44]

It is worth asking, however, whether there is even any normative reason to be silent about what Luc Côté refers to as an 'open secret'.

Given the communicative mechanisms illustrated in this section, it is reasonable to argue that there are quite sound normative reasons *for* the prosecutor to select the few cases that are manageable at the international level in a manner that is not unfair to historical proportions. 'It is not the court's job to write the history of the conflict', notes Serge Brammertz, the current Prosecutor of the ICTY and former Deputy Prosecutor of the International Criminal Court (ICC).[45] 'Still, there is no doubt that the court fulfils an important role in this. For this reason, it is clear that an effort is made to represent different aspects, and regions, of the conflict as far as this is possible.'[46] The ICTR Trial Chamber has even explicitly commended a selection policy 'aimed at shedding light on the events . . . and highlighting the complete landscape of the criminal acts perpetrated at the time',[47] and considering the tribunal's function of confirming 'historical truth', this appears as a sensible approach. After all, it has been highlighted at the outset of this chapter that the clarification of the historical narrative may well be the single most valuable effect that a court of international criminal justice can realistically have at all.

[44] Côté, 'Reflections on the Exercise of Prosecutorial Discretion' (n 3) 176. The author is currently Chief of Prosecutions at the Special Court for Sierra Leone and formerly a member of the ICTR Office of the Prosecutor.

[45] Brammertz interview (14 October 2009, The Hague).

[46] ibid.

[47] Decision on the Prosecutor's Motion to Withdraw the Indictment, *Prosecutor v Ntuyahaga*, Case No ICTR-98-40-T, Trial Chamber 1, 18 March 1999.

Individual Defendants as Representatives?

There is one aspect to this principle, however, which does raise some normative unease. A liberal criminal trial targets individual guilt and nothing else. This remains true even where the crimes at hand are committed collectively.[48] How can it then be acceptable if an indictee is effectively treated as a representative for anyone but himself?

This legal question has been raised particularly at the ICTY. While the overwhelming majority of trials at the ICTY targeted Serbs, some commentators criticised the decision by the ICTY Prosecutor in 2002 to pursue an ailing Croatian general merely out of an apparent desire to 'bring a high-ranking Croat to The Hague',[49] ie to make the selection of cases more representative. Allison Danner criticises that such an ultimately ethnic selection does 'not instil faith in the fairness of international justice' and argues that an international prosecutor should not focus on the nationalities of the accused at all.[50] This argument was also made by one of the defendants in *Prosecutor v Delalić et al (the 'Čelebići case')*, Esad Landžo. Landžo, a Bosnian Muslim, claimed that the Prosecutor was pursuing his case 'simply because he was the only person the Prosecutor's office could find to "represent" the Bosnian Muslims' at that time[51] and thus was pursued purely 'to give an appearance of "evenhandedness" to the Prosecutor's policy.'[52] (The ICTY Prosecutor, in her response, was 'honest and cautious' enough not to deny such an intention, notes Luc Côté.[53])

However, whereas Landžo complained of having been 'singled out, as a Bosnian Muslim',[54] the Appeals Chamber did not find this selection decision to have infringed upon his rights.[55] Rather, the Appeals Chamber pointed to the fact that the selection was in line with the ICTY Prosecutor's pre-announced policy of narrowing in on 'persons holding higher levels of responsibility, or on those who have been personally responsible for exceptionally brutal or otherwise extremely serious offences.'[56] This had, of course, not been denied by Landžo. Rather, what the defendant had objected to was his selection from *within* this narrowed-down group where he had apparently been preferred over Serb suspects of equal noto-

48 For a rich display of theoretical approaches to individual responsibility for collective behaviour see Ambos, *Der Allgemeine Teil des Völkerstrafrechts* (n 5) 523–42.

49 See, eg Daniel Simpson, 'Croatia Protects a General Charged with War Crimes: In Rubble of Village Serb Calls for Vengeance', *New York Times*, 3 December 2002, 10.

50 Danner, 'Enhancing the Legitimacy and Accountability' (n 23) 544.

51 *Prosecutor v Delalić et al* ('*Čelebići* case') Case No IT-96-21-A, Appeals Judgement (20 February 2001) [612].

52 Cryer, *Prosecuting International Crimes* (n 28) 213.

53 Côté, 'Reflections on the Exercise of Prosecutorial Discretion' (n 3) 176.

54 Cryer, *Prosecuting International Crimes* (n 28) 213.

55 See also Côté, 'Reflections on the Exercise of Prosecutorial Discretion' (n 3) 176.

56 *Čelebići case* Case No IT-96-21-A, Appeals Judgement (20 February 2001) [614].

riety, merely for his apparent importance to the Tribunal's desired ethnic narrative.

The Appeals Chamber, however, did allow the Prosecutor to select between suspects of equal notoriety at discretion, thus allowing for the Prosecutor to take the *representative value* of a suspect into consideration:

> The breadth of the discretion of the Prosecutor, and the fact of her statutory independence, imply a presumption that the prosecutorial functions under the Statute are exercised regularly. This presumption may be rebutted by an appellant who can bring evidence to establish that the discretion has in fact not been exercised in accordance with the Statute, here, for example, in contravention of the principle of equality before the law in Article 21. This would require evidence from which a clear inference can be drawn that the Prosecutor was motivated in that case by a factor inconsistent with that principle.[57]

Two reasons support this ruling. Firstly, it is important to note that a representative selection of course does not imply that the accused is *tried* as a representative. Rather, the trial remains exclusively concerned with the individual's guilt. In the case of the ailing Croatian general, for instance, this was the indictee's responsibility for a violent military campaign against Serb civilians in Croatia ('Operation Storm').[58] In Landžo's case also, the accused was not made to answer for anything but his individual guilt – his 'bad luck' merely being that the ICTY Prosecutor had decided not to let the crimes committed by Serbs distract *all* attention from the crimes committed by Bosnian Muslims such as Landžo.

Secondly, in a system as 'expressive' as this one, the selection of cases will send out a message in *any* case.[59] 'One cannot not communicate', as the sociologist Paul Watzlawick famously put it. A decision by the Prosecutor not to deliberately shift some attention towards Muslim perpetrators would inevitably have also sent out a message and this would have been a message that would have even distorted the Prosecutor's own findings on 'historical truth' – hardly a preferable alternative.

In sum, the normative challenge for international prosecutors was described particularly vividly by Payam Akhavan, while working at the ICTY Office of the Prosecutor in 1998, as one of 'constructing the optimal truth':

> In its selection of cases, the ICTY Prosecutor must construct an overall picture of the conflict that provides optimal cathartic and reconciliatory potential. In doing so, the Prosecutor must consider to what extent it can be actuated by such motives without compromising the ICTY's independence and impartiality. But

[57] ibid [611].

[58] For the proceedings in the Bobetko case, compare Peskin, *International Justice in Rwanda and the Balkans* (n 39) 102, 131–35. The case is also highlighted by Del Ponte, *Madame Prosecutor* (n 20) 250–51.

[59] See also Rosalyn Higgins, *Problems and Process: International Law and How We Use It* (Oxford, Clarendon Press, 1994) 5.

> with very limited resources at its disposal, and in view of the overwhelming number of serious crimes that have been committed, there is no way for the Prosecutor to avoid making broader strategic choices. Such choices may include the manner in which case selection will construct an overall truth or narrative of what transpired in the former Yugoslavia and how this may impact reconciliation and peace building in the region.[60]

4. ARE OBJECTIVE SELECTIONS POSSIBLE? THE GRAVITY TEST

With political actors emphatically pronouncing different versions of 'historical truth', where can a court of international criminal justice find the objectivity which other institutions apparently lack in such a situation? What is to prevent a court from adding further harm to 'historical truth' by inadvertently subscribing to a distorted version of 'truth' through a distorted selection of cases? What, in other words, is to guarantee that the court will not become yet another actor in a highly politicised debate over 'historical truth', merely extending authoritative support to one actor whilst weakening another?

Much has been written about the problem of historical objectivity. Hannah Arendt, for instance, was sceptical as to whether a 'true' narration of history exists at all:

> Have not generations of historians and philosophers of history demonstrated the impossibility of ascertaining facts without interpretation, since they must first be picked out of a chaos of sheer happenings (and the principles of choice are surely not factual data) and then be fitted into a story that can be told only in a certain perspective, which has nothing to do with the original occurrence?[61]

'Is not the mere selection of particular facts, let alone their interpretation in a narrative, always filtered through the eyes of a particular people, with a particular historical experience?'[62] asks Payam Akhavan and points to Charles Maier: '*Chacun a sa mémoire.*'[63] Can the selection of cases, essential to the non-distortion of 'historical truth' in this system, then be made in any strictly objective way to avoid these problems?

[60] Akhavan, 'Justice in The Hague' (n 3) 775.

[61] Hannah Arendt, *Between Past and Future: Eight Exercises in Political Thought* (New York, Penguin Books, 1993) 227.

[62] Akhavan, 'Justice in The Hague' (n 3) 768.

[63] Charles S Maier, 'A Surfeit of Memory? Reflections on History, Melancholy and Denial' (1993) 5 *History and Memory* 136.

Focussing on Crimes, not Perpetrators

In an effort to make case selections as objective as possible, the Prosecutor of the UN ad hoc tribunals defined legal selection criteria at an early stage. Since at least 1997,[64] a policy was implemented at the tribunals to focus on persons who were either (1) high-level officials or (2) low-level perpetrators responsible for particularly egregious offences. The only change to this guideline in the meantime has been to narrow the focus down even further. From a temporary 'big fish v small fish' debate at the beginning of the 1990s,[65] the focus has shifted back towards the original Nuremberg approach of targeting 'big fish' exclusively.[66] In his summary of 15 years of practice, the current ICTY Prosecutor recently repeated that '[c]hoices must be made about whom to prosecute' and emphasised the pre-announced policy decision to concentrate impartially (1) on the 'most serious' crimes and, *cumulatively*, (2) on persons of the 'highest responsibility' for those crimes.[67] This policy has since also been adopted at the ICC.[68]

In theory, this programme for selecting cases shifts all attention to the few most serious crimes committed within the court's jurisdiction. Subsequently, one simply follows the chain of command up from there as far as possible to find the 'right' person to indict.[69]

[64] See Danner, 'Enhancing the Legitimacy and Accountability' (n 23) 540.

[65] See Akhavan, 'Justice in The Hague' (n 3) 777–81, noting some debatable arguments in favour of confronting low-level physical perpetrators also. This has recently been reinforced by the ICC Pre-Trial Chamber I, as highlighted by Margaret DeGuzman, 'Gravity and the Legitimacy of the International Criminal Court' (2008) 32 *Fordham International Law Journal* 1427. For the pragmatic perspective that led the ICTY Prosecutor to conduct the very first trial against 'small fish' Duško Tadić, see Del Ponte, *Madame Prosecutor* (n 20) 124. See also Danner, 'Enhancing the Legitimacy and Accountability' (n 23) 543, at note 276, emphasising that most suspects in practice actually lie somewhere in between the schematic 'big fish' and 'small fry'.

[66] Compare Carla Del Ponte, 'Prosecuting the Individuals Bearing the Highest Level of Responsibility' (2004) *Journal of International Criminal Justice* 516.

[67] ICTY Manual on Developed Practices (June 2009) p 14. Available at www.icty.org.

[68] Article 17 Rome Statute, dealing with admissibility, authorises the ICC (which includes the ICC Prosecutor) to dismiss cases that are 'not of sufficient gravity to justify further action by the Court', and the ICC's first Prosecutor, Luis Moreno-Ocampo, has added that he will focus his attention 'on those who bear the greatest responsibility, such as the leaders of the State or organisation allegedly responsible for those crimes.' ICC Office of the Prosecutor, Policy Paper (September 2003) p 7. Available at www.icc-cpi.int. William A Schabas, 'Prosecutorial Discretion v. Judicial Activism at the International Criminal Court' (2008) 6 *Journal of International Criminal Justice* 736–41 shows how the ICC Prosecutor only slowly turned his attention to the issue of 'gravity'.

[69] For example, the ICTY in 2006 put Jadranko Prlić, the former Foreign Minister of Bosnia and Herzegovina, and five other Bosnian Croats on trial – 'an indictment by proxy', as Del Ponte, *Madame Prosecutor* (n 20) 272, openly admits, since the actual *highest*-level Croat leaders around former President Franjo Tudjman had deceased and thus escaped international prosecution.

This clear focus on crimes suggests a neutral act of cognition and a process in which it is only facts which dictate decisions. On this basis, Allison Danner advocates:

> Instead of focusing on the nationality of the offenders, the Prosecutor should use as his primary screening criterion the seriousness of the offense committed. Although measuring 'seriousness' involves philosophical and practical challenges, assessing the harm engendered by a crime is surely a less controversial approach than targeting particular individuals because of their status or nationality. In addition, seriousness of the offense is a commonly accepted criterion for domestic charging decisions. Furthermore, the relative clarity of this standard helps address one of the principal criticisms of prosecutorial guidelines – that they are fundamentally indeterminate. A primary focus on the crimes committed will afford the surest foundation for impartial prosecutorial decision making.[70]

However, does this programme for selecting cases really relieve judicial decision makers of any need to define their own historical perspective on a conflict situation? A closer look at the criterion of 'gravity' (synonymous with 'seriousness'), which this section offers, illustrates some doubts.

What is Gravity?

How can the gravity of a crime be measured objectively? The UN's International Law Commission (ILC), working on a draft ICC Statute, abandoned its attempts to define 'gravity' in the abstract early in its deliberations.[71] This is because, even where the crimes at hand are necessarily *all* of a most egregious type, it is widely accepted that the comparison of their gravity is not simply about counting victims ('quantity'), but obviously also about the 'quality' of crimes.

The ICC Prosecutor argued in 2005 that the number of victims is nonetheless a *relatively* objective factor.[72] More recently, he has agreed, rather emphatically even,[73] with his critics[74] that qualitative considerations are also indispensable.[75] Nonetheless, the problem which the ICC Prosecutor's 2005 argument rightly highlighted remains: where can any degree of

[70] Danner, 'Enhancing the Legitimacy and Accountability' (n 23) 544.

[71] DeGuzman, 'Gravity and the Legitimacy of the International Criminal Court' (n 65) 1456.

[72] Luis Moreno-Ocampo, 'Statement at Informal Meeting of Legal Advisors of Ministries of Foreign Affairs' (24 October 2005) 9, arguing that the number of victims tends to be reported reliably.

[73] For a discussion of the controversial *Abu Garda* indictment see, eg Kevin J Heller, 'Situational Gravity under the Rome Statute' in Stahn Carsten and Larissa van den Herik (eds), *Future Directions in International Criminal Justice* (2009) 11–12.

[74] See, eg ibid.

[75] ICC Office of the Prosecutor, 'Draft for Discussion: Criteria for Selection of Situations and Cases' (June 2006). Available at www.icc-cpi.int.

objectivity be drawn from with regard to 'quality'? To what extent is it possible to rank crimes in terms of 'quality' in the abstract? And to what extent does this actually make selection decisions *in casu* any more predictable?

Attempts at ranking types of international crimes in the abstract have proven difficult. The ICTR, as a tribunal faced with a genocide, has categorised genocide as the 'crime of crimes', which is inherently more serious than crimes against humanity, which in turn are inherently more serious than war crimes.[76] Allison Danner supports this categorical approach and makes even finer distinctions, suggesting four levels of hierarchy between international crimes. In descending order of gravity, these are: 1. Genocide; 2. Persecution-type crimes against humanity; 3. Murder-type crimes against humanity; 4. War crimes.[77] However, each of these core crimes encompasses many different acts that are connected only by context and, in some cases, intention.[78] For instance, the crime of genocide does not necessarily involve an act of killing.[79] Furthermore, the ICTY, a tribunal faced with a multitude of different atrocities, has rejected ranking even these different acts (such as wilful killing, rape and forceful transferral) in the abstract as 'too rigid and mechanistic.'[80]

The ICC Prosecutor has been very careful in suggesting only a very basic hierarchy of crimes in the abstract, echoing only what is probably a consensus among (modern) domestic penal systems: that crimes resulting in death are the gravest and that rape is 'also at the level of highest gravity'.[81] At the same time, the ICC Prosecutor has emphasised that the relative quality of particular crimes – most of which in the context of international criminal justice will cause deaths – is not characterised solely by their abstract 'nature', but also by their 'manner of commission' and 'impact', which cannot be assessed in the abstract but only *in casu*.[82]

Some Historical Perspective is Indispensable...

Instead of clinging to an inflexible, and not always convincing, hierarchy of crimes, international prosecutors have often looked to a different aspect

[76] See, eg *Prosecutor v Musema*, Case No ICTR-96-13-T, Judgment (27 January 2000) [981]; *Prosecutor v Kambanda*, Case No ICTR-97-23-S, Judgment (4 September 1998) [1417].

[77] Allison M Danner, 'Constructing a Hierarchy of Crimes in International Criminal Law Sentencing' (2001) 87 *Virginia Law Review* 470–83.

[78] See also Heller, 'Situational Gravity under the Rome Statute' (n 73) 6.

[79] Article 6 Rome Statute, dealing with genocide, enumerates five alternative acts, including (d) 'imposing measures intended to prevent births within the group', and (e) 'forcibly transferring children of the group to another group'.

[80] *Prosecutor v Furundzija*, Case No IT-95-17/1-A, Appeals Judgment [246].

[81] ICC Office of the Prosecutor, 'Draft for Discussion: Criteria for Selection of Situations and Cases' (June 2006). Available at www.icc-cpi.int.

[82] ibid.

of 'quality': which crimes, among the group of atrocities identifiable as most serious *in casu* cause particular shock and dismay to the international community, thus requiring an expressive response most urgently? In this vein, in 1998, the ICTY Prosecutor chose to indict Dragoljub Kunarac and others for using systematic rape as an instrument of terror against Bosnian Muslims.[83] The indictees were relatively low-level physical perpetrators with a long line of commanders above them and the Prosecutor had numerous other perpetrators responsible for mass *killings* rather than rapes to choose from. Yet, the selection of Dragoljub Kunarac allowed for the ICTY Prosecutor to introduce the subject of crimes of sexual violence into the focus of international criminal justice for the first time, clarifying – in the kind of 'exemplary selective prosecution' commended by Luc Côté[84] – that rape can constitute a crime against humanity.[85]

In *Lubanga*, a case where the ICC Prosecutor indicted the accused 'only' for the conscription of child soldiers whilst perpetrators responsible for mass killings were left unindicted, the ICC Pre-Trial Chamber I reaffirmed this rationale, calling this selection criterion 'social alarm': 'In assessing the gravity of the relevant conduct, due consideration must be given to the social alarm such conduct may have caused in the international community.'[86] This idea has, in fact, guided prosecutors in international criminal justice from the beginning. Each of the four IMT Prosecutors at Nuremberg prioritised, albeit to different extents, on articulating special points of 'alarm' to their particular home audiences.[87] With that however, the inherent problem of basing judicial selections on 'social alarm' is also already apparent.

. . .But Hardly Objective

What the expression of 'social alarm', which refers to the moral outrage of the 'international community',[88] conceals is that the particular societies, of which this figurative community is composed, are by no means homogenous in terms of what alarms them. As Michael Ramsey rightly notes, the 'comfortable rhetoric' of an international community 'disguises the fact that there is no unified "world community" with a simple and easily

[83] *Prosecutor v Kunarac et al*, Case No IT-96-23-T & 23/1-T.

[84] Côté, 'Reflections on the Exercise of Prosecutorial Discretion' (n 3) 175.

[85] This selection decision is also highlighted by DeGuzman, 'Gravity and the Legitimacy of the International Criminal Court' (n 65) 1463.

[86] *Prosecutor v Lubanga*, Case No ICC-01/04-01/06, Decision on the Prosecutor's Application for a Warrant of Arrest, art 58 (10 February 2006) para 46. This criterion is also advocated strongly by Heller, 'Situational Gravity under the Rome Statute' (n 73) 9–14.

[87] See below chapter two, section two.

[88] ibid.

accessible opinion to be had for the asking' but 'only hundreds of societies, with diverse and conflicting national practices'.[89]

Assuredly, even though the international community 'defies a monolithic definition,' certain common *interests*, eg in 'global stability', can be identified.[90] Yet, in asking for feelings of moral outrage, eg at sexual violence or the abuse of children's rights, one must expect priorities to differ. A feminist will more than likely set different priorities than an old-school ethno-pluralist, while Arab States have, in international deliberations, set different priorities than European States. This is not to advocate moral relativism but hopefully to make a sociological point: 'social alarm' is not universal. Neither can it be measured with any degree of 'objective' precision.[91] Ultimately, as the ICC Appeals Chamber rightly criticised, the criterion 'depends upon subjective and contingent reactions to crimes rather than upon their objective gravity.'[92]

For this reason, many commentators have tried to define other criteria for 'quality' ('manner of commission' and 'impact') with more precision in the abstract.[93] Ultimately however, with numerous aspects of gravity to weigh against one another in the case of a particular conflict, it is conceivable that one will, at best, be able to identify a *group* of most serious crimes from within one conflict rather than a mathematically precise 'ranking' of crime sites. This makes a second step in the selection process inescapable.[94]

[89] Michael D Ramsey, 'International Materials and Domestic Rights: Reflections on Atkins and Lawrence' (2004) 98 *The American Journal of International Law* 79.

[90] Sloane, 'Expressive Capacity of International Punishment' (n 1) 53f.

[91] In order to 'prove' a particularly high degree of social alarm in *Abu Garda*, the ICC Prosecutor pointed to statements by the African Union and the UN Security Council, in which both had 'condemned' the attacks against peacekeepers. See ICC Prosecutor, *Situation in Darfur, The Sudan (ICC-02-05-162), Summary of the Prosecutor's Application under Article 58* (20 November 2008) para 7. Available at www.icc-cpi.int. However, the same political organs condemn numerous other crimes also, inside and outside of the Darfur region. Moreover, why should statements by the African Union be any more indicative of the opinion of the 'international community' than statements by, for instance, the States of East Asia?

[92] See *Prosecutor v Ntaganda Dyilo*, Case No ICC-01/04-169, Judgment on the Prosecutor's Appeal Against the Decision of Pre-Trial Chamber I entitled 'Decision on the Prosecutor's Application for Warrants of Arrest, Article 58' (13 July 2006) [72]. For support of this critique, see DeGuzman, 'Gravity and the Legitimacy of the International Criminal Court' (n 65) 1426–29.

[93] See, eg ibid 1451–54. There is an original argument made by Heller, 'Situational Gravity under the Rome Statute' (n 73) 7, that the categorical 'ranking' of crimes along the lines of 'most people's ethical sensibilities' is in fact intuitively guided by an appraisal of their typical 'systematicity' (ie to what extent is the violence integrated into a systematic policy or merely an isolated outburst?), with the most systematic forms of violence being the most serious. Heller suggests focussing on this feature (an aspect, arguably, of the 'manner of commission') instead of on an inflexible abstract hierarchy. This approach offers an additional advantage in that it automatically draws the prosecutorial attention towards crimes which shed a light on larger parts of 'historical truth' rather than on isolated incidents.

[94] See also DeGuzman, 'Gravity and the Legitimacy of the International Criminal Court' (n 65) 1415, noting: 'The Prosecutor may only select cases within a situation for prosecution that meet the gravity threshold for admissibility. The Prosecutor has complete discretion however, in selecting among admissible cases.'

How may the prosecutor prioritise *within* this narrowed-down group of crimes? Which case should he or she begin with and where should each portion of prosecutorial resources be directed? The rationale at this stage, logically, can no longer be 'gravity'. Rather, it becomes inescapable at this stage to make policy choices.[95]

Even though such decisions will naturally always be debatable, to simply avoid making them is, in practice, not an option. Even to decide, in the interest of strict judicial objectivity, not to introduce any prioritisation other than 'gravity' – that is, to process the evidence for the group of 'most serious' crimes purely in the random order as it comes in – would represent a deliberate decision and a rather arbitrary one at that. Certain crimes, for which evidence may be particularly hard to obtain, would not receive adequate attention at all. Judicial resources could be drawn entirely disproportionately to atrocities from only one part of the conflict.

The same challenge is also encountered if we follow the less realistic assumption that an objective and precise 'ranking' between numerous different atrocities (eg from the 'first most serious' to the 'thirtieth most serious' atrocity of a conflict) were indeed possible. Would it then be acceptable normatively, in light of the court's responsibility not to distort 'historical truth', to focus finite resources entirely on the 'top five' atrocities committed only by one party even if the 'ranking' then immediately continues with dozens of atrocities committed exclusively by the other party? Or should one not rather aim to assure that the five trials which are manageable target both parties in some proportional way? In a judicial system dedicated to confirming or at the very least not distorting 'historical truth', some sense of historical perspective arguably cannot be done without at this stage.

In sum, for the normative reasons illustrated in the previous section of this chapter, a fair selection policy ultimately has to be representative of 'historical truth' even if this 'truth' can be portrayed only in very broad brushstrokes. The 'gravity' test for selecting cases, which has been examined in this section, does not afford a mechanism to assure this fairness automatically. Rather, the determination of a representative selection remains the responsibility of the decision maker who selects cases. And this is where it becomes central to ask which particular picture of 'historical truth' this decision maker has.

[95] For an in-depth exploration see ibid 1459–64, interestingly highlighting some scholarly suggestions to include political bodies in the decision process at this stage in order to add legitimacy to these policy choices.

5. THE CRITICAL SYSTEMIC ROLE OF THE PROSECUTOR

As Allison Danner notes, the task of selecting between cases requires prosecutors – in domestic systems just as in the international domain – to 'make judgments about the purpose and priorities of their particular system. Of all the by-products of discretion, this policymaking role has perhaps the greatest systemic consequences for criminal justice.'[96] In the international domain, this is even all the more so since this power remains remarkably unchecked by judicial control, as this section is hoped to show.

Predefined Narratives Inform the Selection Process. . .

It is not judges who determine which version of 'historical truth' the selection of cases at a court of international criminal justice shall be based upon after having weighed all the evidence and having heard the accused, but rather the determination falls upon the international prosecutor long *before* cases ever enter the court arena and only after a purely in-house assessment. At this early stage, prosecutors never find themselves in a position where they have evidence for all the atrocities committed during a whole conflict in front of them and can then trust a simple cross-section through all of these crimes sites to produce an 'objective', representative sample. Rather, as a group of experts commissioned by the UN Security Council in 1999 observed of the UN ad hoc tribunals' work:

> Allegations are brought to the attention of the Office of the Prosecutor and the investigations staff from numerous sources, including victims, witnesses, the media, NGOs, Governments and others. The number of complaints is so great and involves so many widespread geographic areas and individuals that it is physically impossible for the investigations staff to deal with all of them.[97]

Building prosecution cases in such a situation is not a matter of reacting to all calls received but rather of deciding where to start investigations proactively. For this, prosecutors require some idea of what they are hoping to find.

As the current ICTY Prosecutor notes, 'A clear mandate will allow the early development of an investigation strategy, and that in turn will allow evidence to be collected in an organised fashion for particular prosecution

[96] Danner, 'Enhancing the Legitimacy and Accountability' (n 23) 518.

[97] Report of the Expert Group to Conduct a Review of the Effective Operation and Functioning of the International Tribunal for the Former Yugoslavia and the International Criminal Tribunal for Rwanda, UN Doc A/54/634 (1999) [125].

cases.'[98] In the same vein, Louise Arbour contended in 1999 that 'rather than to weed out weak or frivolous complaints' from the unfathomable masses of information received, the real challenge faced by an international prosecutor is 'to choose from many meritorious complaints the appropriate ones for international intervention'.[99]

. . .and are then Reproduced in Court

The order of precedence in which prosecution cases are formed in the international criminal justice system is, thus, quite remarkably different from the ideal that is commonly promoted within domestic systems. First, the international prosecutor needs to develop an overall historical perspective on the incidents in question. Only then can the actual investigations reasonably commence, amassing evidence roughly in the proportions of the prosecutor's predefined strategy.

The consequences of this peculiar situation are visible in the memoir of the former ICTY Prosecutor Carla Del Ponte. On the one hand, Del Ponte complains that members of her office sometimes lacked perspective on the historical 'big picture' before setting out to conduct investigations.[100] On the other hand, Del Ponte's own initial historical perspective on the 'big picture' in Yugoslavia is based on books and media coverage, Del Ponte explains, even noting at one point that

> I could not accept that evidence of linkages between Belgrade and the violence in Croatia and Bosnia did not exist. The press reporting on the war had shown clearly that Milošević bore significant responsibility for the crimes in those two republics.[101]

International press reports on the conflict in the Balkans had, of course, been far from uniform. Had Del Ponte, for instance, been reading Russian newspapers instead of Western ones, she probably would have received quite a different 'overall context of the wars' to start from.

[98] ICTY Manual on Developed Practices (published in June 2009) p 14. Available at www.icty.org/x/file/About/Reports%20and%20Publications/ICTY_Manual_on_Developed_Practices.pdf.

[99] Louise M Arbour, 'Statement to the Preparatory Committee on the Establishment of an International Criminal Court' (8 December 1997), quoted in ibid 520.

[100] Del Ponte, *Madame Prosecutor* (n 20) 129f: 'There was a tendency among personnel of the Office of the Prosecutor to form opinions about the overall Yugoslav conflict based upon what witnesses from one particular village, one region, or one side were telling them. As a result, many staff members were incapable of assessing the relative importance of particular incidents, documents, and targets in terms of how they fit into the overall context of the wars. They were also susceptible to manipulation by interested parties, because they lacked criteria for assessing the witnesses' credibility of the plausibility of the accounts they provided.'

[101] ibid 90.

How can Judges Control the Prosecutor's Selection Policy?

At a later stage in proceedings, and in light of evidence and witness statements, the judges of a tribunal may of course give a factual assessment which differs from that in the indictment, thus correcting the prosecutor's version of 'historical truth'. However, unlike the fine print of indictments, the overall historical 'big picture' which is reflected in the prosecutor's selection of cases is not something which judges at a court of international criminal justice are capable of adequately controlling. Certainly, judges can review the prosecutors' motions for indictments and reject them. The ICC Statute has even strengthened judicial oversight in this respect by introducing a special Pre-Trial Chamber. However, none of the relevant rules allow the judges to get involved in a discussion on whether the ICC Prosecutor's selection of cases is fair to the historical proportions within a conflict. The most that judges could do to correct a selection of cases which they find to be unfair to 'historical truth', in theory, would be to weed out individual cases on the pretence of a lack of evidence – but not for the cases actually being unrepresentative.[102]

Should the prosecutor decide to simply shield one party to the conflict from accountability, judges would be in no position to stop this. For judges to *add* new indictees to a prosecutor's list in order to expand the judicial spotlight, eg to another party to the conflict, is not possible even in theory.[103] Tribunal judges have, accordingly, rejected all such motions: in two instances at the ICTR, the defence lawyers of Hutu *génocidaire* defendants requested that judges order the ICTR Prosecutor to open an investigation into the assassination of Rwandan President Habyarimana in 1994. The judges denied these motions, arguing that the defence had 'failed to establish a legal basis on which the Trial Chamber could order supplementary investigations by the prosecutor in this case. The issue is one solely for the discretion of the prosecutor.'[104] Such a legal basis has not been created at the ICC either.[105]

[102] According to art 61 (7) Rome Statute, before a case can go to trial, the Prosecutor must receive confirmation by the ICC Pre-Trial Chamber that there is 'sufficient evidence to establish substantial grounds to believe that the person committed each of the crimes charged'.

[103] As Schabas, 'Prosecutorial Discretion v Judicial Activism' (n 68) 754f, shows, the same is also true for adding individual charges: 'At the practical level, the ability of judges to direct the outcome of a trial in this way is rather limited.'

[104] See Côté, 'Reflections on the Exercise of Prosecutorial Discretion' (n 3) 167.

[105] Articles 53 (1) (c) and 53 (2) (c) Rome Statute require the ICC Prosecutor only to 'inform' the judges of a decision to decline to pursue a case. And even this rule applies only where the Prosecutor makes use of an exceptional authority to dismiss a case at his or her own discretion 'in the interests of justice'. For criticism see Heller, 'Situational Gravity under the Rome Statute' (n 73) 31–34.

The Limited Perspective from the Judges' Bench

Once a case has found its way into a courtroom and thus into the domain of judges, the judicial decisions are no longer about 'a system, nor history, a historic tendency or an "ism", but a person', as Hannah Arendt notes.[106] More specifically, while there are sound normative reasons for international prosecutors to select cases representatively of larger historical dimensions in the first place, as shown above,[107] there are consequently just as sound normative reasons for judges to treat each individual case only as an individual case.[108] The tension which can arise between these two professional perspectives becomes particularly clear whenever an individual who was selected 'representatively' is acquitted. The ICTY's case of Naser Orić offers an illustrative example.

Orić, a Bosnian Muslim, was indicted in 2003, a decade after his alleged crimes, in an effort by then ICTY Prosecutor Carla Del Ponte to add more balance to the Tribunal's portrayal of 'historical truth', which had until then concentrated mainly on Serb perpetrators. When the ICTY Appeals Chamber in 2008 found Orić innocent, this triggered angry protests in Serbia. The judges' decision was taken to be equally symbolically motivated as the Prosecutor's selection decision had evidently been. 'It is of course especially controversial' whenever a representative of one of the 'smaller' perpetrator groups is acquitted, notes Del Ponte's successor, Serge Brammertz, albeit without referring to a particular case.[109] To fight such misperceptions regarding their intentions as judges, the ICTY Trial Chambers have gone to great lengths to stress to audiences that their perspective is a purely individualist one.[110]

Judges are in no position to 'nominate' defendants whom the prosecutor has not selected, nor are judges in any position to argue the fairness of this

[106] Hannah Arendt, 'Die persönliche Verantwortung unter der Diktatur', konkret 6/1991, 34, 39, quoted in Herbert Jäger, 'Menschheitsverbrechen und die Grenzen des Kriminalkonzeptes: Theoretische Aspekte der Einsetzung eines UN-Kriegsverbrechertribunals' (1993) *Kritische Vierteljahresschrift für Gesetzgebung und Rechtswissenschaft* 263.

[107] See above section three.

[108] For a distinctly prosecutorial perspective, however, see Côté, 'Reflections on the Exercise of Prosecutorial Discretion' (n 3) 175: 'Even if we often hear that international criminal justice is concerned with individual responsibility "which substitutes itself to collective guilt . . . and annihilates the thirst for revenge", one can say that the very limited number of individuals tried by international courts reduces greatly the desired benefit of the individuality of criminal sanction.'

[109] Brammertz interview (14 October 2009, The Hague).

[110] See, eg *Prosecutor v Nikolić*, Case No IT-02-60/1-S, Sentencing Judgment (2 December 2003) [60]: 'by holding *individuals* responsible for the crimes committed, it was hoped that a particular ethnic or religious group (or even political organisation) would not be held responsible for such crimes by members of other ethnic or religious groups, and that the guilt of the few would not be shifted to the innocent'. This view was 'firmly upheld' in *Prosecutor v Radoslav Brdjanin*, Case No IT-99-36-T, Sentencing Judgment (1 September 2004) [43]. See also Akhavan, 'Justice in The Hague' (n 3) 766.

particular selection of defendants with the individuals in the dock – rather, what they are concerned with is only the individual guilt of each defendant. In an attempt to nonetheless introduce a critique of the ICTY's overall portrayal of 'historical truth' into the courtroom itself, the defence in *Prosecutor v Radoslav Brdjanin* innovatively argued in 2004 that the judges had developed an 'unintentional bias . . . against Serbs', resulting out of the fact that the prosecutor had presented them primarily with Serb indictees over the years.[111] The Trial Chamber, however, dismissed this charge as legally 'misconceived and unfortunate' since no substantial evidence could be presented to challenge the impartiality of the judges' bench.[112]

6. CHECKS ON THE PROSECUTOR? THE 'ACCOUNTABILITY V INDEPENDENCE' DEBATE

As the above section has shown, the selection of a tiny fraction of cases from a conflict situation by the international prosecutor can only be controlled by judges to a very limited extent. This is for structural and normative reasons. This leaves us with a remarkable situation given the fact that the shape of the prosecutor's selection defines the overall narrative output of a tribunal to a much larger extent than at any domestic criminal court.[113] If the prosecutor has such great responsibility and power, should he or she not be subjected to at least some form of outside control?

The Need for Democratic Accountability

In the domestic realm, this question is easily answered with yes. The liberal ideal of an independent judiciary refers primarily to the independence of judges. The ideal does not mean however that the prosecutor is independent from government. Rather, in domestic legal systems of most democracies, the policymaking public prosecutor is held personally accountable to an electorate or elected government – for example, the Ministry of Justice or Attorney General.[114] It is society as a whole whom the prosecutor represents in court and that society thus needs to mandate

[111] *Prosecutor v Radoslav Brdjanin*, Case No IT-99-36-T, Trial Judgment (1 September 2004) [39]–[43].

[112] ibid.

[113] See above section three.

[114] A survey of several Western democracies is offered by Danner, 'Enhancing the Legitimacy and Accountability' (n 23) 512f. Although Danner's focus is on prosecutorial independence, she concludes that prosecutors 'generally are regarded as more partisan than members of the judiciary', ibid 523.

him or her for democratic legitimacy. This does not disregard the fact that the prosecutor does not ultimately adjudicate: the mere power to publicly accuse persons ('charging power'), or contrarily to deny vindication to others, is considered reason enough to install some safeguards against the abuse of that power and to call for democratic checks on the prosecutor.

One could argue that this concern applies a fortiori at the international level. After all, the charging power of the international prosecutor is even greater and more prone to abuse here. Allison Danner rightly points out that an international prosecutor has the power to brand an individual a war criminal in the eyes of the international public even if no conviction ensues.[115] Robert Sloane also highlights the power of tribunals to 'disempower elites through stigma and reputational injury', even stating that 'In this regard, the mere issuance of an indictment . . . is itself the "punishment" by which [international criminal law] may deter.'[116] Theodor Meron, shortly before becoming a judge at the ICTY, even asserted that war crimes indictments leave individuals

> with a mark of Cain that serves as some measure of retribution, preventing them from travelling abroad and instilling in them the fear of arrest by an adversary or foreign government. In the absence of many actual trials and judgments, the confirmed indictments come as close as is possible to establishing a credible international record of the indicted persons' offences, one that will discredit them until they stand trial.[117]

Indeed, this is 'not the kind of power one wants to deliver without any restraints'.[118] Since the prosecutor's margin of discretion in selecting cases is much greater in the international context than on the domestic level,[119] shouldn't the democratic argument for accountability have even more purchase here?[120]

Is this Need Reduced here for a Special Reason?

Jürgen Habermas suggests that in the special case of international criminal courts, democratic accountability of the prosecutor may nonetheless be done without. This is because the substantive norms, which the international prosecutor applies, appear particularly deserving of universal consent since they 'are the product of prior learning processes and have

115 ibid 521.
116 Sloane, 'Expressive Capacity of International Punishment' (n 1) 74.
117 Meron, *War Crimes Law Comes of Age* (n 11) 283.
118 Danner, 'Enhancing the Legitimacy and Accountability' (n 23) 516.
119 See above section two.
120 This is supported by DeGuzman, 'Gravity and the Legitimacy of the International Criminal Court' (n 65) 1462; Alexander Greenawalt, 'Justice without Politics? Prosecutorial Discretion and the International Criminal Court' (1996) 39 *NYU Journal of International Law and Politics* 664; Danner, 'Enhancing the Legitimacy and Accountability' (n 23) 525f.

been tried and tested within democratic nation-states. Thus, their normative substance evolved from constitutions of the republican type.'[121] What Habermas is suggesting is that nobody could reasonably object to the application of such valuable norms – why should anyone then object to the prosecutor's work?

However, this arguably blurs two very distinct questions. One of these is: are the substantive norms which the prosecutor applies sufficiently legitimate? The other is: is the prosecutor's rationale for their highly *selective* application legitimate? The prosecutor is a legal policymaker and this task, by definition, exceeds the bare black letter law which we might indeed be able to agree on widely.

Perhaps a second idea can nonetheless relieve us of the need to hold the policymaking prosecutor accountable. Finding the 'truth', unlike exercising good judgement, is usually not something for which we turn to democratic processes; however, fairness to 'truth' is the core challenge in the international prosecutor's representative selection of cases.[122] Where a portrayal of 'truth' is the goal, we usually turn instead to specially appointed, independent persons – ie judges – to 'uncover' it forensically. Could not the same rationale then apply to prosecutors? Unfortunately, it cannot. As much as forensic objectivity is appealing, it must be borne in mind that the overall 'truth' of an entire conflict situation, which the international prosecutor is tasked with illuminating in a fair manner, is necessarily a construction out of countless facts weighed against one another.[123] The decision for one narrative or the other is a policy choice – and no less so where it is made entirely in good faith in this 'truth'.[124]

If one thus maintains that the international prosecutor needs to be held accountable in some way, one is left with the question to whom?

Which Institution Can Best Exercise Democratic Control?

One traditional answer on the international level is the UN Security Council. This was the answer upon which the UN ad hoc tribunals were based.[125] Of course, the UN Security Council's legitimately representing

[121] Jürgen Habermas, *Der gespaltene Westen* (Frankfurt am Main, Suhrkamp, 2004) 139 = Jürgen Habermas, *The Divided West* (Cambridge, Polity, 2006) 140. For 'cosmopolitan law as a paradigm' to soothe democratic concerns in international law, see also Armin von Bogdandy, 'Globalization and Europe: How to Square Democracy, Globalization, and International Law' (2004) 15 *European Journal of International Law* 899f.

[122] See above section three.

[123] See above section four.

[124] See also DeGuzman, 'Gravity and the Legitimacy of the International Criminal Court' (n 65) 1461.

[125] See below chapter four. Undoubtedly, the judges at the UN ad hoc tribunals are independent. The prosecutors however are hand-picked by the UN Security Council and are accountable to that body.

the society of States is, in many respects, a fiction. The 15 members of the UN Security Council – 10 of whom rotate regularly and are chosen to represent different world regions – are indeed the closest there is to a 'world government' at present, but the Security Council is not a democratic body since its five permanent members, who hold the most power, are not dependant on elections. In other words, by making a prosecutor accountable to the UN Security Council, one approaches the goal of democratic legitimacy but ultimately falls significantly short of it.

An alternative to Security Council control would be a full assembly of States like the UN General Assembly, overseeing prosecutorial policy by the principle of 'one country, one vote'. Democratic concerns can be raised here as well. The democratic quality of 'one country, one vote' is doubtful not only because tiny populations can outvote the most populous States – China and India, for example, are reduced to the same voting power as Lesotho or Liechtenstein – but also because many States are not constituted democratically on the inside. The UN General Assembly, therefore, is far from a democratic form. Moreover, on a purely practical level, observers of the UN have pointed out that such a forum of States, while perhaps functional as a legislature to some limited extent, is hardly capable of administering in detail and exercising effective executive oversight,[126] which is why such an assembly would theoretically first have to create a gubernatorial body for practical reasons.[127] Historically, this has been done only once before and it resulted in the UN Security Council. The UN Security Council would hence still appear as the logical choice.[128]

A pragmatist might argue that as much as the present architecture of international law – with the UN Security Council as a quasi-government – is democratically unpleasing, there is no other international body that can yet claim to come any closer to representing the whole society of States with more legitimacy. Forms of supranational representation that have been achieved in regional associations, such as the EU, are not available on a global level (yet).

[126] Danner, 'Enhancing the Legitimacy and Accountability' (n 23) 524: 'On the whole, similar bodies in other international institutions have not proven to be strong oversight mechanisms. Longtime international observers have privately voiced the opinion that the [Assembly of States Parties, which elects the Prosecutor and judges at the ICC] will prove to be a weak body because of internal policy disputes.'

[127] DeGuzman, 'Gravity and the Legitimacy of the International Criminal Court' (n 65) 1462, who favours this model, consequentially advocates a 'more active role' for the Assembly of States Parties to the ICC 'in the selection of situations and/or cases, for example through a standing committee'.

[128] This argument has recently been renewed by Greenawalt, 'Justice without Politics?' (n 120) 664.

The Call for Complete Judicial Independence: An Escape from the Dilemma?

For the controllership over the international prosecutor, there is, of course, nonetheless an alternative to the UN Security Council. This alternative, which has recently been advocated particularly by European States, does not seem to bring us close to the democratic goal *at all* however. It is the idea of holding the prosecutor accountable only to 'humanity' and of making him or her independent of any legal control by States as a consequence. This means that the UN Security Council is not replaced by a preferable institution but simply by a vacuum. This, put simply, is the model adopted by the ICC.

The democratic idea here is that humanity, and not States, constitutes the democratic referent, or *demos*, which the prosecutor represents, whereas States are primarily the potential accused from which humanity requires protection.[129] States' coercive influence on the prosecutor is then undesirable under all circumstances, even if it comes from a representative body like the UN Security Council. This concept is echoed in a fundamentally different conception of the prosecutor's role: instead of being required to represent and be accountable to the society of States (like in the concept of the UN ad hoc tribunals), the ICC Prosecutor now, quite contrarily, 'functions as a counterweight to state power, a role not often played by prosecutors in domestic systems'.[130]

However, how does this 'cosmopolitan' concept meet the need for democratic accountability of a policymaking prosecutor? How can humanity be expected to exercise any effective control if not through political bodies? Humanity presently does not have a democratic voice but through States. And human rights groups and NGOs, which occasionally claim to represent a 'global civil society', lack a formal democratic mandate altogether. A mere 'moral accountability' of the prosecutor hardly means effective legal control since the numerous delicate questions, which the prosecutor is tasked with deciding, are delicate exactly *because* there are so many different relevant opinions within humankind.

An argument similar to mere 'moral accountability' is 'pragmatic accountability'.[131] The idea here is that the 'likelihood of capricious exercise of the prosecutor's discretion' will be lessened by his or her daily need to work with State governments in order to detain suspects.[132]

[129] This change of paradigm – regarding the community of mankind and not the society of states as the *demos* – is the focus of Jason G Ralph, *Defending the Society of States* (Oxford, Oxford University Press, 2007).

[130] Danner, 'Enhancing the Legitimacy and Accountability' (n 23) 518.

[131] See, eg ibid 525f.

[132] Michael J Struett, 'The Politics of Discursive Legitimacy: Understanding the Dynamics and Implications of Prosecutorial Discretion at the International' in Steven C Roach (ed),

However, does this suffice to please the concerns which formed the basis for the need for democratic accountability in the first place? As in domestic law, the test for democratic checks and balances is not whether they function when a prosecutor is happily persuaded by 'built-in incentives . . . to act in ways that can be justified to a broad set of outside observers'[133] but rather when he or she decides otherwise. Are any safeguards in place to account for this case? This question remains and it may even be reinforced whenever the independent ICC Prosecutor is advised to extend investigations not only to weak or failed States but also to powerful ones in order 'for the ICC's legitimacy to grow over time',[134] ie to select cases with the Court's own interest in mind.

Instead of soothing the serious concerns over an independent international prosecutor who is not accountable to those whom he represents, the argument of 'pragmatic accountability' might actually add to these concerns. Already under the institutional design of the UN ad hoc tribunals, the international prosecutor was dependant on national governments for help in collecting evidence and detaining suspects and the 'pragmatic' control which this affords to some States is, of course, directly related to how much those States have to offer to the prosecutor. This mechanism, again, is far from democratic. And even if it might indeed soothe fears of a 'loose cannon' prosecutor to some extent, it does not answer the need for democratic control, which is the reason for calls for institutional accountability in the first place.

One is thus left with a dilemma. Conventional democratic logic requires safeguards to check the potentially hazardous power of prosecutors. The democratic reasoning behind this has been explored at the beginning of this section. Given the fact that the international prosecutor is necessarily involved in particularly delicate questions of policymaking, this requirement is even significantly amplified at the international level. Yet, since '[h]alfway democratic procedures of legitimation have until now been institutionalized only at the level of the nation-state',[135] there is presently no suitable democratic structure available to which one could subject the international prosecutor. The UN Security Council is not a democratic body and other models of institutional oversight by a forum of States are hardly more democratic nor are they capable of exercising a gubernatorial function. The alternative of releasing the prosecutor into complete independence, on the other hand, misses the goal of democratic accountability entirely.

Governance, Order and the International Criminal Court: Between Realpolitik and a Cosmopolitan Court (Oxford, Oxford University Press, 2009) 114.

[133] ibid 124.
[134] ibid 107.
[135] Habermas, *The Divided West* (n 121) 139.

If this situation is unpleasing, it is at least not novel: how to fulfil democratic standards on an international scale is one of the big unsolved problems of international law at the present stage of legal development.[136] Perhaps it is some solace that international criminal justice is not alone with this flaw.

Frequent calls for a reform of the UN Charter, which to date is seen as a rather imperfect 'world constitution', are evidence to this. It is hardly surprising that there is no perfect solution for this general problem in the special case of international criminal justice. At the same time, it is particularly regrettable and problematic in this special case since an instrument as sharp as an international criminal court really is in particular need of democratic legitimacy. This chapter, in the end, does not pretend to offer a solution – merely, it is hoped to have highlighted the problems which arise when one considers how to design an institution of international criminal justice. An honest acknowledgement of these problems is necessary in order to fairly analyse the political debates around the question of how to design international tribunals. These debates will be the focus of the upcoming historical chapters of this book, mostly in chapter four and chapter five (dealing with the UN ad hoc tribunals and the ICC respectively).

7. CONCLUSION

The basic political analysis in this chapter has lead to a clear and familiar answer, yet the normative analysis leaves us with a rather unpleasing, paradoxical situation.

The strongest social and political impact which a court of international criminal justice can (usually) realistically make is through its authoritatively pronouncing the 'historical truth' of a conflict, most notably in respect of the question which party to the conflict bears which portion of responsibility for atrocities.[137] In practice, this portrayal of 'truth' is communicated primarily through the court's representative selection of cases for trial. Out of the hundreds, if not thousands of potential cases within an international tribunal's reach, only very few can be chosen[138] and it is widely accepted that the proportions in the dock should then be representative of a wider 'truth'.[139] A court which places nine Serbs and only one Croat on trial sends an entirely different historical message to a court which places one Serb and nine Croats on trial. However, who decides which selection is fairer? It is impossible, even in theory, to escape the

[136] von Bogdandy, 'Globalization and Europe' (n 121).
[137] See above section one.
[138] See above section two.
[139] See above section three.

difficulties resulting from the fact that historical narrations are always dependant on a particular cultural and normative mindset[140] and the sensitive policy choice is, in practice, ultimately left almost entirely to the prosecutor with very little effective control for judges.[141] This leads us to the first conclusions of chapter one: the prosecutor is the central policy-maker with regard to the function of international criminal justice as a 'referee' between fiercely opposed historical narratives. Hence, to influence this prosecutor should be in the power political interest of any political actor concerned.

The upcoming chapters will examine the relevance of this interest in Germany's politics of international criminal justice. What role did Germany's interest in particular historical narratives play in defining the official political position vis-à-vis international criminal justice? And what role, if any, did Germany's own chances at influencing prosecutorial policies play in defining whether Germany opposed or supported new tribunals? As explained in the Introduction to this book, there is a sense that Germany's 1990s turn towards a proactive role in international law was driven purely by values and not interests. On the basis of the analysis undertaken in chapter one, this book sets out to examine this common assumption more closely.

On a normative level, however, what conclusions can we draw from the analysis undertaken above? Is the desire by political stakeholders to gain influence or control over the prosecutor condemnable? Is there anything sinister about a State actor aiming for influence over the historical narratives produced here? The answer here, as shown above,[142] is more difficult. While a State actor will typically have a *self*-interest in defending its own narrative of 'truth', the pursuit of this interest only gives reason to embarrassment insofar as that narrative of 'truth' is not held in good faith – aside from that, the protection of 'truth' from distortion surely is nothing which even the most liberal of democracies would need to hide. It is important to keep this in mind.

A second normative question also arises from the aforementioned fact that the international prosecutor has the power to strengthen one historical narrative and weaken another. Should the prosecutor, who is vested with such power, be subjected to some form of checks and balances? Or in other words, do States have a democratically legitimate right to pursue their interest in controlling the prosecutor? While there is a common understanding today among all democracies that prosecutors should indeed be subjected to some form of democratic accountability,[143] the opinions on how to best integrate the *international* prosecutor into a

[140] See above section four.
[141] See above section five.
[142] See above section one.
[143] See above section six.

system of checks and balances are diverse. This chapter has brought no real answer to the question to whose control the prosecutor should ideally be subjected. Rather, it has highlighted a regrettable dilemma. Two possible alternatives, which both have their advocates, are equally flawed from a democratic perspective, control of the international prosecutor by the UN Security Council is not democratic. On the other hand, to simply leave the prosecutor independent of all outside control just means that democratic accountability is not achieved at all.

Finally, it is remarkable that State actors at present nonetheless seem to have very clear preferences in this normative 'accountability v independence' debate. This has become practical in the creation of the ICC and is therefore illuminated in more concrete terms in chapter five, which explores Germany's role in the creation of the ICC. Germany was one of the most outspoken advocates of prosecutorial independence at that time. It will be interesting, in chapter five, to see whether any interplay between this normative position and the particular political interests of Germany (and its allies in this debate) can be identified.

2

German Objections to the Nuremberg Trials after 1949

COMPARED TO MANY later tribunals, the practical opportunities to select representative cases for a certain narrative of 'historical truth' at Nuremberg were excellent: with high-level perpetrators from virtually every part of the Nazi system apprehended and with no further military risk for the Allied Forces standing in the way, the International Military Tribunal (IMT) was able to select cases at relative liberty. Amidst the smoking rubble of Europe, the IMT seized this chance to communicate an understandable narrative on 'historical truth' to the world: the groups most responsible for the devastation were represented to audiences by a carefully selected, very small group of high-level Nazi officials which the IMT placed in the dock with the charges against them being kept remarkably focussed and concise.

Germany's initial role at this stage is, of course, easily described: while the narrative conveyed through the prosecution's selection of cases was decided upon almost directly by the four Allied Powers, Germany, after its defeat, was not afforded any chance at influencing prosecutorial policies. However, in the years after Nuremberg, West German policymakers and legal scholars set out to challenge the authority of the IMT's narration of the war through a number of legal arguments.

These revisionist attempts to rebut the Nuremberg narrative are the focus of this chapter. They are remarkable not only because of their clear interplay between law and politics, but also because this initial, harsh criticism of the IMT in Germany would shape – and in some respects even sharpen – German understanding of international criminal justice for decades.

1. THE ALLIES IN CONTROL

While some commentators today still debate whether the IMT can be classified as an international or merely a multinational court,[1] there is no

[1] For example, Robert Cryer, *Prosecuting International Crimes* (Cambridge, Cambridge University Press, 2005) 38f, argues that a truly 'international' character of the IMT is evidenced by the fact that the four Allied Powers were later joined by 19 smaller States

reasonable disagreement that the power to select cases at Nuremberg lay exclusively with 'four national delegations'.[2] All IMT Prosecutors were hand-picked by their respective governments and, while relatively independent from the Allied Control Council that governed Germany after its capitulation,[3] received political guidance directly from their respective governments, which is why William Schabas notes that '[t]o be entirely accurate, these were not "independent" prosecutors but rather representatives of their own governments'.[4] According to Telford Taylor, deputy to the US Chief Prosecutor at Nuremberg, the Soviet Chief Prosecutor regularly responded to the requests of his IMT colleagues by promising 'to call Moscow';[5] the British prosecution team's 'reports to the Foreign Office enabled that august ministry to assert its influence';[6] and France's Chief Prosecutor was an active politician who spent most of the trial time absent in France and left the IMT entirely in 1946 in order to become a cabinet minister in Paris.[7]

Taylor claims that the US prosecution team was the only exception, receiving no official guidance or pressure from Washington.[8] However, a recent study shows how US government intelligence agents were integrated into the US prosecution team up to its highest levels in order to ensure that those Nazis who had cooperated with US forces in the final months of the war would be shielded from prosecution.[9] Also, as Gary Bass has shown,[10] US government negotiators at the pre-trial stage had already shaped the cases presented at Nuremberg to a degree unmatched by any of the other Allies.

2. ALLIED PRIORITIES: SHAPING THE HISTORICAL NARRATIVE

It is the result of no small effort that 'sixty years later, the Nuremberg judgement remains a fixed anchor of our children's education.'[11] In order

recognising the London Charter. For a more critical analysis see Antonio Cassese, *International Criminal Law* (Oxford, Oxford University Press, 2008) 332; also Heiko Ahlbrecht, *Geschichte der völkerrechtlichen Strafgerichtsbarkeit im 20. Jahrhundert* (Baden-Baden, Nomos, 1999) 70.

[2] This expression is used by Telford Taylor, *The Anatomy of the Nuremberg Trials* (Boston, Back Bay Books, 1992) 208.

[3] Cryer, *Prosecuting International Crimes* (n 1) 39.

[4] William A Schabas, 'Prosecutorial Discretion v. Judicial Activism at the International Criminal Court' (2008) 6 *Journal of International Criminal Justice* 732.

[5] Taylor, *The Anatomy of the Nuremberg Trials* (n 2) 209.

[6] ibid 213.

[7] ibid 212.

[8] ibid 216.

[9] Michael Salter, *Nazi War Crimes, US Intelligence and Selective Prosecution at Nuremberg* (New York, Routledge-Cavendish, 2007).

[10] Gary J Bass, *Stay the Hand of Vengeance* (Princeton, Princeton University Press, 2000) 176f.

[11] Mark A Drumbl, *Atrocity, Punishment, and International Law* (Cambridge, Cambridge University Press, 2007) 175.

to convey the IMT's narrative to the world, the Allies tore down a wall of the main courtroom of Nuremberg's *Justizpalast* to seat the international press, the trials were broadcast around the world[12] and, in court, the stage was set for an exploration not only of individual guilt but also of historical dimensions.

A Tribunal to 'Bring Home' a Message

The chance to illustrate a particular historical narrative had been one of the most important political reasons to hold trials at Nuremberg in the first place. To prosecute Nazi war criminals in a court of law instead of going through with the popular notion[13] that the 'worst of the worst' should be summarily executed was an initiative of the United States, with the United Kingdom and the Soviet Union following only grudgingly at first[14] and with France playing hardly any part at all. To these western democracies, there had, of course, been a compelling liberal argument in favour of avoiding summary executions all along, which is rightly highlighted by numerous authors: 'If we stand for all the things we've been saying we stand for, we can hardly refuse to make an inquiry [into individual guilt]', stated Robert Jackson, the US Supreme Court Judge who would later become the US Chief Prosecutor at the IMT.[15]

Even within the US government, however, the political decision whether or not to follow Jackson's approach was very close.[16] The opinion promoted by then Treasury Secretary Henry Morgenthau Jr that executing Nazi leaders without trial would be more helpful in 'preventing World War III'[17] than any softer approach, was actually the prevailing opinion within the United States until September 1944.[18] It was only after the US government overturned Morgenthau's plan and decided in October 1944 to side instead with Jackson and hold a tribunal that Stalin also swayed, surprisingly energetically, in favour of a judicial process, baffling

[12] This is described in detail by Gerhard Stuby, 'Nürnberg 1945/46: Von der Harmlosigkeit des Gedenkens' (2006) *Blätter für deutsche und internationale Politik* 94; also Norbert Frei, 'Der Nürnberger Prozeß und die Deutschen' in Wolfram Wette and Gerd R Überschär (eds), *Kriegsverbrechen im 20. Jahrhundert* (2001) 480.

[13] For surveys of contemporary public opinion in the United States and Britain, see Bass, *Stay the Hand* (n 10) 160f and 183f.

[14] For Britain's initial reservations in light of the negative experiences with the Leipzig trials after World War I, see Arieh J Kochavi, *Prelude to Nuremberg* (Chapel Hill, University of North Carolina Press, 1998).

[15] Quoted in the *Morgenthau Diary* (18 May 1945) vol 2, 1508.

[16] Bass, *Stay the Hand* (n 10), 205.

[17] Morgenthau to Roosevelt, in *Morgenthau Diary*, vol 1, 631f, quoted in ibid 168.

[18] For a vivid account of the 'collapse of the Morgenthau Plan' in September 1944, see ibid 166–69.

Churchill.[19] The merit of Jackson's liberal argument is clear. However, was this really what made the large block of less liberally-inclined policymakers within the Allied governments decide to side with Jackson in 1944?

Stalin was certainly not inclined to soften his position on Nazi war criminals purely on the grounds of Jackson's liberal idealism – even less so than Churchill. As Gary Bass rightly observes, '[P]ower need not have paid reason the tribute of trials at Nuremberg.'[20] Remarkably, 'power' was ultimately persuaded nonetheless and there is some indication that it was not the pure quality of Jackson's liberal argument which convinced Stalin, Churchill or Morgenthau to allow Jackson to go ahead. For Stalin, war crimes trials became interesting for their expressive value: the distinction between moral right and wrong and not merely between the obvious victory and defeat was a central point to make.[21] A trial can achieve something that a summary execution cannot.

The same idea also began to appeal to the three western Allies. In the words of Henry Stimson, then US Secretary of War, a trial would 'bring home to the German people' not only the simple fact of the defeat of their regime but also 'the *wrong*doing done in their name' (emphasis added).[22] If Nazi war criminals were to be punished without trial, 'Germany will simply have lost another war', argued Murray Bernays, one of the proponents of Nuremberg within the US government, in September 1944. 'The German people will not know the barbarians they have supported, nor will they have any understanding of the criminal character of their conduct and the world's judgement upon it.'[23]

The advantage of clarifying 'historical truth' was thus one which appealed to power politicians especially.[24] In a June 1945 memorandum to Robert Jackson, Telford Taylor described what he considered to be the 'most important' goal of these trials besides demonstrating Allied unity after the war:

> To give meaning to the war against Germany. To validate the casualties we have suffered and the destruction and casualties we have caused. To . . . make the war meaningful and valid for the people of the Allied Nations and, it is not beyond hope, for at least some people of the Axis Nations.[25]

[19] ibid 196.
[20] ibid 180.
[21] ibid 202.
[22] Bradley F Smith, *The American Road to Nuremberg* (Stanford, Hoover Institution Press, 1982) 23.
[23] Memorandum by Murray Bernays, Colonel in the US War Department, 'Trial of European War Criminals' (15 September 1944). Quoted in ibid 26.
[24] This point is somewhat missed by Paul Betts, 'Germany, International Justice and the Twentieth Century' (2005) 17 *History & Memory* who notes at 59: 'the Americans . . . and certain key figures within the British Foreign Office convinced their allies about the virtues of avoiding vengeful retribution, and that trying Nazi leaders was the most fair way to dispense lasting justice'.
[25] Compare Taylor, *The Anatomy of the Nuremberg Trials* (n 2), 50.

Selecting Illustrative Defendants

In the trial of major war criminals, the 24 accused were carefully selected to represent the different parts of Germany's elite made responsible for the Nazi regime's crimes.[26] For example, after extensive debates among the IMT Prosecutors, it was decided that the Nazi's financiers and industrial leadership should be placed in the dock as well, represented by one banker and one industrialist. Gustav Krupp, the Reich's largest arms tycoon, was selected as the one person to exemplify the guilt of all German industrialists who had armed and funded the Nazi regime.[27] These representative proportions in the dock were deemed so important that, after Gustav Krupp fell ill, it was even considered by the prosecution to simply replace the indictee with another, equally heavily implicated industrialist: his son Alfried.[28]

This motion by the prosecution to amend the indictment came too late however, leaving Alfried Krupp a 'very lucky man' in Telford Taylor's words.[29] This incident was not only regrettable for the prosecution because Gustav Krupp ended up with impunity but also – and even to a much larger extent – because the prosecution had thereby lost its chance to effectively illustrate its theory of Germany's industry as the 'Third Pillar' of the Nazi Regime (along with the Nazi Party itself and the *Wehrmacht*) in this first and most widely publicised IMT trial.[30] Germany's industrialists would not be in the dock as part of the 'major war criminals' and only appeared in later trials with less symbolic value.

Defendants were again selected representatively for a narrative in the series of 12 subsequent IMT trials which highlighted the complicity of, inter alia, Germany's military, judicial, medical, industrial and administrative elites. Particularly in the trials of the industrial and administrative elites, individual cases were presented to the audience as examples for a larger point to make.[31] As one of Taylor's advisers in an August 1946 memorandum noted:

> [I]t is true that 'German industry and finance' as an abstract is not indictable. But to try separately the largest German corporations and their top executives

[26] For insights into the selection process, see ibid 85 and 89f.

[27] ibid 81.

[28] Compare ibid 151–61.

[29] ibid 94.

[30] See, eg Walter T Schonfeld, *Nazi Madness* (London, Minerva, 2000) 24, regretting a 'gaping hole in the defendants' row'.

[31] For criticism of that strategy, see, eg Frank Gausmann, 'Vergangenheitsbewältigung durch Recht? Kritische Anmerkungen zur Anklagestrategie in den Nürnberger Industriellenprozessen' in Helia-Verena Daubach (ed), *Leipzig – Nürnberg – Den Haag: Neue Fragestellungen und Forschungen zum Verhältnis von Menschenrechtsverbrechen justizieller Säuberung und Völkerstrafrecht* (Düsseldorf, Justizministerium des Landes NRW, 2008).

> without, nevertheless, demonstrating at some point in each trial how German private and semi-public economic organizations consciously and willingly became criminalized is to ignore the immense importance of bringing that ultimate historic fact to the notice of the world.[32]

In his opening statement at the trial against the Nazis' administrative elite, Taylor explained that this group of persons would be symbolised by an exemplary geographic focus on the few bureaucrats seated in Berlin's *Wilhelmstraße*[33] – the individual indictees from this street represented an otherwise rather erratic selection.

Prioritising between Crimes

With the stage thus set, which historical crimes did the IMT aim to illuminate? It has been described as 'one of the great ironies of Nuremberg's legacy'[34] that the IMT is today often remembered as the site of the Holocaust trials. In fact, the charge which the Prosecution at Nuremberg focussed on primarily was Germany's waging a war of aggression ('crimes against peace'). The central message communicated at Nuremberg was thus: World War II had not been 'simply another war' (Bernays) between competing powers, but rather a crime perpetrated by one nation and a justified effort by several other nations to stop it.

In theory, the legal framework of the IMT would have allowed the prosecution to give 'two distinct groups a forum to express outrage: the international community and the actual individual survivors.'[35] However, Mark Drumbl rightly notes that 'these two groups are not necessarily allied'.[36] The Nuremberg IMT is a first and rather clear example of how narrative interests, even between different parts of the group of 'individual survivors', can be highly diverse. Soviet, American and British forces had liberated Auschwitz, Dachau and Bergen-Belsen. They had seen the monstrous atrocities committed there and had realised the desires of the individual survivors there for their plight to be recognised publicly. Yet during the negotiations at the 1945 London Conference, where a statute for the IMT was drawn up, the negotiators decided to prioritise the plight of the survivors back in the United Kingdom, the United States and the Soviet Union. Some eastern European States protested. However, the United States argued strongly in favour of concentrating on Germany's illegal war as such, against which US troops had fought, while 'the other

[32] Quoted in ibid 59f.
[33] See US Government Printing Office (ed), *Trials of War Criminals before the Nuremberg Military Tribunals under Control Council Law No. 10*, vol. XII (1949), 138.
[34] Bass, *Stay the Hand* (n 10) 148.
[35] Drumbl, *Atrocity, Punishment and International Law* (n 11) 3.
[36] ibid.

atrocities' (Jackson)[37] should be given less priority. As Robert Jackson explained:

> Without boring you too much, I will tell you why we are interested in that. It is probably difficult for those of you who have lived under the immediate attack of the Nazis to appreciate the different public psychology that those of us who were in the American Government dealt with. Our American population is at least 3,000 miles from the scene. Germany did not attack or invade the United States in violation of any treaty with us. The thing that led us to take sides in this war was that we regarded Germany's resort to war as illegal from its outset, as an illegitimate attack on the international peace and order.[38]

Narrative Interests of Four Governments

The Soviet Union and the United Kingdom added their own 'public psychologies' to these considerations. The United Kingdom, which had fought Hitler since 1939 and had suffered firebombings, pushed for attention to be given to war crimes committed against British citizens.[39] The Soviet Union took great care to assure that the IMT would portray Hitler's and Stalin's regimes as strict military and moral opposites, averting, for instance, any mention of the August 1939 Hitler-Stalin Pact to partition Poland.[40]

Public pressure in the United States and the United Kingdom did ultimately call for the Holocaust to be included into the Nuremberg prosecution case.[41] However, the respective charges remained peripheral throughout the major war criminals trial.[42] Each of the Allies had fought Nazi Germany from a different position, developing, to some extent, different domestic narratives to justify their war efforts – and in them, the Holocaust had not played a central role to anyone. For the same reason, the Nazis' collaborator regimes in France and eastern Europe – which had helped facilitate the Holocaust but had not pursued aggressive expansionist strategies themselves – were not illuminated at all.[43] Moreover, any attention to allegations that the Allied Forces had committed war crimes

[37] Robert Jackson (19 July 1945). Quoted in Bass, *Stay the Hand* (n 10) 177.

[38] Quoted in ibid 176.

[39] ibid 191–94.

[40] Compare ibid 200. After allegations regarding the Soviet massacre of Polish officers at the Katyn forest became public, the Soviet prosecution team at Nuremberg even explicitly laid the blame on Germany. Compare ibid 201; also Payam Akhavan, 'Justice in The Hague, Peace in the Former Yugoslavia? A Commentary on the United Nations War Crimes Tribunal' (1998) 20 *Human Rights Quarterly* 782.

[41] Bass, *Stay the Hand* (n 10) 178–80.

[42] Weinke, '"Von Nürnberg nach Den Haag"?' in Helia-Verena Daubach (ed), *Leipzig – Nürnberg – Den Haag* (n 31) 28; Betts, 'Germany, International Justice and the Twentieth Century' (n 24) 61.

[43] See Weinke, '"Von Nürnberg nach Den Haag"?' (n 42) 25.

themselves would only have blurred this central message or would even have encouraged those in Germany and elsewhere who advocated an entirely different view of what had transpired in the past six years.

3. GERMANY AND THE *NULLUM CRIMEN* DEBATE

The Nuremberg Trials were initially treated with caution by German legal and political commentators. Between 1946 and 1948, there was even a group of favourably inclined scholars surrounding Gustav Radbruch, the eminent Social Democrat who had briefly served as Germany's Minister of Justice in the 1920s, whose academic career had been stopped abruptly by the Nazis[44] and who now attempted to communicate the historical value of Nuremberg to broader audiences in Germany.[45] However, Radbruch's journal did not survive for long[46] and Radbruch died unexpectedly in 1949. Whereas East Germany soon departed on a separate path in respect to opinions on the Nuremberg IMT,[47] the range of published opinions in West Germany soon became much narrower and much less favourable to the IMT.

Resorting to Rigorous Legal Positivism

In the 1950s, numerous judges and law professors who had built a career under the Nazis were returning to their former professions[48] and the West

[44] Compare eg Horst Dreier, 'Gustav Radbruch und die Mauerschützen' (1997) *JuristenZeitung* 422f.

[45] Ingo Müller, 'Nürnberg und die deutschen Juristen' in Rainer Eisfeld (ed), *Gegen Barbarei: Essays Robert M. W. Kempner zu Ehren* (1989) 262–64; Susanne Jung, *Die Rechtsprobleme der Nürnberger Prozesse* (Tübingen, Mohr, 1992) 156–58.

[46] Müller, 'Nürnberg und die deutschen Juristen' (n 45) 264.

[47] The discourse in East Germany was notably more favourable to the IMT, compare Jung, *Die Rechtsprobleme der Nürnberger Prozesse* (n 45) 2, also Gerhard Werle, 'Von der Ablehnung zur MitgestaltungDeutschland und das Völkerstrafrecht' in Pierre-Marie Dupuy and others (eds), *Common Values in International Law: Essays in Honour of Christian Tomuschat* (Kehl, NP Engel Verlag, 2006) 658–61. Some authors there openly criticised West Germany's attitude as revisionist, compare for instance Stefan Zimmermann, 'Die strafrechtliche "Bewältigung" der deutschen Diktaturen' (1996) *Juristische Schulung* 865–71. This chapter's exclusive focus on West Germany is not to disregard this. However, East German academic and political traditions were abruptly discontinued after the reunification with West Germany in 1990, and it is almost exclusively the West German discourse out of which *current* positions have evolved. For an understanding of Germany's current political position, which this book aims to achieve, a view to West Germany's position after the war is, hence, more indicative.

[48] See Ingo Müller, *Furchtbare Juristen* (Munich, Droemer Knaur, 1989). Specifically for the personnel of West Germany's judiciary, historians have coined the term of near complete 'restauration', see Michael Stolleis, 'Rechtsordnung und Justizpolitik 1945–1949' in Norbert Horn and Helmut Coing (eds), *Europäisches Rechtsdenken in Geschichte und Gegenwart: Festschrift für Helmut Coing zum 70. Geburtstag* (Munich, Beck, 1982); also Hans Wrobel, *Verurteilt zur Demokratie* (Heidelberg, Decker & Müller, 1989).

German debate on Nuremberg was rapidly dominated by aggressive Nuremberg defence attorneys such as Otto Kranzbühler[49] and by sceptical legal scholars.[50] West German policymakers and scholars began to challenge the legitimacy of the IMT and to voice harsh criticism of its jurisprudence after only a brief period of hesitance – and this argumentative position, which shows some remarkable interplay between legal and historical reasoning, would lose little of its edge for almost four decades.[51]

For the most part, legal criticism of the IMT revolved around two lines of argument. Firstly, this was the claim that the IMT had applied its jurisdiction retroactively, thus violating the principle of *nullum crimen, nulla poena sine lege*. This is the focus of this section. Secondly, claims were made that the Tribunal's selection of cases was not fair to 'historical truth', frequently expressed through invocations of *tu quoque*. This is the focus of the next section.

Already in November 1945, the defence at Nuremberg had argued that the prosecution of individuals for acts of State constituted a 'revolution',[52] and thus a violation of the *nullum crimen* principle,[53] thus rejecting the very essence of international criminal law on the grounds of strict domestic legal positivism.[54] The IMT responded that, as a principle of material justice, *nullum crimen* could not shield the accused at Nuremberg from prosecution since they had known that they were violating international law.[55]

Radbruch, who argued in support of Nuremberg, famously added a philosophical argument. According to Radbruch, courts need not consider the Nazi's own laws, which would exculpate Nazi crimes domestically, to be 'law' at all. Where the degree of injustice in these domestic laws was 'manifest' and 'unbearable' to such an extreme extent, Radbruch argued that these laws simply represented 'non-law' and that they should not bind any judge.[56] Initially, this argument was not well received in Germany, as will be shown below. German academia mostly clung to a strongly positivist view that allowed for the IMT to be described as legally illegitimate.

[49] Stuby, 'Nürnberg 1945/46' (n 12) 95.

[50] Jung, *Die Rechtsprobleme der Nürnberger Prozesse* (n 45) 3f lists a total of 12 legal monographs harshly critical of the IMT published by members of Nuremberg defence teams between 1947 and 1953, and a 'flood' of university dissertations in the 1950s which came to their support.

[51] See Werle, 'Deutschland und das Völkerstrafrecht' (n 47) 660.

[52] See Otto Kranzbühler, 'Nürnberg als Rechtsproblem' in Hermann Jahrreiß (ed), *Um Recht und Gerechtigkeit: Festgabe für Erich Kaufmann zu seinem 70. Geburtstage* (Kohlhammer, Stuttgart, 1950) 219.

[53] Joint Defence Motion (19 November 1945), reprinted in Herbert Kraus, *Gerichtstag in Nürnberg* (Hamburg, Gesetz-und-Recht-Verlag, 1947).

[54] Ahlbrecht, *Geschichte der völkerrechtlichen Strafgerichtsbarkeit* (n 1) 79; Jung, *Die Rechtsprobleme der Nürnberger Prozesse* (n 45) 148f.

[55] Ahlbrecht, *Geschichte der völkerrechtlichen Strafgerichtsbarkeit* (n 1) 75.

[56] Gustav Radbruch, 'Gesetzliches Unrecht und übergesetzliches Recht' (1946) *Süddeutsche Juristenzeitung* 107.

Historical Subtexts: A Bid for the Moral High Ground

Some, mainly international, commentators noted the historical irony in this legal debate. The same legal scholars in Germany who had worked so hard at tearing down the *nullum crimen* principle in its entirety during the years of the Nazi regime[57] were now calling upon exactly that principle in defence of their former regime.[58] Although traditionally positivist,[59] Germany's legal scholarship after 1933 had enthusiastically loosened all constraints on the application of laws by the State. For example, one German professor, who had argued in 1934 that criminal courts should be free to abide to their 'healthy prejudice' and should adjudicate in the spirit of their 'political leadership'[60] rather than within the boundaries of black letter law, was now among the most vocal, suddenly positivist critics of Nuremberg.[61]

West German commentators, no less aware of the historical irony of this debate, turned the argument of their critics around however. Some made a point of likening the traditionally slightly less positivist, more flexible approach of common law jurists in respect of *nullum crimen*[62] with the radical disregard previously practised by the Nazis.[63] The author of a 1955 doctoral thesis on *nullum crimen*, for instance, set out by stating that disregard for this principle was one typical feature of authoritarian regimes that have no qualms about 'removing or incapacitating elements that could endanger them',[64] after which the author went on to elaborate on how the IMT had done exactly this.

The president of the regional appeals court (*Oberlandesgericht*) in Celle, during a debate with Radbruch, even ostensibly warned of 'repeating' the Nazis' mistake of placing considerations of 'justice' above black letter law

[57] In 1935, the Nazis had effectively changed the principle of *nullum crimen, nulla poena sine lege* in § 2 of the German criminal code into *nullum crimen sine poena*. The new § 2 read: 'Any person who commits an act which the law declares to be punishable or which is deserving of penalty according to the fundamental conceptions of the penal law and sound popular feeling, shall be punished.' It was the Allies who revoked this change in 1945. Compare Jung, *Die Rechtsprobleme der Nürnberger Prozesse* (n 45) 155.

[58] See, eg RH Graveson, 'Der Grundsatz nulla poena sine lege und das Kontrollratsgesetz Nr. 10' (1947) *Monatsschrift für Deutsches Recht* 278; also Karl S Bader, 'Zum Nürnberger Urteil' (1946) 1 *Deutsche Rechts-Zeitschrift* 140.

[59] Frank Neubacher, *Kriminologische Grundlagen einer internationalen Strafgerichtsbarkeit* (Tübingen, Mohr Siebeck, 2005) 173f.

[60] See Georg Dahm, 'Das Ermessen des Richters im nationalsozialistischen Strafrecht' (1934) *Deutsches Strafrecht* 90.

[61] See Georg Dahm, *Zur Problematik des Völkerstrafrechts* (Göttingen, Vandenhoeck & Ruprecht, 1956).

[62] Ahlbrecht, *Geschichte der völkerrechtlichen Strafgerichtsbarkeit* (n 1) 391.

[63] For further examples see Jung, *Die Rechtsprobleme der Nürnberger Prozesse* (n 45) 156–69.

[64] Dieter Haass, *'Nulla poena sine lege' im nationalen und internationalen Recht* (Heidelberg, Diss. 1955) 5.

out of political motivations or vengeance.[65] In the same vein, a popular German text book on international law attacked the IMT for having aimed to 'eliminate' the leaders of a defeated State primarily for reasons of 'vengeance'.[66]

This rhetorical figure, which reinforced the theme that the two sides to the war were not so different from one another – whereas the defendants at Nuremberg had apparently already moved on to a virtuous, new rule-of-law position – was also echoed in parliament. When the European Convention on Human Rights was introduced in 1950, its article 7 on the prohibition of retroactive prosecution made an exception to allow for judgments of the Nuremberg type (where an act, although not illegal in black letter law, is outlawed by the laws of all civilised nations). Germany's parliament, however, made a reservation to this qualification,[67] brazenly explaining that Germany had previously suffered from similar disregard for the *nullum crimen* principle under the Nazis.[68] Paradoxically, the legal exculpation of Nazi war crimes, which many German commentators at the time were promoting through legal arguments (not without an eye to their own biographies, one may note) was thus combined with a new claim of moral high ground welcomed by many Germans in the early years after the war.

Historical Subtexts: Impunity as a Matter of 'German Dignity'

This constellation was to have a lasting effect on legal doctrine in West Germany. Assuredly, the legal arguments made by the IMT were not entirely ignored nor was Gustav Radbruch's philosophical argument in support of the IMT. Germany's highest criminal court, the *Bundesgerichtshof*, implicitly referred to Radbruch in 1952, stating that domestic laws that allow for crimes against humanity could not excuse these crimes.[69] However, courts made very little use of the consequent legal possibilities in their hands. Radbruch's idea of manifestly unjust law as non-law was invoked, rather indirectly, only in some cases concerning administrative matters like the expatriation of German Jews. It was never directly used as *ratio decidendi* in criminal cases.[70]

[65] Hodo Hodenberg, 'Zur Anwendung des Kontrollratsgesetzes Nr.10 durch die deutschen Gerichte' (1947) *Süddeutsche Juristenzeitung* 113.

[66] Friedrich Berber, *Lehrbuch des Völkerrechts* (München, Beck, 1960) 259.

[67] Neubacher, *Kriminologische Grundlagen* (n 59) 165.

[68] Bundestags-Drucksache Nr. 3338 (1949) 5.

[69] *Entscheidungen des Bundesgerichtshofs in Strafsachen*, vol 2, 234, 237; also vol 3, 357, 262f. Zimmermann, 'Die strafrechtliche "Bewältigung" der deutschen Diktaturen' (n 47) 866 shows how the court actually adopted Radbruch's words.

[70] Compare Dreier, 'Gustav Radbruch und die Mauerschützen' (n 44) 423f.

Rather, courts would only adjudicate Nazi crimes where these could be described as acts of 'excessive force', exceeding even the Nazi's domestic law at the time. Returning to a long-held positivist tradition, but now also radicalising it to a degree unmatched worldwide,[71] West Germany's legal community took up a rigorous view on the *nullum crimen* principle, which would remain largely unchanged until 1989.[72]

In 1958, the *Bundesgerichtshof* was able to quote a whole series of government statements to illustrate that West Germany had not recognised *any* of the IMT judgments.[73] In addition, giving a brief indication of that legal assertion's political deliberateness, the court pointed to a remark by the recent Minister of Justice (1956–57), Hans-Joachim von Merkatz of the national-conservative *Deutsche Partei* (German Party), who had explained that non-recognition was a matter of 'German dignity'.[74] While the Minister of Justice in 1956 insisted on speaking of 'alleged' German war crimes when referring to judgments of non-German courts,[75] the *Bundesgerichtshof* used the term 'so-called' with regard to German war criminals.[76]

Recent historical analyses have agreed in describing the positivist rigour of post-war German scholarship as a temporary *Sonderweg* (particular path) in legal culture,[77] understandable only against a backdrop of 'political-psychological resentment against the jurisdiction of the victors',[78] 'apologetic tendencies'[79] and, generally, a highly-politicised atmosphere in Germany's legal academia in the post-war years.[80]

[71] Markus Kenntner, 'Der deutsche Sonderweg zum Rückwirkungsverbot: Plädoyer für die Aufgabe eines überholten Verweigerungsdogmas' (1997) *Neue Juristische Wochenschrift* 2298.

[72] Michael Walter, 'Zur Reichweite des Konzeptes Kriminalität: Einige Überlegungen zur "Makrokriminalität" Herbert Jägers' (1993) 25 *Kriminologisches Journal* 119.

[73] *Entscheidungen des Bundesgerichtshofs in Strafsachen*, vol 12, 36, 40f.

[74] ibid. For more, similar statements in parliament see Müller, *Furchtbare Juristen* (n 48) 243. A sociological analysis of the social psychology around the few trials of Nazi war criminals in the 1950s is offered by Anne Klein, 'Mentalität, Massenmord, Moral: Rechts- und Geschichtsverständnis der bundesrepublikanischen Nachkriegsgesellschaft' in Frank Neubacher and Anne Klein (eds), *Vom Recht der Macht zur Macht des Rechts? Interdisziplinäre Beiträge zur Zukunft internationaler Strafgerichte* (Berlin, Duncker & Humblot, 2006) 176.

[75] *Entscheidungen des Bundesgerichtshofs in Strafsachen*, vol 12, 36, 41f.

[76] ibid 40f.

[77] Neubacher, *Kriminologische Grundlagen* (n 59) 160f; Claus Kreß, 'Versailles – Nürnberg – Den Haag: Deutschland und das Völkerstrafrecht' (2006) 61 *JuristenZeitung* 986; Werle, *'Deutschland und das Völkerstrafrecht'* (n 47) 125.

[78] Jung, *Die Rechtsprobleme der Nürnberger Prozesse* (n 45) 89.

[79] Neubacher, *Kriminologische Grundlagen* (n 59) 162; also Stuby, 'Nürnberg 1945/46' (n 12) 97.

[80] Norbert Frei, *Adenauer's Germany and the Nazi Past* (New York, Columbia University Press, 2002).

Hans-Heinrich Jescheck: A Lone Dissenting Opinion

Somewhat aside from the positivist rigour of mainstream legal academia in post-war West Germany, a line of notably milder criticism in respect of *nullum crimen* also began to grow. Unlike the jurists who had personally been active in Nazi courts or Nuremberg defence teams, some younger jurists were willing to reassess. The most influential protagonist here was Hans-Heinrich Jescheck, a young scholar who published the first comprehensive study on international criminal law in the German language in 1952. His book, on the accountability of State organs under international criminal law,[81] was edited by three professors heavily involved in the Nazi regime[82] and earned Jescheck an appointment as professor in Freiburg in 1954. Where Jescheck argued in cautious defence of the Nuremberg principles, support came from Wilhelm Grewe, a conservative who had kept his university position throughout the Nazi regime and had become the international law adviser to West Germany's Foreign Office in the 1950s.[83]

On the one hand, both Jescheck and Grewe agreed with the Nuremberg defence attorneys that the charge of 'crimes against peace' at Nuremberg had violated *nullum crimen*.[84] Of course, they did not go as far as the Nuremberg defence attorney Otto Kranzbühler, who had brazenly argued that the only crime against peace had been the United States' intervention in Europe,[85] whilst Germany's attack on the Soviet Union had apparently represented an 'act of defence'.[86] Nonetheless, Jescheck did not see any criminal guilt in Germany's role as an aggressor.[87] Grewe would later call this charge a 'miscarriage of justice' to which Rudolf Hess, Hitler's Party Deputy, had fallen 'victim'.[88]

[81] Hans-Heinrich Jescheck, *Die Verantwortlichkeit der Staatsorgane nach Völkerstrafrecht* (Bonn, Röhrscheid, 1952).

[82] Edmund Mezger had been one of the Nazi regime's most prominent criminal law professors, suggesting to 'exterminate criminal lineages through measures of racial hygiene' in 1944: Edmund Mezger, *Kriminalpolitik und ihre kriminologischen Grundlagen* (Stuttgart, Enke, 1944) 26. Nonetheless, he continued his career at the University of Munich after 1948. Erich Schwinge was the leading commentator on Nazi military law, which was the basis for tens of thousands of executions, and a military judge before returning to the University of Marburg in 1948. Adolf Schönke was one of the leading commentators on criminal law during the Nazi regime, and did not lose his position at the University of Freiburg at any time.

[83] Müller, 'Nürnberg und die deutschen Juristen' (n 45) 273f.

[84] Wilhelm Grewe and Otto Küster, *Nürnberg als Rechtsfrage* (Stuttgart, Klett, 1947) 31 and 45; Jescheck, *Die Verantwortlichkeit der Staatsorgane* (n 81) 414.

[85] Kranzbühler, 'Nürnberg als Rechtsproblem' (n 52) 229.

[86] ibid 227.

[87] Jescheck, Die Verantwortlichkeit der Staatsorgane (n 81) 414.

[88] Wilhelm Grewe, 'Rückblick auf Nürnberg' in Kay Hailbronner (ed), *Staat und Völkerrechtsordnung: Festschrift für Karl Doehring* (Berlin, Springer, 1989) 248. Stuby, 'Nürnberg 1945/46' (n 12) 97 considers Grewe a good representative of the German legal mainstream of his time.

On the other hand however, Jescheck and Grewe argued that the same could not be said about charges of war crimes and crimes against humanity.[89] These were seen as legitimate in principle. Jescheck noted Nuremberg's 'accomplishment' of having 'clearly confirmed' the principle that individuals could be held criminally accountable for war crimes under international law and for crimes against humanity under national law: 'Also, there is nothing wrong with bringing high-level or top-level state officials to justice on this basis.'[90]

With this relative openness, Jescheck would remain the only voice of influence in German academia to pursue an interest in the *future* of international criminal law for several years.[91] By the end of the 1950s, the very vocal group of Nuremberg defence attorneys had largely spoken their mind; the older generation of professors was largely content with placing their protest of the IMT on the record, usually in the form of slim passages in their respective text books; and West Germany's judiciary continued to apply a strictly positivist, and thus effectively apologetic, view on war crimes and Holocaust cases.[92] Jescheck went on to build an academic career as director of the Max Planck Institute for Foreign and International Criminal Law in Freiburg from 1954 to 1982,[93] during which time he would mentor numerous younger scholars.

4. GERMANY AND THE *TU QUOQUE* DEBATE

As much as Jescheck's milder approach to *nullum crimen* distinguished him from many contemporaries, it is important to note what Jescheck *did not* disagree with. The furthest that Jescheck would go in defence of the IMT was that the Tribunal had (partly) got the law right – but the history wrong. 'Of course, a defeated party which has burdened itself with grave guilt will have to be cautious before reproaching others', noted Jescheck, who, in devoting only three pages of his 420-page monograph to the fairness of the Nuremberg IMT's selection policy to 'historical truth', was clearly one of the more moderate voices in this respect. However, with that, the degree of historical revisionism laid out in those three pages and

[89] Jescheck, *Die Verantwortlichkeit der Staatsorgane* (n 81) 241f.

[90] ibid 416.

[91] Compare the appraisals by Otto Triffterer, 'Hans-Heinrich Jeschecks Einfluss auf die Entwicklung des Völkerstrafrechts und auf dessen Durchsetzung' (2004) 116 *Zeitschrift für die gesamte Strafrechtswissenschaft*; Otto Triffterer, 'Völkerstrafrecht im Wandel?' in Theo Vogler (ed), *Festschrift für Hans-Heinrich Jescheck zum 70. Geburtstag* (Berlin 1985); see also Claus Kreß, 'Versailles – Nuremberg – The Hague: Germany and International Criminal Law' (2006) 40 *The International Lawyer* 27f.

[92] For criticism, see Gerhard Werle and Thomas Wandres, *Auschwitz vor Gericht* (Munich, CH Beck, 1995) 28f, 212f.

[93] Until 1966, this had been named the Institute for Foreign and International Criminal Law.

in other passages of Jescheck's 1952 monograph is quite indicative of how widespread these views actually were within Germany's legal community at the time.

Equating the Crimes of 'Both Sides'

Regarding the Wehrmacht's *Vernichtungskrieg* (war of extermination) against the peoples of eastern Europe and the Balkans, Jescheck claimed in 1952 that 'both sides' had 'engaged in a war of ideologies without any trace of mercy'.[94] This not only distracted from the historical proportions, but also flatly ignored the fact that the apparent ideology of one side had actually consisted primarily in defending itself against a foreign aggressor and oppressor.

Such criticism of the IMT's apparent unfairness to 'historical truth' was frequently expressed in invocations of *tu quoque*.[95] This legal objection relies on the fact that both sides of a dispute have committed the same violation. The underlying suggestion that the atrocities of Nazi Germany had not been shocking beyond reasonable comparison but that they had rather been part of a somewhat ubiquitous phenomenon to which all sides to the war had fallen victim to some extent was not only made by some West German historians[96] but also frequently echoed within the legal debate. As noted in the above section, the only crimes which Jescheck was willing to acknowledge legally were crimes committed within the war (violations of *ius in bello*) – and these, he claimed, had simply been committed on all sides. 'However, it is unacceptable to have double standards applied to situations *that are exactly identical*' (emphasis added),[97] Jescheck wrote.

Understating German War Crimes

Claus Kreß ascribes Jescheck's early support for the idea of international criminal law to the 'fresh impression of press reports about German concentration camps which Jescheck had heard during his time as prisoner of war in France'.[98] Indeed, Jescheck considered Holocaust crimes punisha-

[94] Jescheck, *Die Verantwortlichkeit der Staatsorgane* (n 81) 279.

[95] For summaries of the debate see Ahlbrecht, *Geschichte der völkerrechtlichen Strafgerichtsbarkeit* (n 1) 82 and Jung, *Die Rechtsprobleme der Nürnberger Prozesse* (n 45) 91.

[96] See, eg Gerhard Brennecke, *Die Nürnberger Geschichtsentstellung* (Tübingen, Verlag der Deutschen Hochschullehrer-Zeitung, 1970) and Werner Maser, *Nürnberg* (Düsseldorf, Econ, 1977; republished in 2005).

[97] Jescheck, *Die Verantwortlichkeit der Staatsorgane* (n 81) 279.

[98] Kreß, 'Versailles – Nuremberg – The Hague' (n 91) 27.

ble, calling this a question of legal 'conscience'.[99] Yet it is also true that, with regard to war crimes committed by the Wehrmacht in whose ranks Jescheck had served, Jescheck was a lot more lenient, criticising the law applied by the IMT as too strict[100] and defending 'those military leaders of our nation to whom grave injustice has been done' by the IMT.[101]

In his 1952 professorial thesis, Jescheck outlined what he considered a historically fairer prosecution policy: no aggression charges against Germany, only scaled-down war crimes charges against German forces and no trials for crimes against humanity perpetrated against German Jews in the international forum at all.[102] Undoubtedly, the historical message sent out by such a tribunal would have been quite different. Jescheck suggested that a more neutral tribunal, 'a court of the United Nations . . . with renowned experts in criminal law and international law including neutral parties and Germans as judges',[103] would have been more partial to sharing this view. By contrast, the IMT was characterised by Jescheck as a deeply 'politicised' body – a piece of legal camouflage for an essentially political project which 'comes particularly naturally to the Anglo-Saxon mentality'.[104]

The notion of a 'clean Wehrmacht', which has since been thoroughly disproved by historians,[105] was promoted most actively in the post-war years by one of the editors of Jescheck's professorial thesis, the former Nazi military judge Erich Schwinge. Schwinge's own grossly apologetic description of Nazi military justice[106] formed the basis for numerous acquittals in West German courts in the post-war years.[107] And although Jescheck clearly distinguished himself from the majority in legal scholarship in that he did not object to international criminal justice per se, the fact that he was employed by the Ministry of Justice between 1952 and 1954 to assist with policy efforts in defence of German war criminals[108] does illustrate how broad the common ground between this post-war

[99] Jescheck, *Die Verantwortlichkeit der Staatsorgane* (n 81) 356, 373.
[100] ibid 354–62.
[101] ibid 416.
[102] ibid 416f.
[103] ibid 416.
[104] ibid 17.
[105] See, eg Hannes Heer and Klaus Naumann, *Vernichtungskrieg* (Hamburg, Hamburger Edition, 1995); Klaus Naumann, 'Die "saubere" Wehrmacht: Gesellschaftsgeschichte einer Legende' (1998) 7 *Mittelweg 36*; Michael Tymkiw, 'Debunking the Myth of the saubere Wehrmacht' (2007) 23 *Word & Image*; Ben Shepherd, 'The Clean Wehrmacht, the War of Extermination, and Beyond' (2009) 52 *The Historical Journal*.
[106] Otto Schweling and Erich Schwinge, *Die deutsche Militärjustiz in der Zeit des Nationalsozialismus* (Marburg, Elwert, 1978).
[107] The *Bundesgerichtshof* in 1996 acknowledged that its own adjudication of Nazi judicial injustice had been an 'overall failure', see *Entscheidungen des Bundesgerichtshofs in Strafsachen*, vol 41, 317, 339.
[108] Compare Peter Wilkitzki, 'Glückwünsche des Bundesministeriums der Justiz' in Ulrich Sieber and Hans-Jörg Albrecht (eds), *Strafrecht und Kriminologie unter einem Dach: Kolloquium zum 90. Geburtstag von Professor Dr. Dr. h.c. mult. Hans-Heinrich Jescheck* (Berlin, Duncker & Humblot, 2006) 9.

academic and West Germany's conservative policymakers in the 1950s actually was.

5. GERMANY'S OPPOSITION TO NEW TRIBUNALS

To most of Jescheck's West German academic colleagues, the preferable alternative to Nuremberg would simply have been 'no tribunal'.[109] Jescheck, on the other hand, was the first to suggest in 1952 that the core problem of Nuremberg had essentially been an *institutional* one and that this problem could be solved in the future if only the body of the court was designed differently. Jescheck thus supported a new idea which was being debated on the international stage at the beginning of the 1950s:[110] a permanent international criminal court should be under the control of a truly international body in the future. Jescheck's elaborations on this subject are worth exploring not only because Jescheck held the strongest influence on what little literature on international criminal law which was produced during the following decades, but what is more, Jescheck's particular arguments on institutional design had arguably informed the opinion of his harshest opponents in Germany: the vast majority of policymakers who spoke out *against* any new international tribunals. This is the focus of this section.

Jescheck's Lone Argument for a 'UN Court'

When reading Jescheck's 1952 call for an 'impartial' international criminal court, it is hard not to be astonished by its remarkably current sound. It is exactly Jescheck's charge of 'victor's justice' which leads him to argue for a 'UN court' in the future. Jescheck considered a permanent international criminal court under the auspices of the UN to be desirable particularly from a German perspective assuming that 'a court of the United Nations . . . with renowned experts in criminal law and international law including neutral parties and Germans as judges'[111] would have served Germany's interests far better than the IMT.[112] This remarkable point of

[109] Several German commentators had openly argued for amnesty, compare the account by Müller, 'Nürnberg und die deutschen Juristen' (n 45) 257, 266f. This was of course in line with popular sentiment in the early days of the West German State, compare Frei, 'Der Nürnberger Prozeß' (n 12) 480. Even Grewe, who had supported Jescheck's milder line of criticism regarding *nullum crimen*, argued against 'cling[ing] to the failed attempts' made at Nuremberg, Grewe, 'Rückblick auf Nürnberg' (n 88) 248.

[110] For a survey of these early debates, see Otto Triffterer, *Dogmatische Untersuchungen zur Entwicklung des materiellen Völkerstrafrechts seit Nürnberg* (Freiburg im Breisgau, Diss. 1966) 78–84.

[111] Jescheck, *Die Verantwortlichkeit der Staatsorgane* (n 81) 416.

[112] ibid 417–20.

continuity between the charge of 'victor's justice' and the call for a permanent international criminal court has also been highlighted by Claus Kreß.[113]

Perhaps the clearest example for this element of continuity is the fact that in 2006 Jescheck praised the International Criminal Court (ICC) as the fulfilment of his 1952 wishes.[114] From 1974 onwards, Jescheck pursued the project of the ICC as President of the *Association Internationale de Droit Pénale* (AIDP), with Cherif Bassiouni serving as Secretary General.[115]

Germany Opposes New Tribunals

Initially, Jescheck could convince only one of his students, Otto Triffterer, to continue his research on international criminal law in the form of a doctoral thesis, in which Triffterer also supported the idea of a permanent 'UN court' for the future.[116] Aside from that however, the academic landscape had largely been divided into open hostility on the Right – conservative voices remained flatly opposed to any acceptance of international criminal law which would implicitly soften their criticism of Nuremberg – and a peculiar reluctance on the Left.

Assuredly, the United States' involvement in Vietnam did raise some new interest in the idea of an international criminal court with a younger generation of left-leaning legal scholars and criminologists who took up the subject in the 1970s and 1980s. However, this group shared a more sceptical view towards criminal justice altogether and thus ultimately kept their distance from any practical initiatives towards a new international criminal court.[117]

Some younger scholars from outside the 'Freiburg school', among them Herbert Jäger and Gerhard Werle, would take an interest in international criminal law in the 1970s and 1980s based on a far more favourable view of Nuremberg than Jescheck's. However, Jäger and Werle remained exceptions to the rule and they could do little to challenge the predominant feeling in Germany that 'the notion of genuine international criminal law,

[113] Claus Kreß, 'Germany and International Criminal Law: Continuity of Change?' in Herbert R Reginbogin and Christoph J M Safferling (eds), *The Nuremberg Trials: International Criminal Law since 1945: 60th Anniversary International Conference* (Munich, KG Saur, 2006) 239.

[114] Hans-Heinrich Jescheck, 'Schlussworte' in Ulrich Sieber and Hans-Jörg Albrecht (eds), *Strafrecht und Kriminologie unter einem Dach: Kolloquium zum 90. Geburtstag von Professor Dr. Dr. h.c. mult. Hans-Heinrich Jescheck* (Berlin, Duncker & Humblot, 2006) 160.

[115] Triffterer, 'Hans-Heinrich Jeschecks Einfluss' (n 91) 977f; see also Peter Wilkitzki, 'The Contribution of the Federal Republic of Germany and the German Länder to the Work of the ICTY' in Lal C Vohrah (ed), *Man's Inhumanity to Man: Essays on International Law in Honour of Antonio Cassese* (The Hague, KLuwer Law International, 2003) 923.

[116] Triffterer, *Dogmatische Untersuchungen* (n 110) 223.

[117] This is highlighted by Neubacher, *Kriminologische Grundlagen* (n 59) 175.

i.e., of individuals being held accountable directly under international law, had become moot', as Heiko Ahlbrecht observes.[118] This opinion would remain predominant in German academia up until the beginning of the 1990s.[119]

To West Germany's government, the idea of such a court also remained flatly unappealing and perhaps Jescheck's own realist analysis of the IMT (the Tribunal as the long arm of the particular powers which control the prosecution) played more of a part in this than he would have liked to think.

It has often been said that both sides during the Cold War feared that such a permanent international criminal court would create a forum for political attacks from the other side.[120] Even if the apparently 'politicised' nature of the IMT as an institution had then been the only problem of Nuremberg, as Jescheck suggested, the UN during the Cold War certainly did not promise a forum where West Germany could expect its views to be shared by judicial decision makers universally.

In 1980, West Germany expressed to the UN General Assembly 'without great diplomatic clouding'[121] that it had serious doubts about the usefulness of resuming any discussion about the Nuremberg principles.[122] When the UN's International Law Commission (ILC) presented its Draft Code of Crimes against the Peace and Security of Mankind (Draft Code) in 1988, this was again criticised by the government of Germany. In a statement delivered by the representative of West Germany's Foreign Office to the ILC on 9 November 1988, two central objections were made. These two objections bear quoting at length, since the same government, still led by conservative Chancellor Helmut Kohl, would soon play a remarkable role in arguing exactly the opposite effect.[123]

Firstly, regarding the *crime of aggression*, which was included as article 12 of the Draft Code, West Germany argued that no court could be expected to draw the line between just and unjust war with any claim to objectivity:

> It is not without reason that Article 39 of the United Nations Charter makes it the responsibility of the Security Council to determine the existence of any act of aggression. The armed conflicts of recent decades show that the question whether an act of aggression has been committed and by whom has nearly

[118] Christian Tomuschat, 'Sanktionen durch internationale Strafgerichtshöfe' in Deutscher Juristentag (ed), *Verhandlungen des sechzigsten Deutschen Juristentages: Band II/1 – Sitzungsberichte* (Munich, 1994) Q 54.

[119] Werle, 'Deutschland und das Völkerstrafrecht' (n 47) 660.

[120] See, eg Neubacher, *Kriminologische Grundlagen* (n 59) 338–50. This is why West Germany at the time was not the only State to oppose efforts to install a permanent ICC, compare Ahlbrecht, *Geschichte der völkerrechtlichen Strafgerichtsbarkeit* (n 1) 134.

[121] Kreß, *Versailles – Nuremberg – The Hague* (n 91) 27.

[122] UN Doc A/C.6/35/SR. 12, 7 October 1980.

[123] See below the introduction to chapter four.

> always been controversial. As long as this question has not been settled with binding effect on the States concerned, the matter cannot possibly be left in the hands of any judge in any country. In fact one must ask whether any State proceeding to prosecute persons involved would not be interfering in a conflict between other States in contravention of international law. In any event, there is a danger that States will wrongly use such means in pursuit of other political aims.[124]

Secondly, West Germany argued against the principle of *universal jurisdiction*, warning that this would allow judicial actors to discredit those who take different political views:

> Absolute universality, on the other hand, makes it possible for States to attempt to impose their views on other States by means of criminal prosecution. . . . In my view it is not realistic to entertain the prospect of individual judges deciding on the conduct of other States in political matters which are the object of political contention between States, a possibility hitherto unknown on such a scale in international practice.[125]

In a vote taken on 9 December 1988 in the UN General Assembly, West Germany – alongside France, the United Kingdom, the United States and Israel – was part of a minority to speak out against the ILC's continuation of its work on the Draft Code.[126] This was no longer the expression of revisionist sentiment against Nuremberg but arguably of a new and more pragmatic, interest-oriented assessment. West Germany, as a State on the border of the Warsaw Pact countries, had nothing to gain from an international criminal court that would potentially complicate this conflict further and that might even be used to target western policies.

6. CONCLUSION

It is hard to deny that the IMT was under direct and exclusive political control of the four Allied Powers[127] and that these four States took advantage of their means of influence to highlight certain aspects of the war's 'truth' that were of particular interest to their own home audiences.[128] In this sense, the IMT was a victor's court. Also in this sense, it was 'political'. However, as Gary Bass rightly notes, 'the phrase "victors' justice" is in the end a largely uninformative one'.[129] As chapter one has shown, a 'non-political' court of

[124] The full wording is quoted in Clemens Lerche, 'Völkerrechtliche Praxis der Bundesrepublik Deutschland im Jahre 1988' (1990) 50 *Zeitschrift für ausländisches öffentliches Recht und Völkerrecht (Heidelberg Journal of International Law)* 365f. For a summary of the statement see UN Doc A/C.6/43/SR.34.

[125] ibid.

[126] For votes by particular states, see UN Doc A/43/PV/76.

[127] See above section one.

[128] See above section two.

[129] Bass, *Stay the Hand* (n 10) 16.

international criminal justice simply is not imaginable since the selection of cases inescapably requires policy choices to be made; hence, the interesting question really is: does the court apply a *fair* policy or an *unfair* one? As Bass notes, 'The kind of justice one gets depends on the nature of the conquering state.'[130] A victor may well be interested in a fair portrayal of 'historical truth', provided that this 'truth' is nothing to be ashamed of. And in exactly this sense, Nuremberg was, by and large and with the few exceptions mentioned above,[131] fair to historical 'truth'. It served the urgent need (of victims and devastated post-war societies alike) for the fundamental clarification of German guilt and unparalleled atrocity.

The reactions from West Germany's legal scholarship and policymakers were, after a brief period of hesitance, driven by the desire to rebut this historical narrative. West Germany's post-war legal academia departed on a path of legal delegitimisation of Nuremberg, presenting a uniquely rigorous, positivist approach to the principle of *nullum crimen*, which was particular only to Germany[132] (although it was interestingly shared in some respects by jurists in Japan).[133] This allowed for indirect attacks on the legitimacy of the Nuremberg judgments, while the legal invocation of *tu quoque* enabled German legal scholars to challenge the Nuremberg narrative more directly by implying that the Allies had committed atrocities of a comparable gravity to Nazi Germany.[134]

The political core of the legal debate in Germany, which led to the government's speaking out against any international attempts to repeat the 'negative example' of Nuremberg well into the 1980s,[135] is summarised by the historian Norbert Frei:

> In the end, [the debate in Germany] was not just about a few hundred war criminals, but rather about the political morale of millions: The government's policy enabled former [German] soldiers in the 1950s to continue to see a meaning in their wartime sacrifices, even at the cost of historical accuracy. For this reason, the war was followed by a struggle for memory: The inquiry into the criminal character of the German aggression, its barbarity and insanity from the very beginning, which had been so impressively made at Nuremberg – and which had led to a clear answer in the eyes of the international community – was pushed aside. Instead, the Second World War was now presented [in Germany] in similar terms as the First, raising a claim of 'normality' – partly out of ignorance, mostly however with full knowledge and intent – that was entirely out of place in the case of the unparalleled crimes of the Germans.[136]

[130] ibid.

[131] See above section two.

[132] See above section three.

[133] Compare Philipp Osten, *Der Tokioter Kriegsverbrecherprozess und die japanische Rechtswissenschaft* (Berlin, Berliner Wissenschafts-Verlag, 2003).

[134] See above section four.

[135] See above section five.

[136] Frei, 'Der Nürnberger Prozeß' (n 12) 490f.

As much as the legal attacks on Nuremberg were thus driven by revisionist intentions and as ill-founded as many of the legal arguments arguably were, West Germany's realist analysis of the IMT was actually rather precise: scholars and policymakers in post-war West Germany had understood the power of such a tribunal as a tool to authoritatively confirm 'historical truth' (which is why they aimed to attack the authority of that tribunal). This particular perspective shaped the understanding of international criminal law, with which generations of law students in West Germany would then grow up. Even the lone voice of the legal scholar Hans-Heinrich Jescheck, who advocated the creation of a permanent international criminal court early on, was based on a robustly realist analysis of Nuremberg as the long arm of four powers. Jescheck argued that a 'UN court' would be preferable to an IMT, purely from the German perspective – while evidently assuming that the 'historical truth' of World War II would have deserved a portrayal different from that by the Nuremberg IMT.[137]

[137] See above section five.

3

Germany's Own GDR Trials after 1989

AS ILLUSTRATED IN chapter two, Germany's legal scholarship and policymakers in the years after Nuremberg almost unanimously denied the legitimacy of international criminal justice per se – a position which they would abandon abruptly in 1989. This sudden shift is the focus of this chapter. The question with which legal academics and policymakers were faced in 1989 was how to deal with the crimes of the fallen regime in East Germany. Their answer was a call for strict crim inal accountability. This meant a sharp turn away from the previous, rigorously positivist position vis-à-vis the principle of *nullum crimen*.

In chapter two, my analysis shows how the rejection of the Nuremberg principles by the vast majority of Germany's legal scholarship and policymakers in the post-war years was driven by the opposition to the particular historical narrative painted by the Nuremberg IMT. This opposition shaped a predominant understanding in Germany of international criminal justice as a powerful tool to write history with a claim to judicial objectivity. The following exploration in this chapter is hoped to shed light on how the aforementioned German policymakers now put this understanding to use for the first time.

1. WEST GERMANY IN CONTROL

After the fall of the Berlin Wall and the collapse of State communism in 1989, the first East German government to result from free elections chose to dissolve the East German State, the *Deutsche Demokratische Republik* (German Democratic Republic, hereinafter: GDR), and merge its territory with the established legal framework of West Germany. This reunited, larger German State remained under the continued chancellorship of West German conservative Helmut Kohl and within this legal and political framework, the old East German elites were rapidly put on trial. From 1989 until 1999, approximately 100,000 functionaries of the GDR were officially investigated for State crimes. More than 500 were ultimately sentenced.[1] While the rigorous prosecution policy, largely conducted by a

[1] Klaus Marxen and Gerhard Werle, *Die strafrechtliche Aufarbeitung von DDR-Unrecht* (Berlin, de Gruyter, 1999) 234f.

West German judiciary, evoked some charges of 'victor's justice' among supporters of the old East German regime,[2] the major difference in this respect, of course, was that there were never any serious grounds for criminal charges against the party of the accuser. Crimes of the magnitude committed by the East German regime had simply not taken place in West Germany. West German political stakeholders thus had little to lose from such trials.

Still, if need be, the possibility of political influence over courts' prosecution policy was there: The German government would have been able to exert influence over prosecutorial policies by granting partial amnesties, by hand-picking prosecutors and by binding prosecutors to executive guidelines in the German tradition of strong prosecutorial accountability.[3] When members of the Kohl government carefully suggested granting partial amnesty to former GDR spies working against the West,[4] both chambers of parliament, the *Bundestag* and the *Bundesrat*, objected.[5] Instead, the *Bundestag* passed legislation allowing for more GDR cases to be prosecuted. It lifted the statute of limitations from acts of murder committed in the GDR in 1993.[6] The same decision had previously taken West Germany's parliament 30 years to reach with respect to Nazi crimes.[7] Moreover, East Germany's first democratic government after 1989 did not hesitate to use its capacities to exert control over prosecutors, firing two Attorney Generals within less than one year for being too 'soft' on the old regime.[8]

After the total dissolution of the GDR in 1990, prosecuting efforts were coordinated in a less centralised fashion by the District Attorney of Berlin, who was tasked with the bulk of the cases,[9] and by each of his colleagues in office in the five former East German *Länder*.[10] Nonetheless, all GDR cases were still handled by high-level prosecutors directly accountable to

[2] Paul Betts, 'Germany, International Justice and the Twentieth Century' (2005) 17 *History & Memory* 69.

[3] For a comparison of this tradition with other States which place less emphasis on prosecutorial accountability, see, eg Allison M Danner, 'Enhancing the Legitimacy and Accountability of Prosecutorial Discretion at the International Criminal Court' (2003) 97 *American Journal of International Law* 515.

[4] Compare Klaus Kinkel, 'Wiedervereinigung und Strafrecht' (1992) *JuristenZeitung* 486; Wolfgang Schäuble, *Der Vertrag* (Stuttgart, Deutsche Verlags-Anstalt, 1991) 286.

[5] Kai Rossig and Antje Ross, 'Alternativen zur strafrechtlichen Ahndung des DDR-Systemunrechts' in Albin Eser and Jörg Arnold (eds), *Criminal Law in Reaction to State Crime: Comparative Insights into Transitional Processes* (Freiburg im Breisgau, Max-Planck-Institut für Ausländisches und Internationales Strafrecht, 2000) vol 2, 525.

[6] Marxen and Werle, *Die strafrechtliche Aufarbeitung von DDR-Unrecht* (n 1) 6f.

[7] This is highlighted by Frank Neubacher, *Kriminologische Grundlagen einer internationalen Strafgerichtsbarkeit* (Tübingen, Mohr Siebeck, 2005) 381.

[8] Marxen and Werle, *Die strafrechtliche Aufarbeitung von DDR-Unrecht* (n 1) 149f, see particularly at note 755.

[9] Compare ibid 202.

[10] ibid 156–61.

the new Ministers of Justice in their respective *Länder*. GDR cases were all handled by newly-created, special prosecutorial departments.[11]

2. WEST GERMAN NARRATIVE INTERESTS

Why was Germany's government interested in such trials, while neighbouring, post-communist countries were evidently not interested to the same degree? Hungary, the Soviet Union, Poland, Bulgaria and Czechoslovakia had all experienced state-administered oppression and crimes against their population, oftentimes more grave than in East Germany. Yet they largely concentrated on rehabilitating perpetrators and compensating victims. While some other post-communist States assuredly conducted sporadic criminal trials after 1989, they largely allowed for de facto amnesties in the interest of reconciliation.[12] At least empirically, this should not surprise us: A tendency towards 'cold amnesties' is common in most political transitions to democracy, where the new elites aim to pacify a society in a state of political upheaval, even at the cost of 'selling justice short'.[13]

Germany after 1989, however, was the exception to this rule.[14] Germany was the only State after 1989 to show a strong interest in illuminating the communist past in the particular forum of criminal trials rather than in other forums. Why?

The Call for Expressive Trials

In the debate within Germany as to whether or not to hold criminal trials for the former GDR regime, one fundamental fact was clear on all sides: courts would be able to target only a small fraction of the crimes of this 40-year regime and any subsequent trials could thus satisfy an exemplary

[11] ibid.

[12] Poland is an example of a post-communist State which conducted a small number of trials for selected parts of its history, compare Albin Eser and Jörg Arnold (eds), *Criminal Law in Reaction to State Crime: Comparative Insights into Transitional Processes* (Freiburg im Breisgau. Max-Planck-Institut für Ausländisches und Internationales Strafrecht, 2000) vol 1, 223–31. In Russia on the other hand, criminal prosecution was entirely negligible, compare ibid 247–57, also XXXI. Compare also Rossig and Ross, 'Alternativen zur strafrechtlichen Ahndung' (n 5).

[13] The various courses of domestic reaction to State crimes after phases of political transition were the subject of a research project at Freiburg's Max Planck Institute for Foreign and International Criminal Law in the late 1990s. According to this survey, numerous States that experienced political transitions in the second half of the twentieth century chose what the researchers dubbed the 'clean break model' (*Schlussstrich-Modell*). With respect to communism, Germany is the only State to have chosen the 'criminal prosecution model' at all, see Eser and Arnold (eds), *Criminal Law in Reaction to State Crime* (n 12) vol 1, XXXI.

[14] See Rossig and Ross, 'Alternativen zur strafrechtlichen Ahndung' (n 5) 523.

function only.[15] It was from this outset that many German commentators argued against holding such trials at all. Some preferred a solution more similar to the 'clean breaks' (*Schlussstriche*) which were quietly being implemented elsewhere in Europe at the time.[16] Also, even though many victims were calling for the punishment of their former tormentors,[17] calls for amnesty were also common, even among former GDR dissidents.[18]

Ultimately, the inner-German debate was won by those who warned against blurring the historical fact that the GDR had been a *criminal* rather than merely a 'different' political system.[19] Of course, public funding for archival work would be important in creating an accurate historical record. However, the additional forum of *criminal* courts would be indispensable in order to make this particular qualitative point.

In September 1991, Helmut Kohl's then Minister of Justice, Klaus Kinkel (who had previously served as head of West Germany's foreign intelligence service), stated to a conference of judges:

> Now the people [in the East] have the *Rechtsstaat* (system of rule of law) which they longed for, and now their rightful expectation is that the perpetrators will be punished rapidly. . . . I trust in the German judiciary. We must succeed in delegitimising the GDR regime.[20]

Before West Germany's government announced its clear policy choice, former GDR dissidents, now in power in East Germany, had already begun to initiate criminal trials. The first democratically-elected East German government, which was in power only briefly and was led by political conservatives supported by Helmut Kohl's West German party,

[15] For a critical perspective see, eg Thomas Hillenkamp, 'Offene und verdeckte Amnestie – über Wege strafrechtlicher Vergangenheitsbewältigung' (1996) *JuristenZeitung* 179; Günther Jakobs, 'Vergangenheitsbewältigung durch Strafrecht? Zur Leistungsfähigkeit des Strafrechts nach einem politischen Umbruch' in Ulrich Battis and others (eds), *Vergangenheitsbewältigung durch Recht: Drei Abhandlungen zu einem deutschen Problem* (Berlin, Duncker & Humblot, 1992) 63; later also Horst Dreier, 'Gustav Radbruch und die Mauerschützen' (1997) *JuristenZeitung* 434. The expressive function of the GDR trials was highlighted affirmatively by eg Kinkel, 'Wiedervereinigung und Strafrecht' (n 4) 487; later also Marxen and Werle, *Die strafrechtliche Aufarbeitung von DDR-Unrecht* (n 1) 245f, 260.

[16] Compare the surveys of this debate by Rossig and Ross, 'Alternativen zur strafrechtlichen Ahndung' (n 5) 521–24 and 525–27; Marxen and Werle, *Die strafrechtliche Aufarbeitung von DDR-Unrecht* (n 1) 255f.

[17] Neubacher, *Kriminologische Grundlagen* (n 7) 373, suggests that the victims in East Germany voiced these calls with more determination than in other post-communist countries.

[18] Compare Rossig and Ross, 'Alternativen zur strafrechtlichen Ahndung' (n 5) 525.

[19] Compare ibid 526 fn 27.

[20] Klaus Kinkel, 'Ansprache auf dem deutschen Richtertag im September 1991' (1991) *Deutsche Richterzeitung* 5. See also Friedrich Dencker, 'Strafrechtliche Aufarbeitung des DDR-Unrechts und Rechtskultur' in Hendrik Hansen (ed), *Aufarbeitung totalitärer Erfahrungen und politische Kultur: Die Bedeutung der Aufarbeitung des SED-Unrechts für das Rechts- und Werteverständnis im wiedervereinigten Deutschland.* Politisches Denken. Jahrbuch 2009 (Berlin, Duncker & Humblot, 2009) 202.

began immediately to prosecute its communist predecessors in 1989.[21] More than half of the former government cabinet (*Politbüro*) were temporarily arrested, mainly on charges of corruption and abuse of power.[22]

Germany's Post-War History: A Clash of Interpretations

This came out of a rather unique political situation. After 1989, most transitional governments in Europe were creating new, and still volatile, political identities as democracies in newly independent States. In Germany, by contrast, a *pre-existing* identity, that of West Germany, was simply expanded towards the east. 'Unlike elsewhere, post-communist institutions did not need to be built from scratch there; on the contrary, West German institutions, personnel and constitutional rules were ready-made to pursue retributive justice', notes Paul Betts.[23] A 'mild' treatment or partial integration of the old elites did not appear necessary to assure stability and there was no pragmatic need to compromise the wishes of victims or to 'sell justice short' at all. On the contrary, the new leadership would even have pragmatic reasons *for* targeting the former communist elites in expressive trials.

This is because the political system of West Germany had previously been exposed to (mutual) attacks on its political legitimacy by the GDR for decades. The governments in East Germany and West Germany had each narrated Germany's post-war history differently, portraying the opposite system as oppressive. The chance of holding expressive trials for GDR crimes now promised to set this record straight.

Throughout the past decades, the communist East German leadership had styled itself as the true antithesis to Germany's common Nazi past, claiming to have purged all Nazi officials from public office[24] and to have immunised the newly founded East German State against all purported (pre)fascist tendencies – most notably, capitalism. By contrast, West Germany was shamed for its apparent points of continuity with Nazism. In this portrayal, the Berlin Wall, erected by the GDR government in 1961 to stop its citizens from emigrating to the wealthier West, was styled an 'anti-fascist protection wall' (*Antifaschistischer Schutzwall*) in official propaganda and the GDR in 1963 staged a symbolic criminal trial *in absentia* against Hans Globke, a West German cabinet minister who had previously served as a high-level Nazi bureaucrat responsible for the racist Nuremberg Laws.[25]

[21] Marxen and Werle, *Die strafrechtliche Aufarbeitung von DDR-Unrecht* (n 1) 148–56, 232.

[22] ibid 151.

[23] Betts, 'Germany, International Justice and the Twentieth Century' (n 2) 66.

[24] Some notable historical doubts are illuminated by Henry Leide, *NS-Verbrecher und Staatssicherheit* (Göttingen, Vandenhoeck & Ruprecht, 2008).

[25] See Claus Kreß, 'Versailles – Nürnberg – Den Haag: Deutschland und das Völkerstrafrecht' (2006) 61 *JuristenZeitung* 984.

By contrast, the West German narrative, and particularly the version held dear by conservative policymakers in the Kohl government, emphasised how West Germany had distanced itself more clearly from the common Nazi past by becoming a liberal democracy. Moreover, the East German system was portrayed as little more than a new shade of 'totalitarianism', with this notion being used as a common denominator to include both fascists *and* communists. This narrative was even officially made a guideline for West German history teachers in 1962.[26] The concept of 'totalitarianism' as a monolithic opposite to democracy was promoted, particularly by political conservatives during the Cold War and had emerged as a central motif of conservative efforts to refocus Germany's 'national identity' by the 1980s.[27]

Reaffirming the Western Narrative

In a moment of exaggeration and in their struggle for legitimacy in 1989/90, some former GDR dissidents even proposed to hold a 'tribunal' reminiscent of Nuremberg for the GDR[28] – the implied equation of communism with Nazism could not have been clearer. This idea never gained much support and trials were held in domestic courts instead. Yet while Kinkel had explicitly warned against simplistic comparisons between the GDR and the Nazi regime, he did name the Nuremberg IMT as an apparent 'historic parallel' for trials.[29]

The most serious crime of the East German regime, referred to by Kinkel as the 'most horrible part of GDR injustice',[30] had been the use of deadly force against East Germans who had attempted to cross the border to the West. An estimated 246 GDR citizens[31] were killed over the course of 28 years. Obviously, this pales in comparison with the atrocities of the Nazi regime. For this reason, Wolfgang Wippermann, among others, criticises attempts at historically equating the 'two German dictatorships' as a 'demonization by comparison' of the GDR – a distortion of historical proportions.[32]

Picking up on this, Erich Honecker, the former East German Head of State, defiantly declared at the beginning of his planned trial in 1992:

[26] See Jürgen Peter, *Der Historikerstreit und die Suche nach einer nationalen Identität der achtziger Jahre* (Frankfurt am Main, Peter Lang Verlag, 1995) 62.

[27] See ibid 37, 48.

[28] Compare Rossig and Ross, 'Alternativen zur strafrechtlichen Ahndung' (n 5) 529.

[29] Kinkel, 'Wiedervereinigung und Strafrecht' (n 4) 487.

[30] ibid 489.

[31] Estimates by historians differ however and go up to 938, compare Marxen and Werle, *Die strafrechtliche Aufarbeitung von DDR-Unrecht* (n 1) 8 fn 29.

[32] Wolfgang Wippermann, *Dämonisierung durch Vergleich* (Berlin, Rotbuch, 2009).

> There were no concentration camps in the GDR, no gas chambers, no political executions, no Volksgerichtshof, no Gestapo, no SS. The GDR did not launch a war or commit war crimes or crimes against humanity.[33]

Nonetheless, proponents of a strict prosecution policy after 1989 argued that the mistakes made in dealing with the Nazi past – that is, ludicrous acquittals before German courts – should not be 'repeated' in the case of the GDR.[34]

3. THE U-TURN ON *NULLUM CRIMEN*

Elaborating on the legal difficulties faced by Germany in bringing GDR crimes to court, Klaus Kinkel noted in 1992 that 'our criminal law is not designed for such State-administered crimes'.[35] Kinkel, who at this point had been promoted from Minister of Justice to Minister of Foreign Affairs, pointed particularly to West Germany's rigorous positivism with respect to *nullum crimen*. He pleaded for the GDR's domestic law not to stand in the way of the criminal prosecution of GDR functionaries.[36] While Kinkel was diplomatic not to speak directly of a *change* in West German legal policy on *nullum crimen* – rather, merely, of applying a rationale previously applicable to Nazi atrocities also[37] – the legal community that Kinkel was addressing clearly understood the problem.[38]

Unlike the guideline-bound prosecutors, judges were of course entirely independent in their judgment of cases. And given the legal status quo at the beginning of the 1990s – and particularly the tradition of rigorous positivism since Nuremberg – it was far from clear whether they would ultimately allow a conviction of GDR functionaries at all or whether all GDR functionaries acting in accordance with the GDR's domestic laws would have to be acquitted.

The Positivist Position

As previously mentioned, the most serious crime of the GDR regime had been the use of deadly force against East Germans who had attempted to

[33] Erich Honecker, Politische Erklärung vor der 27. Großen Strafkammer des Berliner Landgerichts am 3. Oktober 1992, 1415.

[34] See, eg the essays in Bernd Faulenbach, Markus Meckel and Hermann Weber, *Die Partei hatte immer recht* (Essen, Klartext-Verlag, 1994); also Klaus Sühl, *Vergangenheitsbewältigung 1945 und 1989* (Berlin, Volk und Welt, 1994).

[35] Kinkel, 'Wiedervereinigung und Strafrecht' (n 4) 486.

[36] ibid 487.

[37] Kinkel refers – without citation – to judgments by the Bundesgerichtshof concerning Nazi crimes, compare ibid.

[38] See also Dencker, 'Strafrechtliche Aufarbeitung des DDR-Unrechts und Rechtskultur' (n 20) 202.

cross the border into the West. These acts had been legal under the GDR's domestic law[39] and their illegality under international (criminal) law was much less clear than it had been in the cases of many Nazi atrocities.[40] To uphold West Germany's strictly positivist view on *nullum crimen*, which had allowed only for the gravest of Nazi crimes to be prosecuted, would have meant that the shootings at the inner-German border might not have met this threshold at all.[41] A small number of legal scholars, who had defended the traditional positivist reading of *nullum crimen* at the beginning of the 1990s, made exactly this argument.[42]

One West German scholar for instance, Günther Jakobs, found that there was no sufficient basis for the conviction of GDR functionaries under West Germany's legal status quo. Jakobs commented that the government's request to nonetheless proceed – against its own prior position on *nullum crimen* – was essentially about 'choosing certain perpetrators as symbols for a political direction . . . and figuratively indicting their politics with them.'[43] Jakobs went on to criticise:

> [F]or those who have not been victimised personally, the desire to punish seems to be the result of a rather dangerous understanding of the Western political order. This order does not seem to be understood as a well-designed building, the statics of which need to be adjusted occasionally, but rather as a quasi-natural or quasi-logical construction that is valid over time and, moreover, over

[39] Para 27 of the GDR's 'border law' (*Grenzgesetz*) had allowed for the use of force against persons who 'violate' the border, see Marxen and Werle, *Die strafrechtliche Aufarbeitung von DDR-Unrecht* (n 1) 8.

[40] Kai Ambos, 'Nuremberg revisited: Das Bundesverfassungsgericht, das Völkerstrafrecht und das Rückwirkungsverbot' (1997) *Strafverteidiger* 42; Günther Jakobs, 'Untaten des Staates – Unrecht im Staat: Strafe für die Tötungen an der Grenze der ehemaligen DDR?' (1994) *Goldtammer's Archiv für Strafrecht* 3, and Dreier, 'Gustav Radbruch und die Mauerschützen' (n 15) 425; all three authors point out that (customary) international criminal law did not apply. Otto Triffterer, 'Was kann das Völkerstrafrecht zur Bewältigung der Regierungskriminalität in der DDR beitragen?' in Ernst-Joachim Lampe (ed), *Deutsche Wiedervereinigung: Die Rechtseinheit. Vol 2: Die Verfolgung von Regierungskriminalität nach der Wiedervereinigung* (Cologne, Arbeitskreis Strafrecht, 1993) 156f, shows that the use of deadly force to 'protect' a border had even deliberately not been included in the codification of crimes against humanity – unlike eg the crime of Apartheid. One of the rare voices to nonetheless argue to the opposite effect is Silke Buchner, *Die Rechtswidrigkeit der Taten von 'Mauerschützen' im Lichte von Art. 103 II GG unter besonderer Berücksichtigung des Völkerrechts* (Frankfurt am Main, Lang, 1996) 253, 302.

[41] A concise survey of this debate is offered by Ambos, 'Nuremberg revisited' (n 40) 41f. See also Dreier, 'Gustav Radbruch und die Mauerschützen' (n 15).

[42] Compare eg Gerhard Dannecker and Kristian F Stoffers, 'Rechtsstaatliche Grenzen für die strafrechtliche Aufarbeitung der Todesschüsse an der innerdeutschen Grenze' (1996) 51 *JuristenZeitung*; Jörg Arnold, 'Die "Bewältigung" der DDR-Vergangenheit vor den Schranken des rechtsstaatlichen Strafrechts' in Institut für Kriminalwissenschaften (ed), *Vom unmöglichen Zustand des Strafrechts* (Frankfurt am Main, Land, 1995) 306f; Bernhard Schlink, 'Rechtsstaat und revolutionäre Gerechtigkeit' (1994) 10 *Neue Justiz* 434f. For a thorough analysis that examines the different underlying rationales within this position, compare Stefan Zimmermann, 'Die strafrechtliche "Bewältigung" der deutschen Diktaturen' (1996) *Juristische Schulung* 868f.

[43] Jakobs, 'Untaten des Staates' (n 40) 19.

space. This apparent self-evidence is to be *illustrated* in a trial. Assuredly, there is no reason to doubt that [the Western] political order is more adequate to our day and age than the perished State socialist orders were . . . However, this does not justify adding criminal trials against individuals, who never actually subscribed to this Western order, to the *poena naturalis*.[44]

The Surprising Revival of Radbruch

German courts, and with them the majority of legal scholars, struck a new path, however, in order to make adjudication more easily possible. Whereas West German judges had worked for a 'cold amnesty' of Nazi war criminals in the 1950s and 1960s with an eye to their own tainted biographies, the judges at the beginning of the 1990s held no such qualms in dealing with the former political foes from the communist East.[45] In a series of decisions beginning in November 1992,[46] the *Bundesgerichtshof* confirmed criminal convictions of GDR border patrolmen and their commanders, regardless of the domestic legality of their acts. In 1994, the *Bundesgerichtshof* also decided to discontinue its earlier legal doctrine that had protected numerous physical perpetrators of the Holocaust from lifetime sentences by classifying SS perpetrators as mere aiders and abettors who were executing a plan whose only actual authors were apparently Hitler and Himmler:[47] With respect to GDR crimes, the court now allowed for direct perpetrators *and* distant GDR bureaucrats to be punished for the authorship of one and the same act of murder,[48] thus widening the prosecutorial scope considerably.

Most fundamentally, however, courts now relied directly on a substantive qualification to *nullum crimen*, as first advocated in Germany by

[44] ibid.

[45] This sociological aspect is highlighted by Neubacher, *Kriminologische Grundlagen* (n 7) 375. In respect of the political climate in the judiciary, Dreier, 'Gustav Radbruch und die Mauerschützen' (n 15) 430, notes an atmosphere of 'human rights euphoria' at the beginning of the 1990s, to contrast the Cold War atmosphere that had influenced previous proceedings.

[46] See Marxen and Werle, *Die strafrechtliche Aufarbeitung von DDR-Unrecht* (n 1) 12–16. For a concise analysis see also Zimmermann, 'Die strafrechtliche "Bewältigung" der deutschen Diktaturen' (n 42) 868f.

[47] Compare eg Adalbert Rückerl, *NS-Verbrechen vor Gericht* (Heidelberg, Müller Juristischer Verlag, 1984) 274f. To accomplish this technically, courts had raised special *mens rea* requirements. See particularly *Entscheidungen des Bundesgerichtshofs in Strafsachen* vol 18, 87, 94. For in-depth criticism see, eg Barbara Just-Dahlmann and Helmut Just, *Die Gehilfen* (Frankfurt am Main, Athenäum, 1988).

[48] *Entscheidungen des Bundesgerichtshofs in Strafsachen* vol 40, 218, 230. See Günter Heine, 'Täterschaft und Teilnahme in staatlichen Machtapparaten: NS- und DDR-Unrecht im Vergleich der Rechtsprechung' (2000) 55 *JuristenZeitung*; Neubacher, *Kriminologische Grundlagen* (n 7) 380. The contrast to previous jurisprudence with respect to Nazi crimes is also highlighted by Marxen and Werle, *Die strafrechtliche Aufarbeitung von DDR-Unrecht* (n 1) 22f.

Gustav Radbruch in 1946, in referral to the horrors of the Nazi regime:[49] the idea that 'manifestly and unbearably unjust' exculpatory laws of the former GDR should simply be treated as 'non-law'. This idea was applied to the GDR's infamous *Grenzgesetz* ('border law').[50]

As illustrated above in chapter two, Radbruch's philosophic formula had largely been ignored by Germany's legal scholarship for decades[51] and had never actually been used by the German judiciary as ratio decidendi in Nazi cases.[52] In fact, Radbruch's idea had been reduced to a small school of philosophical thought by the end of the 1980s.[53] Only now, in dealing with GDR crimes, was the 'Radbruch formula' suddenly retrieved and employed by German courts for the first time. Forty years after Radbruch's death, the rationale which the eminent Social Democrat had unsuccessfully advocated for the domestic adjudication of Nazi atrocities was applied to the GDR's crimes instead.

The crude historical subtext – an implied equation between the two historical criminal complexes – initially made German courts hesitate.[54] Rather than having recourse to Radbruch's 1946 natural-law rationale directly, the courts sought, somewhat awkwardly, to base their legal arguments primarily on international law. In what was usually the first stage of argument, courts would examine whether the GDR border patrolmen had acted in excess of their domestic laws or superior orders,[55] which would then make their acts illegal even under GDR law and thereby avoid the problem of *nullum crimen* altogether. In a second stage, however, where patrolmen had acted in compliance with GDR law, their acts were declared illegal on account of this law's violating *substantive justice*,[56] as apparently evidenced by the rather cloudy formulations in the International Covenant on Civil and Political Rights[57] and the Universal Declaration of Human Rights.[58]

[49] Gustav Radbruch, 'Gesetzliches Unrecht und übergesetzliches Recht' (1946) *Süddeutsche Juristenzeitung* 107. See above chapter two, section three.

[50] *Entscheidung des Bundesgerichtshofs in Strafsachen, Neue Juristische Wochenschrift* 1994, 2708f.

[51] See above chapter two, section three.

[52] Dreier, 'Gustav Radbruch und die Mauerschützen' (n 15) 424, points out that the rationale had previously been directly applied only in administrative cases, concerning eg the expatriation of German Jews. See also Gerhard Werle, 'Die Entwicklung des Völkerstrafrechts aus deutscher Perspektive' in Gerd Hankel (ed), *Die Macht und das Recht: Beiträge zum Völkerrecht und Völkerstrafrecht am Beginn des 21. Jahrhunderts* (Hamburg, Hamburger Edition, 2008) 109.

[53] Dreier, 'Gustav Radbruch und die Mauerschützen' (n 15) 424.

[54] ibid 425.

[55] Marxen and Werle, *Die strafrechtliche Aufarbeitung von DDR-Unrecht* (n 1) 17.

[56] ibid 18.

[57] *Entscheidungen des Bundesgerichtshofs in Strafsachen* vol 39, 1, 14f.

[58] ibid vol 40, 241, 245f. Neubacher, *Kriminologische Grundlagen* (n 7) 379 considers this 1990s approach to be more refined than Radbruch's original approach.

In clear terms, Germany's federal constitutional court, the *Bundesverfassungsgericht*, began to apply Radbruch's 1946 formula directly in 1996. Whereas other crimes of the GDR, such as the systematic stealing from West German packages by the government postal service, were not deemed sufficiently grave,[59] the GDR's border regime was held to satisfy Radbruch's threshold of 'manifest and unbearable' injustice.[60]

The majority of legal scholars in Germany supported this new approach[61] and with that, Germany's longtime *Sonderweg* ('particular path') of rigorous positivism in respect of *nullum crimen* came to an end.

4. CONCLUSION

Otto Triffterer, who had been one of the few German professors with any active interest in international criminal law throughout the years preceding 1989, was invited in 1993 to elaborate on the question: 'How can international criminal law contribute to dealing with the State crimes of the GDR?'[62] At this point, Triffterer could offer little except praise for the German courts – they had apparently incorporated all the 'lessons of Nuremberg' into domestic law, albeit after several decades of delay.

It is hoped that this chapter has given some insight into the important part which the political interest by West Germany's elites in a particular historical narrative played in making this belated policy shift possible. As illustrated at the outset of this chapter,[63] German policymakers only opened up to the legal rationales of Nuremberg 'at a time where this no longer infers any costs to them', as Gerhard Stuby comments.[64] On the other hand though, they could also expect a gain from opening up to these legal rationals. After 40 years of political rivalry with the communist East Germany, the West German government now had an interest in scoring a point in a struggle for interpretative authority over 'historical truth' and since the government had all the judicial means to assure that this point would be made by courts in the desired form,[65] it rapidly seized the chance, together with former GDR dissidents, to delegitimise the GDR regime in the forum of criminal justice.[66] In previous decades when faced with the crimes of the Nazi regime, West German jurists and policymak-

[59] *Entscheidungen des Bundesgerichtshofs in Strafsachen*, vol 40, 8, 16; vol 40, 169, 180; vol 41, 187, 194.

[60] ibid vol 95, 96, 131f.

[61] See Zimmermann, 'Die strafrechtliche "Bewältigung" der deutschen Diktaturen' (n 42) 869.

[62] Triffterer, 'Was kann das Völkerstrafrecht' (n 40).

[63] See above section one.

[64] Gerhard Stuby, 'Nürnberg 1945/46: Von der Harmlosigkeit des Gedenkens' (2006) *Blätter für deutsche und internationale Politik* 99.

[65] See above section one.

[66] See above section two.

ers had largely adhered to a set of legal arguments shielding German perpetrators from prosecution.[67] However, now faced with the crimes of the GDR regime, such legal doctrines were dropped.[68]

There are at least two aspects which made such expressive trials advantageous to West German power politics in the early 1990s. Firstly, such trials would add legitimacy to Germany's particular, rather unique mode of reunification: The Kohl government at the time was criticised for a simple 'takeover' of the East, not only by proponents of the old East German regime but also by some members of the left-of-centre opposition in West Germany. To reinforce the theme that the GDR had been an illegitimate and oppressive system meant adding legitimacy to the Kohl government's narrative of 'liberation'. Secondly, a resolute prosecution policy would also demonstrate to the rest of the world that the reunified German State was not a *new* political creature staffed with members of a formerly communist establishment (like so many eastern European neighbours at the time), but rather a smooth continuation of the familiar West Germany. This promised to preserve the political status which West Germany had worked so hard to earn within the West.

[67] See above chapter two.
[68] See above section three.

4

German Support for the UN Ad Hoc Tribunals in the 1990s

AFTER OPENING UP to the principal idea of international criminal law following 1989, Germany was in a position to join a new international debate. Throughout the Cold War, governments both in the East and the West had been reluctant to endorse the practical realisation of new Nuremberg-style courts, fearing a 'politicisation' or, in other words, a court that would legally support the political narratives of the adversary. As a result, the political project had effectively been dormant for decades. The beginning of the 1990s, however, brought rapid change. With the Cold War at an end, the ideas of international criminal justice gained new momentum and Germany, which had previously been one of the most rigorous opponents of international criminal justice, now took a remarkably proactive role. This surprising new German role is the focus of this chapter.

In the early 1990s Germany took to the international stage, emphatically arguing for the creation of new, Nuremberg-style tribunals – first for Saddam Hussein and then for war crimes in the former Yugoslavia. The International Criminal Tribunal for the former Yugoslavia (ICTY), which the UN Security Council created in 1993, enjoyed Germany's unconditional support even though it was under the exclusive control of the UN Security Council, where Germany largely stood to the side. It would thus appear that Germany supported this Tribunal *without* having any chance of controlling it despite the fact that Germany's own stakes were actually rather high at this Tribunal, as will be shown below. Is this an example of new human rights idealism in the freshly reunified German State? Had German policymakers, who had only recently warmed to the Nuremberg Principles in order to allow for the domestic adjudication of the communist East German regime, become overzealous converts, promoting the 'lessons of Nuremberg' on the international stage without any interest of their own?

1. THE UN SECURITY COUNCIL IN CONTROL

The first President of the ICTY, Antonio Cassese, praised the institutional design of the ICTY in 1994: 'This is a truly international institution. . . . It is an expression of the entire world, not the long arm of four powerful victors.'[1] However, as Cassese, who had personally experienced the frustrating search for the first Prosecutor of the ICTY, would come to know better than anyone else, control here had in fact merely shifted from the four Allied Powers to the 15-member UN Security Council and particularly to the five veto-wielding permanent members of that body (also known as the P5). Both the ICTY in 1993 and the International Criminal Tribunal for Rwanda (ICTR) in 1994 were created as subsidiary organs of the UN Security Council[2] and its five permanent members could exert direct control and thus influence the UN ad hoc tribunals' portrayal of truth through a number of channels.

Influence over the Prosecutor's Mandate

Firstly and most basically, the UN Security Council can influence the tribunals' portrayal of truth through the design of tribunal mandates. It is a well-known line of criticism that the UN Security Council in creating tribunals prioritised between conflicts as it pleased. As Robert Cryer notes:

> Where there is agreement on the acceptability of a tribunal among the permanent five members of the Security Council, the possibility of an international tribunal is there. Where it is not, either because there is insufficient interest to make proposals for a Tribunal or if the interests of any one of these powers is implicated, then quite simply there will not be a Tribunal.[3]

It is less well-known that this power also enabled the Security Council to pre-select cases *within* a conflict to a certain degree by simply tailoring the judicial mandate. Assuredly, the ICTY's scope of jurisdiction includes the entire territory of the former Yugoslavia and the entire period after 1991. At the ICTR, however, the temporal scope was tailored exclusively to the year 1994 and to the territory of Rwanda only. This is the result of a clash

[1] Antonio Cassese, Speech at the UN, 14 November 1994, quoted in *ICTY Yearbook 1994*, 136f.

[2] Referring to an initial US suggestion that the ICTY be supervised by an administrative council composed of the members of the Security Council, Frédéric Mégret, 'The Politics of International Criminal Justice' (2002) 13 *European Journal of International Law* 1275, comments that this 'was simply more than public opinion would have been ready to stomach. The ICTY might be a subsidiary organ of the Security Council, but it could not simply be merged with it, or the bluff would be exposed.'

[3] Robert Cryer, *Prosecuting International Crimes* (Cambridge, Cambridge University Press, 2005) 211.

of narrative interests at the level of the UN Security Council, as Victor Peskin has highlighted.[4] As for the time before 1994, France had no desire to allow for any illumination of its own military support for the former Hutu regime in the years leading up to the genocide. As for the time after 1994, the United States and the United Kingdom had no desire to allow for any illumination of acts of vengeance committed by Tutsi rebels of the Rwandan Patriotic Front (RPF) against Hutu civilians after the end of the 1994 genocide. These latter massacres of vengeance, which were of a different quality and much smaller scale than the genocidal campaign by Hutu *génocidaires*,[5] had largely been left out of the accounts by most western journalists and scholars[6] and the United States and the United Kingdom, still mindful of the West's guilt for its complacency during the genocide and therefore strongly supportive of the new, post-genocide regime, had no intention of distressing the Tutsi-led government of Paul Kagame with this particular part of 'truth'.[7]

Influence over the Prosecutor

Secondly, inside the Office of the Prosecutor (the position originally included the responsibility both for the ICTY and the ICTR), the UN Security Council held 'almost everything short of suzerainty, notably by controlling all key nominations'.[8] Gary Bass gives a particularly vivid account of the Security Council's hand picking of an international prosecutor in 1993–1994, which amounted to a 'protracted, politicized fiasco'.[9] Richard Goldstone of South Africa, who would ultimately be appointed as the first ICTY/ICTR Prosecutor in 1994, was the candidate of compromise following a yearlong 'tug of war' between western members of the Security Council and Russia. During this time, Russia succeeded in blocking any candidate put forward by a member of NATO, which at the time was protecting a no-fly zone in Bosnia and launching air strikes against Serbian forces. 'Moscow made clear it did not want anyone from a NATO member, fearing bias against the Serbs', the *New York Times* noted.[10] The compromise candidate, Richard Goldstone, pursued Serb suspects only

[4] Victor Peskin, *International Justice in Rwanda and the Balkans* (Cambridge, Cambridge University Press, 2008) 162.

[5] ibid 192.

[6] ibid 193, 210.

[7] ibid 162, 194.

[8] Mégret, 'The Politics of International Criminal Justice' (n 2) 1275.

[9] Gary J Bass, *Stay the Hand of Vengeance* (Princeton, Princeton University Press, 2000) 217.

[10] Paul Lewis, 'South African is to Prosecute Balkan War Crimes', *New York Times*, 9 July 1994: 'At various moments in the search, Russia blocked a Canadian candidate from Sri Lanka, Christopher Amerasinghe, and two American candidates, Cherif Bassiouni, an Egyptian-born law professor in Chicago who led the commission collecting evidence, and Charles E. Ruff, an early Clinton Administration candidate for Deputy Attorney General.'

very slowly at the beginning of his term and made it a policy not to pursue the Tutsi RPF in Rwanda at all.[11]

Goldstone's careful, diplomatic style made it possible for him to propose a successor from a NATO member State, Louise Arbour of Canada, in 1996. After Arbour indicted Slobodan Milosevic in 1999, however, in the midst of NATO's Kosovo intervention to which Russia strongly objected, Russia again insisted on a prosecutor from a 'neutral' country.[12] Carla Del Ponte of Switzerland was brought in by the Security Council in 1999 after Arbour resigned to take a position at the Supreme Court of Canada. To the Council's surprise, however, Del Ponte would test the political tolerance of the UN Security Council members more than both her predecessors.

Del Ponte's vigorous attempts to investigate suspects from the Tutsi RPF[13] and to break up the West's 'pro-RPF narrative'[14] finally led to her removal from the ICTR in 2003, at which time the United States and the United Kingdom intervened to restructure the Office of the Prosecutor,[15] leaving only Del Ponte in charge at the ICTY and installing a successor at the ICTR, Hassan Jallow of Gambia, who has since made no efforts to target Tutsi suspects.[16] After Del Ponte spent another four years at the ICTY, during which time she put considerable pressure on Serbia to extradite fugitive war criminals, Russia blocked the renewal of Del Ponte's Yugoslav mandate.[17] Although in 2007 the entire senior prosecution staff at the ICTY reacted by sending a joint letter to the UN Secretary General requesting that Del Ponte's Deputy, David Tolbert of the United States, continue the job, with some senior staff members even threatening to resign otherwise,[18] Serge Brammertz of 'neutral' Belgium was brought in instead. The UN Security Council once again made its control over the prosecution staff clear.

Influence over the Judges?

Although judges can only influence a tribunal's selection policy to a very limited extent, which is why their influence on the historical narrative of a

[11] Peskin, *International Justice in Rwanda and the Balkans* (n 4) 189: 'My attitude . . . was to give priority in investigations and prosecutions to the most guilty,' Goldstone told me in the interview. 'We didn't have enough resources to investigate all the nines and tens,' he said, referring to a hypothetical ten-point scale of atrocitiy. 'And the RPF, who acted in revenge, were at ones and twos and maybe even fours and fives.'

[12] Carla Del Ponte, *Madame Prosecutor* (New York, Other Press, 2009) 29.

[13] Peskin, *International Justice in Rwanda and the Balkans* (n 4) 208–31.

[14] ibid 210.

[15] ibid 220–22. See also Del Ponte, *Madame Prosecutor* (n 12) 231-36.

[16] Peskin, *International Justice in Rwanda and the Balkans* (n 4) 225–31.

[17] Brammertz interview.

[18] Ed Vulliamy, 'War Crime Lawyers Fight UN on Top Job', *The Observer*, 23 September 2007.

tribunal is less interesting than that of the prosecutor,[19] it is nonetheless worth noting that their *nomination* is under similar control at the UN ad hoc tribunals as that of the prosecutors.[20] Judges, like the prosecutor, are hand-picked by political stakeholders. Few legal practitioners from inside the tribunals are as honest as Michael Bohlander in criticising the common practice by States of nominating professors or diplomats without any forensic credentials,[21] often primarily to reward political loyalty.[22] The same criticism has been raised by Wolfgang Schomburg of Germany, who served as a judge at the ICTY from 2001–2008.[23] Schomburg describes how he was interviewed by diplomats from dozens of States before being elected to the bench.[24]

On the other hand, however, the current ICTY judge Theodor Meron strongly emphasises judges' subsequent complete professional independence from political bodies, which still distinguishes their position from that of the Prosecutor to a considerable extent.[25]

2. GERMANY'S NARRATIVE INTERESTS ON THE BALKANS

In 1991, Croatia called for the creation of an international tribunal to highlight the victimisation of ethnic Croats by Serb forces[26] and in December 1992, the US government reacted by presenting a list of leaders and politicians from the Balkans, among them Serbian President Slobodan Milošević, who should face their judges at a 'second Nuremberg'.[27] The ICTY was created in 1993 by a resolution of the UN Security Council, of which Germany was not a member. Yet far from merely standing aside,

[19] Compare above chapter one, section four.

[20] Pursuant to art 13*bis* ICTY Statute, candidates for the position of permanent judges are short-listed by the UN Security Council and then elected by the UN General Assembly. Available at www.icty.org.

[21] Michael Bohlander, 'The International Criminal Judiciary: Problems of Judicial Selection, Independence and Ethics' in Michael Bohlander (ed), *International Criminal Justice: A Critical Analysis of Institutions and Procedures* (2007) 326f.

[22] ibid 328.

[23] Verbatim at the conference 'Der Internationale Strafgerichtshof (IStGH) in der Praxis', hosted by the German Section of the International Commission of Jurists in Berlin on 13 March 2009.

[24] Quoted in Michael Bohlander, 'The International Criminal Judiciary: Problems of Judicial Selection, Independence and Ethics' in Michael Bohlander (ed), *International Criminal Justice: A Critical Analysis of Institutions and Procedures* (2007) 329. Most recently, this practice of politicised selections, exemplified by International Criminal Court (ICC) and International Court of Justice (ICJ) selections, has been criticised in detail by Ruth Mackenzie and others, *Selecting International Judges* (Oxford, Oxford University Press, 2010).

[25] Theodor Meron, *The Humanization of International Law* (Leiden, Martinus Nijhoff, 2006) 163–77.

[26] Compare Peskin, *International Justice in Rwanda and the Balkans* (n 4) 98–100.

[27] Elaine Sciolino, 'U.S. Names Figures It Wants Charged With War Crimes', *New York Times*, 17 December 1992.

Germany's vocal support for the creation of this tribunal was prominent: As early as September 1992, Kinkel spoke out internationally in support of Croatia's request for a tribunal.[28]

Germany's Own Role on the Balkans

Germany did not initially participate in international peacekeeping efforts in the Balkans – yet it was nonetheless part of this conflict in a very real way. From the beginning of the hostilities in the Balkans, Germany had sided strongly with Croatia, denouncing Serbia as the aggressor and encouraging Croatia's nationalist leadership on its path to independence by becoming the first State to recognise Croatia's independence in December 1991. (The United States held reservations that this step would spark new violence and the European Community was only convinced of this one month later.)[29] By contrast, Russia advocated a narrative that was entirely opposed to Germany's. To Russia, the Serb-dominated Yugoslav government was confronted with Croatian 'separatists' who were now receiving political support from Croatia's old World War II ally, Germany.

Germany continued to argue its side in the case and was joined in this by other NATO countries. When Croatia came out as the winner of the war for the Krajina region in 1995 after a brutal campaign of 'ethnic cleansing' against ethnic Serbs, the United States and Germany refrained from condemning Croatia's 'Operation Storm' in a show of support for the outcome.[30] Moreover, in 1999, Germany became directly involved in the conflict, bombing Serbian targets as part of NATO's military intervention in support of the autonomy of the Albanian-dominated Kosovo region.

Again, the narrative was highly controversial: Russia spoke of illegitimate Kosovar separatism and sided again with Serbia. Even members of NATO, which were now operating as de facto allies of the Albanian Kosovo Liberation Army (KLA), had, only a year earlier, classified the KLA as a terrorist organisation. Even within Germany, the West's pro-Kosovar intervention was highly controversial. The intervention put the new German government composed of Social Democrats and Green Party members (in office 1998–2005) to its first serious test. The German government reinforced its narrative of Serbia as the true aggressor: Germany's new Foreign Minister, Joschka Fischer of the Green Party, went as far as to

[28] Compare Klaus Kinkel, Speech delivered at the London Conference in general debate, 9 September 1992, in ICTY (ed), *The Path to The Hague: Selected Documents on the Origins of the ICTY* (The Hague, United Nations, 2001) Doc 8. See also Peter Wilkitzki, 'The Contribution of the Federal Republic of Germany and the German Länder to the Work of the ICTY' in Lal C Vohrah (ed), *Man's Inhumanity to Man: Essays on International Law in Honour of Antonio Cassese* (The Hague, Kluwer Law International, 2003) 924.

[29] Compare Peskin, *International Justice in Rwanda and the Balkans* (n 4) 99.

[30] ibid 103.

compare the Serb President Milošević to Hitler in order to underline the legitimacy of Germany's military intervention on behalf of the KLA.[31]

The Clash of Interpretations

The question for the newly reunified Germany, which had made its first daring steps onto the international political stage by recognising Croatia's independence in 1991, was precarious: Would an international tribunal add authenticity to Germany's narrative – or would it rather portray Germany as having poured oil into the Balkan fire? Slobodan Milošević, in his later trial at the ICTY, would argue exactly this point several times, claiming that Germany had aimed to maximise its regional influence over a partitioned Yugoslavia. Moreover, would the Tribunal make NATO itself the target of criminal investigations, seeing as NATO air strikes had caused civilian deaths and given the fact that the ICTY's broad mandate allowed for the prosecution of all sides of the conflict?

In terms of the ICTY's function as 'bearer of the "official discourse of the truth"'[32], the stakes for Germany were accordingly high. Unlike for some of Germany's NATO allies, this narrative interest was arguably the single most important interest for Germany.

The political impulse that set policymakers in the United States and, to a lesser degree, France in motion in 1992 in favour of creating the ICTY has often been described as their unwillingness to intervene effectively in the Balkans. To many political observers, the ICTY appears to have primarily been 'a fig leaf for inaction',[33] designed to soothe public dismay at an otherwise largely inactive West.[34] In the specific case of Germany, however, which was eagerly in favour of a tribunal for Yugoslavia at the time, this is not a sufficient explanation. Assuredly, Germany also showed an ambition to demonstrate its ability to handle this European problem and in this sense, a tribunal to intervene post facto would of course be better than nothing.[35] However, unlike the US government which was under

[31] See the critique by Jutta Ditfurth, 'Fischer relativiert NS-Vergangenheit: Der Außenminister trieb die Grünen schrittweise in den Krieg', *Focus* 17/1999.

[32] Pierre Hazan, *Justice in a Time of War* (Station, Texas A&M University Press, 2004) 176.

[33] Peskin, *International Justice in Rwanda and the Balkans* (n 4) 38.

[34] See Geoffrey Robertson, *Crimes against Humanity* (London, Allen Lane, 1999) 286; also Payam Akhavan, 'Justice in The Hague, Peace in the Former Yugoslavia? A Commentary on the United Nations War Crimes Tribunal' (1998) 20 *Human Rights Quarterly* 744f. Yves Beigbeder, *Judging War Criminals* (New York, St. Martin's Press, 1999) 171, calls the Tribunal a 'post-facto substitute for an effective, timely, military intervention by the UN Security Council'. The United States envoy to the Balkans, Richard Holbrooke, is even quoted as having called the ICTY 'little more than a public relations device' by Howard Ball, *Prosecuting War Crimes and Genocide* (Lawrence, University Press of Kansas, 1999) 141.

[35] 'This is the hour of Europe, not the Americans', the President of the Council of Ministers of the European Communities, Jacques Poos of Luxembourg, had famously assumed in 1991. Quoted in Hazan, *Justice in a Time of War* (n 32) 10.

public pressure to act, Germany was in no great need of international face-saving: nobody at the time expected the newly reunified German State to intervene anywhere militarily. Rather, as explained above, Germany had *already* played a part in the conflict in the Balkans. Naturally, the German government would now have an interest in defending and promoting its own narrative of this conflict. For this reason, it is not surprising that Germany's bid to nominate a permanent judge to the ICTY in 1998, while hostilities were still virulent, was voted down several times in the UN General Assembly. As the then German candidate, Peter Wilkitzki of the German Ministry of Justice, assumes, doubts as to the political neutrality of a German government officer on this position probably played a part.[36]

Comparable narrative interests of Germany are not apparent in the parallel case of Rwanda, whose government also demanded a tribunal in 1994 to highlight Tutsi victimhood.[37] For this reason, it is perhaps not surprising, judging from the records of Germany's official diplomatic statements on the international stage, that Germany did not show a notable interest in the creation of the ICTR in 1994.

However, given Germany's narrative interests in the Yugoslavia conflict, Germany's unconditional support of the ICTY does remain puzzling. Important decisions regarding the ICTY's illumination of the Balkan wars could be influenced by the P5 (four of which held their own stakes in the conflict), yet Germany, as an outsider to the Council, would largely have to watch with its hands tied. Did Germany thus entrust its sensitive political interests to that tribunal blindly? Did it rely on the 'objectivity' of the ICTY to *automatically* reflect Germany's perspective on 'truth'? Or is Germany's unwavering support despite its lack of control perhaps an indication that Germany's policy here was, in fact, not driven by self-interests at all but rather by pure human rights idealism?

3. WESTERN PRIORITIES: SHAPING THE HISTORICAL NARRATIVE

Germany's narrative interests in the Balkans were largely aligned with those of the three NATO members in the UN Security Council: the United States, the United Kingdom and France, who all could exert considerable control over the ICTY's prosecution policy through a number of channels of influence. The United States, as the initiator of the ICTY, had made its own perspective on 'historical truth' clear from the beginning: As early as

36 Wilkitzki interview (24 April 2010 by telephone).

37 See Peskin, *International Justice in Rwanda and the Balkans* (n 4) 159.

December 1992, the list of Balkan leaders proposed by the United States for a 'second Nuremberg' showed a clear focus on leaders of the Serb forces,[38] in contrast with the assertion made by Russia that all parties to the conflict shared the same guilt. As illustrated in the above section, this focus on Serb leaders by the US was exactly the point that Germany had also hoped to make.

A Focus on Serbs as Perpetrators

Although Richard Goldstone, the compromise candidate for first ICTY Prosecutor, was less vigorous in pursuing investigations than the US would have liked, Goldstone's focus in selecting from 'many thousands of significant targets'[39] was firmly set on Serbs. As Theodor Meron, the eminent New York professor who would later be nominated by the United States as an ICTY judge, explained in 1997, 'Since the Serbs committed more atrocities than any other party . . . justice required that any indictments of Serbs be prepared and launched without waiting for parallel indictments of Croats and Muslims.'[40] This factual assessment – although heavily contested by Russia – was applied in Goldstone's initial allocation of resources for investigations: In order to collect evidence in an organised fashion, the Prosecutor divided the investigations section into 11 teams, only one of which was assigned to Bosnian Muslim perpetrators and two to Croatian perpetrators. A total of seven out of 11 investigation teams were devoted to collecting and processing evidence for crimes committed by Serbs. Needless to say, '[d]ecisions made by the investigation managers . . . largely predetermined which cases would be brought and in what form' (Del Ponte).[41]

Assuredly, if the early indictments at the ICTY concentrated almost exclusively on Serbs, then it was not only due to policy but also to the fact that the Serbian government's strict non-cooperation with the Tribunal made it especially difficult for ICTY investigators to collect evidence or interview witnesses of crimes committed *against* Serbs. Even if the ICTY Prosecutor aimed for more balanced proportions in the dock at times, 'representative selections are only feasible if the practical situation allows for it', insists the current ICTY Prosecutor Serge Brammertz. 'First of all, the availability of evidence, and the feasibility of investigations in the field are decisive factors.'[42]

[38] Elaine Sciolino, 'U.S. Names Figures It Wants Charged With War Crimes', *New York Times*, 17 December 1992.

[39] ICTY Press Release GR/P.I.S./642–e, Address by Carla Del Ponte, Prosecutor of the ICTY, to the UN Security Council (27 November 2001).

[40] Theodor Meron, *War Crimes Law Comes of Age* (Oxford, Oxford University Press, 1998) 282. The respective chapter is the reprint of a 1997 article.

[41] Del Ponte, *Madame Prosecutor* (n 12) 126.

[42] Brammertz interview. Similarly, at the ICTR, Rwanda's Tutsi-dominated government systematically obstructed investigations against Tutsi suspects, see Peskin, *International Justice in Rwanda and the Balkans* (n 4) 190.

However, as the ICTY's long-time Deputy Prosecutor, Graham Blewitt, also candidly acknowledged, the Tribunal's interest in non-Serb perpetrators was originally rather an indirect one. As Gary Bass notes, 'The tribunal tried to get these indictments [against Croat suspects] out before Dayton, Blewitt says, to defuse accusations of anti-Serb bias.'[43] The Tribunal was meticulous in combating the Serb forces' own historical narrative. 'For instance, when a Bosnian Serb shell killed scores of civilians in Sarajevo's Markale market in 1994, [Serb leader] Karadžić claimed that the Bosnians had faked the incident with corpses from the morgue.'[44] Shortly afterwards, the ICTY made it a priority to adjudicate exactly this isolated incident for its 'particular historical resonance'.[45]

Germany supported the ICTY's investigative efforts. With numerous Balkan refugees coming to Germany in the early 1990s, Germany's Federal Prosecutor General initiated his own investigations into Balkan war crimes based on the principle of universal jurisdiction,[46] soon to be joined by the Prosecutor General of Berlin.[47] This was at a time when the ICTY still lacked adequate investigative resources.[48] More importantly, however, once the Tribunal's investigations became functional, Germany helped to get actual court proceedings started.

The arrest of a suspected Serb war criminal, Dusko Tadić, in Munich on 12 February 1994 was the result of an initiative by Bavaria's then Minister of Welfare.[49] It catapulted Germany to the centre stage of international criminal justice for a moment:[50] A 'stroke of luck' for Goldstone,[51] the arrest of Tadić meant that the ICTY would finally be able to bring a first suspect to trial. German diplomats advocated a rapid extradition to The Hague. Yet two conservative-led ministries, the Ministry of Defence and of the Ministry of the Interior, initially raised concerns about a different aspect of German interest: Both cabinet ministers insisted that no precedent be created by which German nationals would run the risk of being

[43] Bass, *Stay the Hand* (n 9) 244. For a different view, see Peskin, *International Justice in Rwanda and the Balkans* (n 4) 48, who highlights that Serbia's government was not entirely unwilling to allow for investigations of crimes committed against Serbs on a case-by-case basis from 1996 on.

[44] Bass, *Stay the Hand* (n 9) 302

[45] Graham Blewitt, former Deputy Prosecutor of the ICTY, quoted by Allison M Danner, 'Enhancing the Legitimacy and Accountability of Prosecutorial Discretion at the International Criminal Court' (2003) 97 *American Journal of International Law* 543.

[46] See Peter-Tobias Stoll, 'Völkerrechtliche Praxis der Bundesrepublik Deutschland im Jahre 1994' (1996) 56 *Zeitschrift für ausländisches öffentliches Recht und Völkerrecht (Heidelberg Journal of International Law)* 1165.

[47] See Axel Buchwald, *Der Fall Tadić vor dem Internationalen Jugoslawientribunal im Lichte der Entscheidung der Berufungskammer vom 2. Oktober 1995* (Berlin, Berliner Wissenschafts-Verlag, 2005) 52.

[48] See Michael P Scharf, *Balkan Justice* (Durham, Carolina Academic Press, 1997) 79–84.

[49] 'Die Qual dauerte Stunden', *Der Spiegel* 8/1994 (21 February 1994).

[50] See also Claus Kreß, 'Versailles – Nürnberg – Den Haag: Deutschland und das Völkerstrafrecht' (2006) 61 *JuristenZeitung* 986.

[51] Hazan, *Justice in a Time of War* (n 32) 57.

subjected to international criminal justice in the future.[52] In addition, Bavaria and North Rhine-Westphalia, the two largest *Länder*, insisted that Germany reserve the right to decide for or against extraditions to the ICTY on a case-by-case basis, even if the suspects were non-nationals.[53]

Ultimately, the process of passing legislation in Germany to allow for judicial cooperation with the Tribunal took a full 14 months, during which time the Prosecutor and President of the ICTY repeatedly pressured Germany to hurry.[54] Germany drew considerable criticism for this delay.[55] The German law on judicial cooperation with the ICTY was finally passed in April 1995 and Tadić was extradited to The Hague shortly after this. Before that, however, the German government had to reassure sceptics within Germany that this law would never be applied to German nationals.[56]

Only towards the end of the 1990s, with the dust in the conflict region slowly settling and with international pressure mounting on the ICTY to reflect more fairly the complexity of the multiparty conflict, a smaller number of Croat, Muslim and Albanian suspects were also targeted in The Hague. Just like at the ICTR, Carla Del Ponte made it her most important goal to target suspects from all sides. This became the policy project for which she came to be the most admired and attacked . Del Ponte 'took care to select cases based on evidence collected and representing the magnitude of the crimes committed', notes Brammertz of her achievements. 'At the same time, it was necessary to provide for some balance, in order to show that the conflict is not merely black-and-white.' [57]

The Case of NATO

NATO's 1999 military intervention in Kosovo stirred up particular international controversy. NATO lacked a mandate by the UN Security Council. NATO argued that atrocities being committed by Serb forces against the Albanian population in Kosovo justified a 'humanitarian intervention' nonetheless and that Slobodan Milošević was orchestrating atrocities. In this heated international debate, the ICTY went on to play a role with which NATO member States, Germany among them, would ultimately be quite pleased.

Louise Arbour has maintained that her decision to indict Milošević in the midst of NATO's bombing campaign against Serbia, although seen by

[52] Wilkitzki interview.
[53] ibid.
[54] ibid.
[55] See, eg Scharf, *Balkan Justice* (n 48) 101.
[56] For the political debate around this law, see Buchwald, *Der Fall Tadić* (n 47) 54.
[57] Brammertz interview.

Russia as a 'politicised' decision,[58] was not due to outside pressure.[59] Nonetheless, the remarkable timing of this indictment, which added legitimacy to NATO's controversial claims,[60] was no pure coincidence either. This highlights the subtle influence which States can exert through the transmission of information: When negotiations with Milošević over the status of Kosovo failed in early 1999, NATO members, Germany among them,[61] suddenly began to transmit incriminating intelligence for which the ICTY had been waiting for years.[62]' What is more, NATO's subsequent military intervention against Serbia, which lacked approval of the UN Security Council members Russia and China, was followed by a resolution of the UN Security Council 'urging' the ICTY to collect evidence of crimes committed in Kosovo, which NATO had claimed to be intervening against.[63]

When Frédéric Mégret observes that the ICTY's 'financial balance sheet closely followed its political popularity with major funders',[64] this is not only true for the United States[65] but also for Germany. Germany made its first voluntary contribution of $100,000 to the Tribunal in 1999 (which still did not rival the support of the United Kingdom, which provided $3 million in 1999, or the United States, which provided $2 million).[66] Also, similarly to several other NATO member States at the time, Germany sent a group of 17 'gratis personnel' to The Hague for the first time in 1999, the year of the first Kosovo proceedings.[67]

With respect to alleged crimes by NATO itself, much has been written about the decision by Carla Del Ponte to discontinue investigations, a decision of which the ICTY Prosecutor informed the UN Security Council on 2 June 2000. Given the limited scope and gravity of the alleged NATO crimes *in bello*, there is a strong argument that Del Ponte was justified in not applying the same scrutiny to these as to campaigns of 'ethnic cleansing',[68] in line with the pre-announced legal policy of concentrating

[58] Hazan, *Justice in a Time of War* (n 32) 145.

[59] Michael Ignatieff, *Virtual War* (London, Vintage, 2001) 124.

[60] The narrative relevance of the indictment is summarized nicely by Peskin, *International justice in Rwanda and the Balkans* (n 4) 57: 'Milošević the statesman had now become Milošević the villain.'

[61] Hazan, *Justice in a Time of War* (n 32) 130.

[62] Peskin, International justice in Rwanda and the Balkans (n 4) 58.

[63] This resolution is discussed by Cryer, *Prosecuting International Crimes* (n 3) 213.

[64] Mégret, 'The Politics of International Criminal Justice' (n 2) 1276.

[65] ibid.

[66] The Annual Reports of the ICTY, available at www.icty.org, give a detailed record of voluntary contributions by States and non-State actors. For the numbers mentioned here, see ICTY Annual Report 1999 para 197.

[67] ICTY Annual Report 1999 para 195.

[68] Charles Trueheart, 'Taking NATO to Court: Tribunal Reviews Professors' Charges That Alliance Committed War Crimes', *Washington Post*, 20 Jan 2000, speaking of 'an exercise in dangerous relativism'.

on high-level offenders and particularly heinous offences.[69] At the same time, however, it is important to note that each member of the UN Security Council also had the power to *ensure* that Del Ponte would not take a different course of action. The Tribunal's very existence rested on the Council's continued support. As a subsidiary body to the UN Security Council, the Tribunal could theoretically be shut down at a moment's notice. Even if one assumes that Del Ponte's decision not to treat allegations against NATO with the same scrutiny as cases of mass rape or genocide was fair and in good faith, it is fair to assume any different decision on this question would have come at a high price.

The Case of the Kosovo Liberation Army

Regarding the Albanian Kosovo Liberation Army (KLA), which had only recently been rebranded freedom fighters and made informal allies by NATO, Del Ponte has described her war crimes investigations as a deliberate effort to demonstrate the Tribunal's impartiality.[70] Del Ponte complains, however, that the United States would not respond to requests for assistance in investigations against KLA members in 2002[71] and that the European-led United Nations Interim Administration Mission in Kosovo (UNMIK) also began to actively obstruct proceedings against a high-level KLA suspect in 2004.[72]

That high-level suspect, Ramush Haradinaj, suspected of commanding atrocities against ethnic Serbs in Kosovo, was one of UNMIK's choices for political partners in the region. UNMIK allowed Haradinaj to continue his political work in Kosovo even after he was indicted by the ICTY and the Prosecutor warned that this would allow him to intimidate witnesses. Haradinaj was acquitted in 2008, causing an outrage in Serbia, as nine of the 10 witnesses originally willing to testify against him had died of unnatural causes. The ICTY surprisingly decided in 2010 to partially repeat the trial since the original trial had been marred by witness intimidation.

[69] This is supported by eg Danner, 'Enhancing the Legitimacy and Accountability' (n 45) 540; Michael J Struett, 'The Politics of Discursive Legitimacy: Understanding the Dynamics and Implications of Prosecutorial Discretion at the International' in Steven C Roach (ed), Governance, Order and the *International Criminal Court: Between Realpolitik and a Cosmopolitan Court* (Oxford, Oxford University Press, 2009) 110.

[70] Del Ponte, *Madame Prosecutor* (n 12) 88: 'I was determined to present indictments against [Kosovo Liberation Army] leaders implicated in criminal activity. The tribunal's credibility depended on this. A war crimes tribunal that tries the accused from only one side of a given conflict is dispensing only a victor's justice.' See also 276.

[71] ibid 281.

[72] ibid 295–98.

4. GERMANY'S INTERESTS IN NEW TRIBUNALS

Germany's narrative interests vis-à-vis the Yugoslav conflict, as illustrated above,[73] help to explain Germany's strong support for the creation of the ICTY, a tribunal which was (rightly) expected to focus its attention primarily on aspects of the conflict that were particularly important to the western narrative.[74] But there is more to Germany's remarkable new support for international criminal justice after 1990. Germany now took an active interest in international tribunals quite generally, not just in the ICTY. This was in sharp contrast to its previous outspoken scepticism.[75]

Promoting an Iraq Tribunal and the International Criminal Court

In 1990, the United States and the United Kingdom had briefly tabled the idea of applying the Nuremberg principles in order to authoritatively denounce the Iraqi invasion of Kuwait.[76] Both States subsequently went on to stop that invasion by force. While Germany participated in this 1991 UN intervention only financially, not militarily,[77] the idea of creating a tribunal for Iraq evidently resonated particularly well in Germany: In April 1991, Germany's Foreign Minister, Hans-Dietrich Genscher, convinced the other 11 member States of the European Community to join his proposal for a 'Nuremberg-type procedure' to judge Saddam Hussein.[78]

Genscher's successor, Klaus Kinkel, continued to voice this idea even after the United States and the United Kingdom had 'quietly dropped' the idea in 1991,[79] seeing as Hussein had not been ousted from power. Still pointing to the case of Saddam Hussein in 1992, Kinkel noted, 'It should perhaps be considered to create, through international treaties, a criminal law regime that would be better equipped [than domestic courts] to prosecute State crimes.'[80] Kinkel no longer spoke of an imminent threat of politicised justice, as his diplomats had done as recently as 1988,[81] but

[73] See above section three.

[74] ibid.

[75] See above chapter two, section five.

[76] William A Schabas, 'United States Hostility to the International Criminal Court. It's All About the Security Council' (2004) 15 *European Journal of International Law* 707.

[77] For Germany's political calls for an intervention, see Thilo Marauhn, 'Völkerrechtliche Praxis der Bundesrepublik Deutschland im Jahre 1991' (1993) 53 *Zeitschrift für ausländisches öffentliches Recht und Völkerrecht (Heidelberg Journal of International Law)* 963f.

[78] Hazan, *Justice in a Time of War* (n 32) 9f; also Schabas, 'United States Hostility' (n 76) 707. Genscher's advocacy of a tribunal is documented in detail by Marauhn, 'Völkerrechtliche Praxis der Bundesrepublik Deutschland im Jahre 1991' (n 77) 957, 1082.

[79] Elaine Sciolino, 'U.S. Names Figures It Wants Charged With War Crimes', *New York Times*, 17 December 1992.

[80] Klaus Kinkel, 'Wiedervereinigung und Strafrecht' (1992) *JuristenZeitung* 487.

[81] See above chapter two, section five.

rather of 'helping to secure global peace with the means of the law' as 'a fascinating idea'.[82]

Moreover, Germany now also showed a lively interest in facilitating 'Nuremberg-type' procedures elsewhere. With a view to the next step in the development of international criminal justice, Germany's representative to the UN began to take the floor in 1991 to support the long-dormant project of creating a *permanent* international criminal court – the same project which Germany had voted against only three years earlier.[83] When the UN's International Law Commission (ILC) presented its Draft Code of Crimes in 1991, this was welcomed by Germany, although still in careful terms.[84] In 1992, Germany already called upon the ILC to rapidly complete its work on a Draft Statute for an international criminal court.[85] Germany now argued that:

> [T]he process of establishing the ad hoc-Tribunal provides ample evidence for the necessity of a *permanent* court. Although the legal department of the UN Secretariat and the Security Council acted with admirable efficiency and speed it will take some time until the ad hoc-Tribunal for the former Yugoslavia will open its proceedings. . . . [W]e feel that it would be a fallacy to assume that emergency measures like Security Council Resolution 827 already provide an answer to the underlying problem, namely the general lack of prosecution of international crimes. This lacuna needs to be filled by a permanent tribunal. Permanence in this context does not necessarily require a full-time standing body but at least a well-defined structure that could be called into operation without delay if need arises.[86]

[82] ibid. See also Otto Triffterer, 'Was kann das Völkerstrafrecht zur Bewältigung der Regierungskriminalität in der DDR beitragen?' in: Ernst-Joachim Lampe (ed), *Deutsche Wiedervereinigung: Die Rechtseinheit. Vol 2: Die Verfolgung von Regierungskriminalität nach der Wiedervereinigung* (Cologne, Arbeitskreis Strafrecht, 1993) 138, supporting the idea of criminal tribunals for both the 1991 Gulf War and the Yugoslavia conflict.

[83] See above chapter two, section four.

[84] Germany's representative to the UN argued for a strict focus on core crimes and on high-level perpetrators, criticising the Draft Code's provisions targeting 'any individual who commits or orders the commission' of a war crime as too broad. UN Doc A/C.6/46/SR.29, 21–22.

[85] See Statement by the Representative of Germany to the 6th Committee of the UN General Assembly (UNGA), UN Doc A/C.6/47/SR.23 (29 October 1992), arguing, inter alia: 'International criminal law, if it is ever to become effective, needs a trial mechanism capable of prosecuting those who are responsible for its violations.' See also Christine Langenfeld, 'Völkerrechtliche Praxis der Bundesrepublik Deutschland im Jahre 1992' (1994) 54 *Zeitschrift für ausländisches öffentliches Recht und Völkerrecht (Heidelberg Journal of International Law)* 820f and 1009f.

[86] Quoted in Christian Walter, 'Bericht über die Völkerrechtliche Praxis der Bundesrepublik Deutschland im Jahre 1993' (1995) 55 *Zeitschrift für ausländisches öffentliches Recht und Völkerrecht (Heidelberg Journal of International Law)* 1102f.

The 'New' Germany and Human Rights Virtues

Germany's narrative interests in the Balkans have been illustrated above,[87] yet what narrative interests could possibly have been connected to the political support for new tribunals *in general*? In the case of Iraq, it could be argued that Germany, quite like the United States or the United Kingdom, had a point to make – that is, that Germany had narrative interests in that particular situation. But considering the much wider support from Germany for the creation of new ad hoc and permanent institutions of international criminal justice, as illustrated in the above subsection, it is worth exploring a more general kind of narrative interest on the side of Germany.

Frédéric Mégret describes the political rhetoric that led up to the creation of the ICTY in 1993 as 'a bizarre and frantic race for historical legitimacy' between France and the United States:

> Each of these states seemed to calculate that, if an international criminal tribunal were to be created at all, it would be in their interest to be associated with the aura of reviving the idea, while not pushing it so far ahead that it would get out of hand.[88]

US State Department officials were reportedly infuriated after France 'pull[ed] the rug under us [ie the State Department] and [stole] our thunder'.[89] 'By the time the creation of the ICTY became inevitable, even Mitterrand', who had previously been sceptical of the whole project, 'would seek to portray himself as one of its promoters',[90] notes Mégret. Germany – eager to step out of the shadow of Nuremberg and to re-enter the world stage after 1990 – fits this pattern. To be associated with the idea of reviving Nuremberg, for the newly reunified German State, would be a welcome gain in political and moral legitimacy. As Paul Betts notes, 'even if Germany had been at the very centre of discussions of international justice from 1919 to 1989, its status was mostly as its object'.[91] Now however, Germany suddenly received the chance to change that, by joining its western allies in the defence of the Nuremberg principles on the international stage and by making sure that audiences would take notice.

In a statement delivered to Germany's parliament in 1994, the German Foreign Office brazenly claimed that the ICTY had been an idea of none

[87] See above section two.
[88] Mégret, 'The Politics of International Criminal Justice' (n 2) 1273.
[89] Quoted by Scharf, *Balkan Justice* (n 48) 52.
[90] Mégret, 'The Politics of International Criminal Justice' (n 2) 1273.
[91] Paul Betts, 'Germany, International Justice and the Twentieth Century' (2005) 17 *History & Memory* 75.

other than Klaus Kinkel.[92] The Ministry of Justice in later years made more moderate efforts to enhance the visibility of Germany in this project. As Peter Wilkitzki of the Ministry of Justice underlined in a 2003 article, Germany as the third largest contributor to the Tribunal with approximately $8,400,000 in contributions in the year 2000, 'contributes more than its due share to the budget'.[93] 'Unfortunately', noted Wilkitzki, 'this fact, as well as Germany's considerable political and financial commitment as far as the problems of the region are concerned . . . is not reflected in the proportion of German nationals employed at the ICTY'.[94] At this point in 2003, Germany had at least, finally, been successful in bringing the first German to the ICTY judges' bench. This judge was a former prosecutor and officer of the German Ministry of Justice, Wolfgang Schomburg.[95] Even though Germany is not a member of the UN Security Council, an informal agreement later assured that Schomburg's seat was again given to a German national, Christoph Flügge, in 2008.

5. CONCLUSION

This chapter has focussed on an episode that is highly puzzling from the perspective of a realist analysis of the politics of international criminal justice. When the ICTY was created in 1993, it was designed in a way that would afford the UN Security Council considerable control over the Tribunal's prosecution policy;[96] very broadly speaking, the UN Security Council took roughly the same place within the institutional design at The Hague that the Allied Powers had previously taken at Nuremberg. Why then did Germany – which was not among the powerful permanent members of the UN Security Council but rather had to largely stand back and watch others exert influence – still support this tribunal so vigorously?[97] Germany even had more reasons than other States to approach such an institution with particular caution since Germany's own role in the Yugoslav conflict had been a matter of controversy even in the west.[98] Why then take this risk? Why welcome such an institution?

As the exploration undertaken in this chapter indicates, Germany's government did not entrust its particular interests to the ICTY blindly.

[92] *Bundestags-Drucksache* 12/6816, 2. By contrast, Wilkitzki, 'The Contribution of the Federal Republic of Germany' (n 28) 924, notes only that Kinkel 'played a decisive role' in getting the UN Security Council Resolutions 808 and 827 of 22 February and 25 May 1993, which established the ICTY and formulated the Tribunal's Statute, 'off the ground'.

[93] ibid 928–31.

[94] ibid 932.

[95] For the first nomination of a German to that bench in 1998, see above section two.

[96] See above section one.

[97] See above section two.

[98] See above section two.

Rather, Germany's government understood the workings of the Tribunal, with its particular channels of influence leading from the UN Security Council in New York to the Office of the Prosecutor in The Hague, quite well. And Germany was in the fortunate position of having three of its NATO allies among the five permanent members of the UN Security Council. With these three, Germany shared its interest in a particular portrayal of the 'historical truth' of the Balkan conflict and hence Germany could expect that these narrative interests would be taken care of.[99]

While the ICTY's prosecution policy turned out to be a welcome enhancement of the authenticity of Germany's own controversial narrative of the conflict, Germany's good relationship with the Tribunal also allowed the newly reunified German State to show itself as a promoter of human rights on the international stage.[100]

[99] See above section three.
[100] See above section four.

5

Germany's Role (and Stake) in the Creation of the ICC

IN 1995, AFTER the two UN ad hoc tribunals were installed and the debate turned to the creation of a new, permanent International Criminal Court (ICC), Germany's position on international criminal justice shifted again. Whereas Germany had not voiced any objections to the influence of the UN Security Council on international prosecutors before, it now began to argue strongly against any such influence. The predominant idea of a 'UN court' – that is, a court whose prosecutor is mandated and controlled by the UN's 'executive branch', the UN Security Council – was now rejected by Germany. This policy shift on the part of Germany is the focus of this chapter.

The aim of this chapter is to assess both the conceptual shift in Germany's legal arguments presented at the international stage and the power political consequences which these arguments entailed. If the particular alleys of influence of the Security Council's five permanent members should be capped, as say the German negotiators, then two key questions arise: who would then take the Council's position? And would other States gain the influence which the Security Council would lose?

1. WHO SHOULD BE IN CONTROL?

As explored in chapter one, a court of international criminal justice is able to shape a historical narrative through its selection of cases, with the prosecutor being the most powerful figure in this respect. Applying this set of facts to the ICC, the policy question arises: should the ICC Prosecutor, who can use this power on a much larger geographic scale than his predecessors at the regional tribunals, be under the oversight of a political institution in order to add democratic legitimacy to his or her necessary policymaking? This question of 'prosecutorial accountability v independence' was central to the heated debates around the creation of the ICC.

New Degrees of Selectivity

With a larger territorial scope, the gap between legally possible and practically feasible prosecutions is, if anything, even wider in an institution like the ICC than at regional tribunals.[1] The Nuremberg trials altogether placed near to 200 suspects in the dock; the UN ad hoc tribunals in the 1990s were at least able to select a few dozen suspects from each conflict situation. By contrast, the ICC has, to date, been forced to distill the first conflict situations before it – those of Uganda, the Democratic Republic of Congo, Darfur, the Central African Republic, Kenya and Libya – down to a maximum of five indictments each. How does one choose five persons to represent the entire systemic crime committed in a conflict region? The question how to prioritise *within* a conflict situation is obviously more challenging – and more open to policymaking – at the ICC than ever before.

In addition to prioritising within conflict situations, a permanent world court also needs to prioritise *between* situations. This accounts for an extra dimension in the selection process. As Serge Brammertz notes, 'Before you can even start comparing different crime bases within one situation, you are forced to compare different situations with one another.'[2] This second dimension of selectivity has recently caught the attention of commentators.[3]

The prioritisation of a few conflict situations (out of many) will inevitably focus audiences on one particular global narrative: for instance, the decision by the UN Security Council to create tribunals only for Yugoslavia and Rwanda in the 1990s expressed to audiences that Yugoslavia and Rwanda were the most important scenes of atrocities at that particular

[1] Victor Peskin, *International Justice in Rwanda and the Balkans* (Cambridge, Cambridge University Press, 2008) 255. Scarce resources are under even more pressure here, since the problems of logistics, language and diplomacy inevitably multiply where investigations are spread out all over the globe, compare Allison M Danner, 'Enhancing the Legitimacy and Accountability of Prosecutorial Discretion at the International Criminal Court' (2003) 97 *American Journal of International Law* 511 at fnn 4 and 519. The ICC's early proceedings are already drawing criticism for being far more resource-consuming than previous trials at the UN ad hoc tribunals. See, eg Guénaël Mettraux, *The Cost of Justice – Is the ICC Living Beyond its Means?* International Criminal Law Bureau (6 August 2009). Available at www.internationallawbureau.com.

[2] Brammertz interview (14 October 2009, The Hague).

[3] See Mohamed El Zeidy, 'The Gravity Threshold under the Statute of the International Criminal Court' (2008) 19 *Criminal Law Forum* 39; William A Schabas, 'Prosecutorial Discretion v. Judicial Activism at the International Criminal Court' (2008) 6 *Journal of International Criminal Justice* 734: 'There was no selection of a "situation" either at Nuremberg or before the ad hoc tribunals. This had been done for them in their enabling instruments, by the powers that created the institutions.' Also Frédéric Mégret, 'The Politics of International Criminal Justice' (2008) 13 *European Journal of International Law* 1283: '[t]he ICC may eventually simply displace the problem of selectivity, transferring it from the 'external' one of tribunal creation to the "internal" one of caseload selection.'

moment in history, an assertion which is assuredly debatable. The same communicative mechanism is also already visible at the ICC: the fact that all six of the first six situations pursued by the ICC are located in Africa is already drawing criticism for apparently expressing to audiences that atrocities are solely an African problem.[4] Although this criticism of the ICC Prosecutor is not entirely fair,[5] what it does illustrate is the great expressive impact of the Court's prioritisation between conflicts and the normative need to prioritise pursuant to equal standards, however difficult this may actually be in practice.

Chances for 'Objectivity': Slimmer than Ever

Which scenes of atrocity around the globe deserve the ICC's most urgent attention? Which portion of resources should be directed towards the investigation of which conflict? And which situations should be left out of the Court's focus altogether? In reaching a decision that is as objective as possible, the ICC Prosecutor is basically faced with the familiar need to draw comparisons on the grounds of gravity.[6] However, for all the reasons illustrated above,[7] the chances of deciding such questions objectively are once again highly doubtful.

William Schabas gives a very detailed critique of the fairness of the ICC Prosecutor's selection of cases thus far[8] and Kevin Heller's criticism of the ICC Prosecutor's decision to prefer African cases over a case against the British army in Iraq[9] is equally noteworthy. Whether or not one agrees with these authors' particular arguments, they do nicely illustrate the serious difficulty in reaching universal agreement on the question of

[4] Compare Charles Jalloh, 'Regionalizing International Criminal Law? Prospects and Challenges for Africa and the International Criminal Court' (2009) 9 *International Criminal Law Review* 445, noting that 'the international criminal justice regime anchored on the ICC may be undermined, or perhaps even falter, if it is perceived as having a biased, politicized or insensitive application to a single region of the world'.

[5] In reality, it is probably too early to assess a selection *policy* by the ICC, since the first four African conflict situations taken up by the ICC were not selected by the Court but rather referred to it by others. See also Schabas, 'Prosecutorial Discretion v Judicial Activism' (n 3) 740f.

[6] Assuredly, other considerations besides gravity may also be relevant to the selection between situations. For instance, one policy that was decided upon by the ICC Prosecutor at an early stage was to give priority to situations where violence is ongoing, in the hope that it is not too late to achieve some deterrent effect on the actors there – as opposed to other regions where hostilities have ceased, meaning that judicial proceedings can contribute only to creating a historical record. However, the question of gravity is one that is raised in *every* selection decision. Brammertz interview (14 October 2009 in The Hague).

[7] Compare above chapter one, section four.

[8] ibid 747–51.

[9] Kevin J Heller, 'Situational Gravity under the Rome Statute' in Carsten Stahn and Larissa van den Herik (eds), *Future Directions in International Criminal Justice* (The Hague, Kluwer Law, 2009) 1–3.

which situations around the globe deserve to be viewed as most important. Schabas, for example, argues:

> [The ICC Prosecutor's] analysis hinged essentially on the fact that there were thousands of deaths in central Africa, whereas British forces were charged with responsibility for war crimes occasioning loss of life in only 10 or 20 cases in Iraq. . . . The methodology of the comparison between Central Africa and Iraq seems flawed. The Prosecutor could not have been comparing the total number of deaths in Iraq with the total in the DRC or Uganda, because he might have been forced to conclude that the situation in Iraq is more serious.

The ICC Prosecutor, to date, has had very few chances to make selections between situations, whereas the UN Human Rights Council is faced with the same need to prioritise selections but has fewer restraints in doing so. For this reason, the Human Rights Council's work is perhaps illustrative of the problems ahead of the ICC Prosecutor once he or she may begin to select at more liberty in the future. The UN Human Rights Council is tasked with reporting the same kinds of human rights violations which the ICC is tasked with investigating and the Council's mandate, similarly to the mandate of the ICC, emphasises objectivity above all else. The Council is mandated by the UN General Assembly to report on human rights violations worldwide 'based on objective and reliable information . . . in a manner which ensures universality of coverage and equal treatment with respect to all States'.[10] Nonetheless, priorities have to be made.

For instance, the UN Human Rights Council presently allocates a great portion of its attention to charges against one State: Israel. Whether one agrees or disagrees with the fairness of this particular prioritisation, it is clear that the prioritisation itself does not depend merely on simple quantitative arguments, which can be seen by the number of victims in the Israeli-Palestinian conflict paling in comparison with the victims of atrocities committed at the same time in Darfur. Obviously, the UN Human Rights Council is prioritising on the basis of *qualitative* arguments, which is inescapable to a certain degree[11] – even for an institution bound by the principles of 'universality, impartiality, objectivity and non-selectivity'[12] – but obviously debatable in every case.

Once the ICC Prosecutor takes up the difficult business of selecting between conflicts with less restraints, his or her particular decisions, much like those of the Human Rights Council, can be expected to be a matter of even more heated debate. There is clearly the concern that the cultural and political backgrounds of judicial decision makers, instead of purely 'objective' standards, will play some role at this stage (as is the case, in the eyes of many critics, with the UN Human Rights Council). This is why the

[10] UN Doc A/RES/60/251 (3 April 2006) 3.
[11] Compare above chapter one, section four.
[12] UN Doc A/RES/60/251 (3 April 2006) 2.

question of whether the ICC Prosecutor should be subjected to some form of political oversight deserves so much attention.

2. ORIGINALLY, GERMANY FAVOURED UN SECURITY COUNCIL CONTROL

Germany Favoured Security Council Control

Initially, all participants in the debate on the institutional design of a permanent international criminal court in the early 1990s agreed that an international prosecutor should be accountable to the UN Security Council. Germany's stance, which is the focus of this section, was particularly favourable to such accountability to the UN Security Council.

The 1994 Draft Statute: A Permanent UN Tribunal

In November 1992, while the debate over the creation of the ICTY was still lively, the UN General Assembly requested that the UN International Law Commission (ILC) begin to draft a statute for a permanent international criminal court. The 34 legal scholars assembled in the ILC (chaired at the time by Christian Tomuschat of Germany) were advisers only and so it was understood that their aim would primarily be to reflect and summarise the potential for consensus in order to prepare the ground for a later political debate. The ILC emphasised this by arguing strictly from the perspective of its assessment of the 'present stage of development of the international legal system'.[13] The ILC Draft Statue, presented on 1 September 1994, captured this moment and allows for an interesting insight into which shape the ICC might have assumed had events not taken an unexpected turn. The driving force behind the ILC's work on the ICC was Special Rapporteur Professor James Crawford of Australia, an ICC enthusiast who would later play an important role in arguing for an independent ICC Prosecutor. Nonetheless, in 1994, the ILC was very cautious in proposing only 'what was in effect a permanent ad hoc tribunal, perfectly subordinate to the Security Council and interlocked with the Charter of the United Nations'.[14]

[13] Draft Statute for the International Criminal Court, with commentary, in Report of the International Law Commission on the Work of its Forty-sixth Session, UN GAOR, 49th Sess., Supp No 10, 43, UN Doc A/49/10 (1994). Available at www.un.org/law/ilc/index.htm. See commentary to art 25, 46. Reprinted without commentary in M Cherif Bassiouni, *The Statute of the International Criminal* Court (Ardsley, Transnational, 1998) 657–76.

[14] William A Schabas, 'United States Hostility to the International Criminal Court. It's All About the Security Council' (2004) 15 *European Journal of International Law* 701.

The 1994 Draft Statute proposed a position of strong control for the UN Security Council. While upholding the idea that individual States are sovereign in dealing with human rights atrocities within their borders, the Draft Statute allowed *only* for the UN Security Council to pierce this sovereignty by allowing the ICC Prosecutor to intervene. Though the ICC's jurisdiction would, in principle, be limited to States that have consented to the Statute, the UN Security Council would nonetheless be able to refer situations to the Court universally.[15] 'This right, being totally independent of the acceptance of the Court's jurisdiction by any State, provides a means for the waiver of the jurisdictional requirements when the interests of the international community so require', one contemporary commentator explained,[16] making the conceptual underpinning of this arrangement nicely visible. While the ILC Draft Statute considered all members of the international community as sovereign and equal, it regarded the UN Security Council as the closest there is to a rightful representative of that *whole* community. Thus, only the Council can claim to rightfully stand above individual sovereignty. And an international court that claims authority 'over' State actors can draw its legitimacy only from that body.

By the same token, the ILC Draft Statute also reserved a right for the Security Council to shield a State's sovereignty as a matter of exception. The Draft Statute provided for the ICC Prosecutor to require the Council's prior authorisation in the form of a resolution for any investigation into a situation with which the Council is already 'dealing',[17] thus effectively enabling the Security Council's five permanent members to block any investigation with the help of their veto power.

As a consequence, the explicit consent by States by way of a treaty – one innovation which the ILC offered[18] – would merely be important in giving the international criminal justice system new legitimacy. Technically, though, this would not make any difference. The UN Security Council would be able to continue to initiate proceedings without State consent, as had also been the case in the system of UN ad hoc tribunals. Also, while the Draft Statute introduced the right of States Parties to refer situations to the Prosecutor independently,[19] a second noteworthy innovation, the Council's ability to shield States would assure that any activity by the ICC Prosecutor would continue to rely, at a minimum, on the UN Security

[15] Art 23 (1) Draft Statute.

[16] Satu Suikkari, 'Debate in the United Nations on the International Law Commission's Draft Statute for an International Criminal Court' (1995) 64 *Nordic Journal of International Law* 205–21, 213.

[17] Art 23 (3) Draft Statute.

[18] The ILC offered several alternative options. Other 'possible ways whereby a permanent International Criminal Court might enter into a relationship with the United Nations' outlined by the Draft Statute included setting up the Court as an organ or subsidiary organ of the UN. See Draft Statute, appendix III, 73.

[19] Art 25 Draft Statute.

Council's non-objection. In sum, the UN Security Council could continue to decide in favour or against criminal prosecutions case-by-case ('ad hoc'), with the creation of a permanent court merely providing for a more appropriate structure.

Clearly, this Draft Statute was not a suggestion for change. The essential innovation, which the ILC's 1994 Draft Statute suggested, was merely to *permanently* add international criminal justice to the UN Security Council's peacekeeping instruments. This relative caution by the ILC can be attributed to the novelty of international criminal tribunals at the time. The ICTY in 1994 had not yet begun a single trial and the UN ad hoc tribunals thus still appeared as an experiment with an uncertain future.

Germany Advocates Prosecutorial Accountability

Germany emphatically welcomed the 1994 Draft Statute's vision of a permanent 'UN court'.[20] Regarding a central role for the UN Security Council, Germany's representatives at the UN argued that this control by the Council would be 'essential' if the crime of aggression were to be included into the Court's jurisdiction,[21] a measure which Germany strongly favoured.[22] Moreover, in discussions within the German government in 1994, the Ministry of Justice even expressed that the role of the ICC Prosecutor outlined by the Draft Statute 'raise[d] concerns' only for being *too* independent from the Security Council.[23] This was at a time when the Prosecutor's proposed role was considerably less independent than it would later become: the 1994 Draft Statute did not yet grant the Prosecutor the right to investigate situations out of his or her own initiative (*proprio motu*),[24] but rather the Draft Statute afforded the ICC Prosecutor latitude only in deciding, after receiving a situation, whether or not to indict individuals[25] and left the President of the Court with no effective means to overturn this decision.[26] This would enable the ICC Prosecutor, in theory, to block particular cases. A minority of scholars in

[20] *Bundestags-Drucksache* 12/6816 (Antwort der Bundesregierung auf die Kleine Anfrage der Abgeordneten Gerhard Reddemann (CDU), Robert Antretter (SPD) u.a.).

[21] Position of Germany 1995, quoted in Rainer Grote, 'Völkerrechtliche Praxis der Bundesrepublik Deutschland im Jahre 1995' (1997) *Zeitschrift für ausländisches öffentliches Recht und Völkerrecht (Heidelberg Journal of International Law)* 1122–24.

[22] Position of Germany 1995, quoted in ibid.

[23] Nine-page memorandum signed by Wolfgang Birke, Ministry of Justice, sent to the Head of the Division for International Law, Ministry of Foreign Affairs, on 18 October 1994, 2. On file with the author.

[24] Of the ILC's 34 expert members, only one had favoured introducing this possibility. Compare Draft Statute with commentary (UN Doc A/49/10 (1994)) 46. Available at www.un.org/law/ilc/index.htm.

[25] Art 26 (4) Draft Statute.

[26] Art 26 (5) Draft Statute.

the ILC had raised concerns against this power of the ICC Prosecutor. They had argued that the judges at the ICC should at least have the power 'to annul decisions shown to be contrary to law'.[27] Germany joined this criticism by an independent ICC Prosecutor.

In a memorandum to the German Ministry of Foreign Affairs in October 1994, the Ministry of Justice maintained that the ICC Prosecutor's selection policy should not merely be submitted to the effective control of the ICC judges but rather directly 'to the decisions of an organ of the UN, for example the Security Council or a subsidiary body established by it' in order for his or her authority in selecting cases to be acceptable.[28] To give the ICC Prosecutor independence from the community of states by subjecting him or her only to judicial control would otherwise allow for the ICC to work as a 'closed system' with no accountability or checks and balances in place, the German Ministry of Justice warned.[29]

Within the 'accountability v independence' debate, illustrated in chapter one, section VI, Germany thus placed itself clearly at the 'accountability' end of the spectrum. The German Ministry of Justice argued that the ICC Prosecutor should be made accountable to the society which he represents, especially if he or she is to be vested with the power to exercise discretion in selecting cases, which under the Rome Statute would become true to a great extent.[30] Germany assumed that this society was the society of States,[31] rather than a cosmopolitan community of humankind.

Prosecutorial Accountability in German Domestic Law

For Germany to take this position in favour of prosecutorial accountability is not surprising given that Germany's domestic penal system emphasises the need for such accountability in a relatively rigid manner. Whereas many legal systems grant prosecutors some independence from the executive branch in order to ensure their political neutrality,[32] Germany's legal system places prosecutors under relatively strong control. The

[27] Draft Statute with commentary, UN Doc A/49/10 (1994) 47 para 7f. Available at www.un.org/law/ilc/index.htm.

[28] Nine-page memorandum signed by Wolfgang Birke, Ministry of Justice, sent to the Head of the Division for International Law, Ministry of Foreign Affairs, on 18 October 1994, 2. On file with the author.

[29] ibid.

[30] Richard Goldstone describes the degree of the ICC Prosecutor's independence as a 'fundamental departure' from the UN ad hoc tribunals, particularly since art 53 (2) (c) of the Rome Statute gives the ICC Prosecutor the authority to decline to pursue an investigation when such an investigation is not 'in the interests of justice': Richard J Goldstone and Nicole Fritz, '"In the Interests of Justice" and Independent Referral: The ICC Prosecutor's Unprecedented Powers' (2004) 13 *Leiden Journal of International Law* 657.

[31] This is expressed explicitly at the end of the Ministry of Justice's 1994 critique (see above n 23, 3).

[32] Danner, 'Enhancing the Legitimacy and Accountability' (n 1) 515.

government in Germany can directly control prosecutors' use of discretion with directives,[33] a right that is considered a safeguard against renegades and political activists in the prosecutor's office.

In this spirit, the case for subjecting the ICC Prosecutor to the control of a (at least somewhat) legitimised body like the UN Security Council – that is, for adhering to an institutional design similar to that of the UN ad hoc tribunals – was phrased by Germany's Ministry of Justice in October 1994 not as an argument for 'politicising' the judiciary, but contrarily as a prerequisite for the rule of law. This initial position was never voiced by Germany on an international level however. Instead, an agreement was soon reached in internal discussions in Germany to argue exactly the opposite effect.

3. THEN, GERMANY ARGUES FOR 'INDEPENDENCE' INSTEAD

Beginning in 1996, Germany began to voice concerns that a 'UN court' as envisioned by the ILC's 1994 Draft Statute would perpetuate unjustified privileges for the five veto-wielding members of the UN Security Council. Along with a group of smaller and middle-sized States, Germany began to advocate a new concept. The new idea was to completely detach the ICC Prosecutor from the UN Security Council. In the spectrum of the 'accountability v independence' debate, Germany shifted its position radically from the 'accountability' to the 'independence' end.

Germany at PrepCom (1996–98)

Political negotiations on the shape of a future ICC started in March 1996 in New York, where the UN Preparatory Committee (PrepCom) convened for the first of six sessions, which were to last until June 1998. Governments from 120 States were represented, although, as participants noted, only approximately 30 States had sent delegations to PrepCom staffed in a way that enabled them to participate actively. The setting of the debate, at least in its initial phase, was thereby one of few speakers and many listeners. Most of the 30 vocally active States were developed western democracies and among them, a core group of about 15 States soon took the lead in exchanging the most important arguments. Germany joined this core group. Germany had initially sent a delegation of only two officers to New York throughout the year 1996, while France, for example, was rep-

[33] The scope of discretion is, in turn, relatively slim though. Acknowledging that society is represented by the prosecutor, but that it is nonetheless not free to exercise selective justice towards suspects, the law in Germany requires the prosecutor to prosecute, in theory, all felonies for which there is sufficient evidence (*Legalitätsprinzip*).

resented by a team of five to six.[34] Germany, however, began to participate more actively in 1997. The new Head of the Ministry of Foreign Affairs' International Law Department, Hans-Peter Kaul, assigned a higher political priority to the ICC negotiations after taking office at the end of 1996, sending a group of seven delegates to New York.

There, the United States, which had been the driving force in reviving international criminal justice after the Cold War, proposed to proceed swiftly on the basis of the 1994 Draft Statute, in other words: to install a permanent 'UN court'. This proposal was supported by the other four permanent members of the UN Security Council (Russia, China, France and the United Kingdom). US negotiators would later explain that the ICC Prosecutor should be controlled by the international community, drawing on the democratic principle of accountability.[35] The conceptual arguments, essentially, were those which Germany had shared until shortly before. To many smaller States which had only recently or reluctantly accepted the political experiment of war crimes tribunals altogether, this 'conservative' US concept even appealed as a relative improvement. A permanent court, instead of ad hoc tribunals, would save costs and prevent tribunal fatigue.[36]

At the same time, political opposition to this concept materialised for the first time. A small number of middle powers, among them Canada, Argentina, Australia and Germany, joined to form a so-called 'like-minded group' and voiced criticism of the status quo of Security Council primacy over international criminal justice, which until then had been championed mainly by NGOs.[37] Instead of a 'UN court', they argued for a court that would be free of the influence of the UN Security Council and particularly its five veto-wielding permanent Council members (the P5).

The group acted as a uniform caucus and undertook concentrated efforts to win majority support for its positions. From 1997, these efforts were formally coordinated by a bureau. Soon, all member States of the European Union, with the notable exception of France and the United Kingdom, had joined the group, which then gradually won the support of numerous developing countries.

[34] Kaul interview (6 August 2009, The Hague).

[35] See the programmatic speeches by eg Marc Grossman, Under Secretary for Political Affairs, 'American Foreign Policy and the International Criminal Court: Remarks to the Center for Strategic and International Studies', 6 May 2002. Also John R Bolton, Under Secretary of State for Arms Control and International Security, 'The United States and the International Criminal Court', Remarks to the Federalist Society, 14 November 2002.

[36] Caroline Fehl, 'Explaining the International Criminal Court: A Practice Test for Rationalist and Constructivist Approaches' in Steven C Roach (ed), *Governance, Order and the International Criminal Court: Between Realpolitik and a Cosmopolitan Court* (Oxford, Oxford University Press, 2009) 85.

[37] Silvia A Fernández de Gurmendi, 'The Role of the International Prosecutor' in Roy S Lee (ed), *The International Criminal Court: The Making of the Rome Statute; Issues, Negotiations, Results* (The Hague, Kluwer Law International, 1999) 177.

Germany Spearheads the Call for Prosecutorial Independence

Germany now took a particularly strong stance in arguing for prosecutorial independence. In the like-minded group's division of labour, the debates on the role of the ICC Prosecutor at PrepCom had been assigned to Argentina's negotiators as a focal point, yet the delegates of Germany also became strongly involved. As Hans-Jörg Behrens of the German Ministry of Justice reported from New York in August 1997, Germany's objective was to grant UN Security Council members 'no potential whatsoever to set limits to the work of the Prosecutor'.[38] Germany proposed at PrepCom to give the Security Council only a right to refer situations to the ICC Prosecutor – which was of little practical significance since all individual State Parties were to be granted the same right – but no authority to intervene in the ICC Prosecutor's decision making.

Initially, this call for prosecutorial independence was only supported by a small minority of States. While many States agreed with Germany and Argentina in trying to avoid privileges for the P5, the notion of completely detaching the ICC Prosecutor from any UN control also raised concerns. In fact, the P5 were not alone in asking whether an ICC Prosecutor lacking any effective accountability towards the society of States might end up a 'lone ranger running wild', as the Head of Argentina's PrepCom delegation recalls.[39] Discussions were, therefore, controversial even within the group, which had pre-agreed on an independent ICC Prosecutor as one of its negotiating objectives.[40]

The most important concession which Germany and Argentina offered to sceptics within the group was to create a Pre-Trial Chamber which would exercise some control over the ICC Prosecutor's selection policy. This proposal was made by Germany and Argentina in March 1998[41] and was ultimately implemented in article 15 of the Rome Statute. However, it only provides for the institutional design that Germany's Ministry of Justice had earlier criticised in October 1994 as a 'closed system':[42] with this concept, the ICC Prosecutor's power to select cases remains without

[38] Hans-Jörg Behrens, Negotiation Report for the Ministry of Justice, 28 August 1997. On file with the author.

[39] ibid 181.

[40] The like-minded group's set of six pre-agreed 'guiding principles' is discussed by Fanny Benedetti and John L Washburn, 'Drafting the International Criminal Court treaty: Two Years to Rome and an Afterword on the Rome Diplomatic Conference' (1999) 5 *Global Governance* 21.

[41] Morten Bergsmo and Jelena Pejić, 'Article 15: Prosecutor' in Otto Triffterer (ed), *Commentary on the Rome Statute of the International Criminal Court: Observers' Notes, Article by Article* (Baden-Baden, CH Beck, 1999) 362.

[42] See nine-page memorandum signed by Wolfgang Birke, Ministry of Justice, sent to the Head of the Division for International Law, Ministry of Foreign Affairs, on 18 October 1994, 2. On file with the author.

any effective checks and balances by a democratically legitimised body outside the Court.[43] Moreover, for structural reasons, this provides only for a weak type of control. As argued above in chapter one, section VI, the fairness of the prosecutor's overall selection of cases is something which judges – who are required to take an individual perspective on each case rather than an overall perspective on historical fairness – can only control to a very limited extent. While the ICC Pre-Trial Chamber can weed out frivolous cases brought to it by the ICC Prosecutor, it cannot compel the Prosecutor to bring cases that he or she chooses to frivolously ignore.[44]

The concerns within the like-minded group against the German-Argentine goal of an ICC Prosecutor subject only to such weak checks were addressed by a suggestion for compromise tabled by Singapore. Singapore suggested that the UN Security Council should keep some influence, albeit much less than at the two UN ad hoc tribunals. Instead of the ICC Prosecutor requiring the UN Security Council's approval before investigating a situation (which the P5 had suggested), he or she should be free to proceed unless the Council defers a situation by resolution, ie by an affirmative vote by nine of its fifteen voting members. By turning the question on the Council around, Singapore's suggestion thus renders the P5's veto powers ineffective at blocking investigations. Instead of making investigations that are of special interest to any of the P5 unlikely, the effect of the presence of five veto powers on the Council is, if anything, the opposite. A single veto is enough to topple any attempt at a blockade.

This concept does not deny the UN Security Council a special role in relation to the ICC. Nonetheless, it clearly reduced the privileges of the P5 since a permanent member's affirmative vote on whether a particular situation should be deferred from the ICC weighs no more than that of any other Council member. A member of the P5 who wishes to shield an allied State from being investigated by the ICC would, according to Singapore's proposal, have to campaign for support like any other Council member.

On second look, though, Singapore's proposal still leaves some advantage to the P5. The pure fact of the permanence of their membership leaves the P5 with more chances to influence the ICC Prosecutor than the remaining 183 UN members waiting in line to rotate onto the remaining 10 Security Council seats. Germany spoke out against Singapore's suggestion for compromise, arguing that the institutional design of the ICC should not give *any* chance to the UN Security Council to create obstacles

[43] Considering the importance of prosecutors' accountability to the Ministers of Justice in Germany's domestic system, it is surprising that a later German Minister of Justice, Herta Däubler-Gmelin, even argued that there is 'no difference' between the need for complete independence in the national and international judiciary. Herta Däubler-Gmelin, 'Internationaler Strafgerichtshof: Erfolge und Defizite: Zum zehnten Jahrestag des Römischen Statuts' (2008) 53 *Blätter für deutsche und internationale Politik* 83.

[44] For cases which the Prosecutor decides not to investigate, art 15 (6) Rome Statute merely requires that 'he or she shall inform those who provided the information'.

for the Prosecutor. However, given the P5's strong opposition, the price to pay for Germany's goal of an entirely independent ICC Prosecutor, from the perspective of the German negotiators, would have been to accept the P5's 'not joining the Statute in the initial phase'.[45] This was not desirable given the importance of the support by the United States, Russia, China, France and the United Kingdom. For this reason only, and only as a 'fall-back position', Germany ultimately supported Singapore's suggestion for compromise at PrepCom.[46] Singapore's suggestion would ultimately become the wording of article 16 of the Rome Statute.

Germany's Role within the Like-Minded Group

Germany never chaired the like-minded group[47] nor did it send the most delegates to international negotiations.[48] Nonetheless, Germany was by far the largest member of the group in terms of economic strength and population. Germany held this position from the very beginning – when the group consisted of only about a dozen States – and it did not lose this position until the end of the Rome Conference in 1998, by which time the group had grown to a total of 60 members.

Germany and Canada both took special roles in that their delegations became involved in practically all policy debates surrounding the ICC, whereas most other members of the group chose to allocate their limited resources to certain selected debates only.[49] And in terms of policy, Germany was the more rigorous advocate of independence between the two: while Canada chaired the group throughout PrepCom and was thus responsible for the enormously difficult task of moderating between a growing group of geographically and politically diverse States, Germany was more at liberty to concentrate on the debates and to advocate positions at the independence end of the spectrum that were controversial even within the group.[50]

Compared with the total number of States represented at the negotiations in New York and Rome, the 60 like-minded members at Rome were far from a majority. The secret to this group's success, however, was to gain the support of undecided voters, ie the large number of developing

[45] This account is given by Hans-Jörg Behrens in his internal report on the fourth session of PrepCom to the Ministry of Justice, 28 August 1997. On file with the author.

[46] ibid.

[47] This role was originally taken up by Canada. After the Head of the Canadian delegation, Philippe Kirsch, became Chairman of the Committee of the Whole at the Rome Conference in 1998, chairmanship of the like-minded group went to Italy.

[48] To the Rome Conference, Germany sent 18 delegates, the United Kingdom 19, Russia 21, France 32 and the United States more than 40. Kaul interview (6 August 2009, The Hague).

[49] Kreß interview (6 September 2010, by telephone).

[50] Kaul interview.

States and former Soviet republics which pursued no particular policy and decided to join no particular group during the negotiations. Based on an analysis of PrepCom negotiations and UN press statements from 1996 to 1998, a recent study shows that the percentage of States which supported the 'like-minded' suggestion of an independent ICC Prosecutor jumped from 16 to 80 per cent during that short time.[51] This was the result of a remarkable lobbying effort by the group, which continued at the Rome Conference in 1998 when the ICC Statute was founded.

Teaming Up with Small States

One important strategy for winning the support of undecided States was to offer practical support to the delegates of poorer States. Many States had sent only one or two delegates to New York, meaning that they were dramatically understaffed for the complicated negotiations which often took place in several parallel working groups. The UN General Assembly had created a trust fund in 1996 in order to make the participation of poorer States possible. Nonetheless, they were not able to gain any notable influence in the debates.[52] However, when it came to the inevitable show of hands at the end of each debate, the principle of 'one country, one vote' naturally gave them considerable importance: in terms of numbers, even the tiniest delegation became important and gaining their support was thus a central objective of the ambitious like-minded group. To convince developing States, the like-minded group also held a series of regional conferences in developing States, where they made their case for an independent ICC.[53] As Hans-Peter Kaul notes, 'We [the "like-minded" States] needed this group, and on the other side, small States needed legal guidance and political support by well-respected States. So it was a dynamic relationship which worked both ways.'[54]

Perhaps the most striking example was given in May 1998 before the beginning of the Rome Conference. Five core members of the group – Sweden, Norway, Argentina, Canada and Germany – met in Germany's capital of Bonn to discuss drafts from the previous PrepCom meetings. The group went through the proposed Statute, article by article, and created a copy of the draft in which all the bracketed alternatives which they favoured were bolded, while all the remaining alternatives were kept in regular type.[55]

[51] Nicole Deitelhoff and Eva Burkard, *Europa vor Gericht* (Frankfurt am Main, Hessische Stiftung Friedens-und Konfliktforschung, 2005) 18.

[52] ibid 11f.

[53] Compare ibid 13.

[54] Kaul interview.

[55] *Draft Statute Informal Illustrative Paper* (unpublished, on file with Judge Hans-Peter Kaul) 12 May 1998. The introductory words to this paper state that '[i]t is hoped the paper may provide some guidance in the preparation for the Conference in Rome.'

The result was a song book. The draft was mailed from Bonn to Germany's permanent mission to the UN in New York, where it was copied and distributed to all members of the group and to numerous smaller States which lacked the resources to study all the legal details on their own.

Disrupting Competitors

A second important strategy by the like-minded group was to attempt to break the unity of any other competing blocks. France, which never joined the group, tried at one point in Rome to form a caucus of francophone States. Germany's delegates to the Rome Conference learned of this plan and decided that they, too, qualified as francophone, since seven out of 18 delegates were capable of speaking French. The German delegation then turned up at a francophone meeting in Rome, hosted by France, and addressed the numerous African States assembled there. The German delegation offered Germany's support to all developing States and emphasised that the important decisions at hand should not be left to the powerful P5. This appearance naturally infuriated the French delegation[56] and France never came to play a notable part as the leader of a francophone caucus.

Another block which the group attempted to reach out to would not break up as easily however. The large group of Arab States (with the notable exception of Jordan under its western-educated Prince Abdullah) was opposed to many aspects of the ICC.[57] Efforts were made by the group to assuage their concerns and to win their support. For example, in response to a request by Egypt and Syria,[58] the group even supported the inclusion of the 'indirect transferral of an occupant's population onto occupied territory' into the catalogue of war crimes.[59] This legal novelty was clearly directed at Israel's settlement policy and the decision by the Rome Conference to penalise this alongside genocide and crimes against humanity left Israel alienated.[60] The inclusion ultimately did not suffice to earn the support of the Arab block, however, which had numerous other desires unacceptable to the majority at Rome. Why then did Germany, as a like-minded State, support that legal novelty at all? While the inclusion

[56] Behrens, Kaul interviews (15 April 2010, by telephone and 6 August 2009, The Hague).

[57] Lebanon apparently also considered changing its position, but Egypt's delegation kept a firm grip on the entire caucus. Behrens interview.

[58] Ruth Wedgwood, 'The International Criminal Court: An American View' (1999) 10 *European Journal of International Law* 99. Egypt and Syria were promoting a decision by the Conference of Arab Ministers of Justice: Compare 'Decree regarding the Arab Model Law Project on Crimes within ICC Jurisdiction', available at www.iccnow.org.

[59] This would later become art 8 (2) (b) (viii) Rome Statute.

[60] See the finishing statement by the delegation of Israel, '[L/ROM/22] UN Diplomatic Conference concludes in Rome with decision to establish permanent International Criminal Court', 17 July 1998, available at www.un.org/icc.

of the provision on 'indirect transferral' was considered a valuable bargaining chip in negotiations with the large group of more than 40 Arab States at Rome, Israel was only one State, participants of Germany's negotiation team explain, and since Israel was not expected to be earnestly willing to join the Statute anyway, its negotiating position at Rome was regarded as relatively weak.[61]

Partnering with NGOs

The third strategy, lastly, was to team up with NGOs. The like-minded group was 'influential because it framed its agenda in terms of the high moral ground of legalism over the traditions of national selfishness and exceptionalism', as Antonio Franceschet observes.[62] It should be remembered that Germany itself had favoured a 'UN court' with an accountable ICC Prosecutor until only shortly before,[63] but the group now succeeded in framing this idea, which the United States continued to advocate through 1998, as 'a type of alibi institution, weak, with insufficient powers, and capable of action only where the States concerned or the Security Council allow this'.[64] The public support by NGOs like Amnesty International and Human Rights Watch played a key role in enhancing the credibility of this narrative. A group of NGOs that supported the like-minded States, the Coalition for an International Criminal Court (CICC), already numbered 200 at the time the bureau of the like-minded group reached out to it in 1997[65] and both sides began to hold regular 'dialogue and coordination meetings' after that. Germany's representation at the UN hosted these meetings and Hans-Peter Kaul was able to co-chair these with William Pace of the CICC.

Soon, the CICC also began to receive a substantial part of its funds from the like-minded group,[66] notably via the European Union.[67] The presence of NGOs provided several strategic advantages. Most NGOs were clearly in favour of the like-minded position and helped this group, quite simply, with (almost) free expertise and manpower. Moreover, their image as

[61] Behrens, Zimmermann interviews (15 April 2010, by telephone and 18 August 2010, by telephone).

[62] Antonio Franceschet, 'Four Cosmopolitan Projects: The International Criminal Court in Context' in Steven C Roach (ed), *Governance, Order and the International Criminal Court: Between Realpolitik and a Cosmopolitan Court* (Oxford, Oxford University Press, 2009) 200.

[63] See above section II.

[64] Hans-Peter Kaul, 'Auf dem Weg zum Weltstrafgerichtshof: Verhandlungsstand und Perspektiven' (1997) 45 *Vereinte Nationen* 181.

[65] Deitelhoff and Burkard, *Europa vor Gericht* (n 51) 11.

[66] William R Pace and Mark S Thieroff, 'Participation of Non-Governmental Organizations' in Roy S Lee (ed), *The International Criminal Court: The Making of the Rome Statute; Issues, Negotiations, Results* (The Hague, Kluwer Law International, 1999); Marlies Glasius, *The International Criminal Court: A Global Civil Society Achievement* (London, Routledge, 2006).

[67] Deitelhoff and Burkard, *Europa vor Gericht* (n 51) 25.

politically impartial idealists helped transport the positions of the group to undecided delegations and the international media.

By the end of the PrepCom meetings in June 1998, the like-minded group had become the single most dominant group of States in ICC negotiations. When the Rome Conference finally convened in July 1998, the group's coordinator at PrepCom, Canada's Philippe Kirsch, became Chairman of the Committee of the Whole. Kirsch took care to officially invite NGOs and even give them access to all official committees at Rome. The P5 particularly had come to Rome to argue that the society of States as organised in the UN should keep close control over legal policy in the realm of international criminal justice – but the stage was clearly not set for their argument. Instead, the 'global civil society' on which the other side of the debate rested its core arguments was assembled all around.

4. REMARKABLY, IDEALIST AND REALISTS IN GERMANY HAD JOINED HANDS

While Germany originally advocated direct control of the system of international criminal justice by the UN Security Council, it began to argue against any such control and for complete judicial independence instead in the mid-1990s. This remarkable change in policy has been the focus of the above sections. Yet, how did this sudden policy shift come about? Perhaps the most remarkable aspect of the policy debate within Germany, which preceded Germany's official shift, is the fact that it was short. The political left and the political right in Germany agreed to sway in favour of complete judicial independence relatively quickly.

This was unusual when compared to other western democracies of a similar size. Usually, national debates on whether or not to support the radical shift of the system of international criminal justice from the UN-controlled system of the ICTY and ICTR towards an independent system in place at the ICC were divisive and long-lived. In admittedly very simple terms, proponents of traditional, geostrategic foreign politics on the right were usually sceptical of the idea of succumbing national sovereignty to a 'world court' beyond State control, while human rights enthusiasts on the left were usually more supportive of this novel idea of an independent ICC. For instance, Canada's liberal Minister of Foreign Affairs at the time, Lloyd Axworthy, had made the independent ICC a centrepiece of his 'human security agenda',[68] which his conservative

[68] Jan E Schulte, 'Nationale Erfahrungen – Internationale Folgen: Die Verfolgung von "Nazi War Criminals" und die Unterstützung des Internationalen Strafgerichtshofs durch Kanada' in Helia-Verena Daubach (ed), *Leipzig – Nürnberg – Den Haag: Neue Fragestellungen und Forschungen zum Verhältnis von Menschenrechtsverbrechen justizieller Säuberung und Völkerstrafrecht* (Düsseldorf, Justizministerium des Landes NRW, 2008) 203.

opponents in Canada criticised as unhelpful to national interest.[69] Likewise, the cautious support by the United Kingdom and, initially, the United States for the ICC was closely linked to left-of-centre governments. The United Kingdom's Conservative Party, which had at the beginning of the 1990s debated fiercely over yielding any sovereignty to the European Community, strongly opposed the idea of an independent ICC. The United Kingdom joined the group of ICC enthusiasts only in 1997 after Tony Blair's New Labour came into power promising an ethical foreign policy. This was the empirical rule with Germany being an interesting exception.

Helmut Kohl's conservative government in Germany was initially not expected to be inclined towards sacrificing newly-found German sovereignty: assuredly, the Kohl government had supported the UN ad hoc tribunals in 1993 and 1994. However, these tribunals had been regionally limited to the Balkans and Rwanda, thus posing no threat to German sovereignty, and had remained under close control of the UN Security Council. An independent ICC would be different. One scene which took place on 30 June 1997 is particularly illustrative of the astonishment in Germany when the Kohl government actually showed its support for the human rights enthusiasts' vision of an independent ICC.

On that day, the Green Party, along with members of the Social Democrats, held a small conference on the subject of the ICC in Germany's capital of Bonn. There to represent the Kohl government was Hans-Peter Kaul, the Head of the International Law Department in the Ministry of Foreign Affairs. Kaul was asked if the Kohl government would support an ICC Prosecutor with the power to investigate universally, independently of State consent. Kaul's answer was yes. Intent on proving the Kohl government's weak stance on human rights – and aware of the government's recent advocacy of UN Security Council control[70] – the Green Party tried to corner Kaul, asking if the Kohl government would support the right of the ICC to open cases *proprio motu*. Kaul again answered yes. They then asked if the Kohl government would advocate the right of the ICC even to adjudicate the question of its own jurisdiction (*Kompetenz-Kompetenz*). To the Green Party's general astonishment, Kaul's answer was: yes, of course.[71]

The fact that liberal idealists, interested in promoting global norms, would prefer an independent ICC Prosecutor over one that is under the control of the UN Security Council is perhaps not very intriguing – even though it is also far from self-explanatory. In chapter one, I argued that

[69] ibid.

[70] See above section three.

[71] Hans-Peter Kaul, 'Establishment of a Permanent International Criminal Court: A Report on the State of Negotiations Presented at a Hearing Conducted by the Green Party in Bonn on 30 June 1997' (available from Judge Kaul on request).

both the idea of subjecting an international prosecutor to the control of the UN Security Council *and* the idea of giving him or her complete independence can be seen as problematic in democratic terms.[72] The group of young, liberal jurists with whom Hans-Peter Kaul staffed the German PrepCom delegation was aware of that dilemma. According to participants, the risk of an independent ICC Prosecutor running wild was ultimately seen as a lesser evil than a court which would be seen from the beginning as distributing unequal justice.[73] What is far more intriguing, then, is how the numerous policymakers of a more realist, even robustly geostrategic orientation within the Kohl government ever came to agree with this concept of an independent ICC – and so emphatically.

5. GERMAN REALISTS HAD NOTHING TO LOSE FROM THE SHIFT TOWARDS INDEPENDENCE

To depart from the 'UN court' concept of the 1994 Draft Statute and to argue for an independent ICC Prosecutor instead appears detrimental to Germany's national interest at first glance. To sway towards this new idea of an independent international criminal justice system in the mid-1990s meant snubbing Germany's most important military ally: the United States. Moreover, an independent ICC would rid Germany of an advantage previously held: the control by the UN Security Council over the system of international criminal justice had served Germany quite well. With the United States, the United Kingdom and France, three of Germany's closest NATO allies wielded veto powers in the UN Security Council and it can hardly have been beyond hope in the mid-1990s that their exercise of this power would benefit Germany in the future as well. Why then did the proponents of realist national interest within the conservative-led German government – represented most strongly within the Ministry of Defence – agree to support the novel, idealist vision of an entirely independent ICC nonetheless?

It is the considerable accomplishment of Hans-Peter Kaul, Head of the International Law Department in the German Ministry of Foreign Affairs from the end of 1996 to the summer of 1998, to have convinced policymakers on the realist end of the spectrum in Germany that an independent ICC would not only please liberal ideals but actually also best serve their interests. This is the focus of this section. Two arguments were particularly central to Kaul's efforts in inner-governmental debates.[74] First was the ICC's principle of complementarity, which would effectively shield German nationals from prosecution. Second was Kaul's promise

[72] See above chapter 1, section 6.

[73] Wilkitzki, Behrens interviews.

[74] Behrens, Kaul, and Zimmermann interviews.

that the ICC's substantive law of war crimes would not exceed unequivocal *lege lata* and thus would not create any new obligations for German soldiers.

Complementarity: A Shield for Sovereignty

As the inner-governmental debate on Germany's position vis-à-vis a future ICC picked up speed in 1996 and 1997, the Germany Ministries of Justice and Foreign Affairs, both led by politicians of the Liberal Party in the mid-1990s, were already arguing in favour of an independent ICC at PrepCom in Germany's name. This was already the case throughout the years 1996 and 1997 at a time where there was actually still considerable disagreement back in Bonn. The inner-governmental controversy had first become visible in March 1995 when the Ministry of Foreign Affairs had invited a small group of representatives from the Ministries of Justice, Defence and the Interior to consult in relation to the PrepCom negotiations beginning in New York.

The Ministries of Defence and the Interior, two political powerhouses led by high-profile members of Helmut Kohl's conservatives at the time, were sceptical of the entire idea. An Undersecretary of State (*Staatssekretär*) at the German Ministry of Defence in Bonn made it clear that the Ministry of Defence would oppose any foreign court gaining jurisdiction over German soldiers.[75] The Ministry of the Interior joined in, arguing the same point. While the Ministry of Justice had previously suggested that the surrender of German nationals to the ICC would have to be made legally possible by a change to article 16 of the German *Grundgesetz* (Constitution),[76] which guaranteed the non-surrender of German nationals, the Ministry of the Interior now emphasised that this constitutional provision could under no circumstances be 'waived' in upcoming ICC negotiations.[77] (Later, the Ministry of the Interior would give up this insistence. Today, article 16 of the *Grundgesetz* includes a qualification that allows for the surrender of nationals to other member States of the European Union and to international courts 'insofar as due process is guaranteed'.)

For the German Ministry of Defence to insist in this manner on the protection of German nationals was, of course, not unique. In France, for instance, similar inner-governmental negotiations took place at the time and there the Ministry of Defence demanded that French nationals be legally exempt from prosecution in The Hague for at least seven years.

[75] Kaul, Zimmermann interviews.
[76] Letter from Wolfgang Birke, Ministry of Justice, to the Ministry of Foreign Affairs, Division for International Law, 18 October 1994. On file with the author.
[77] Letter from Mr Heyn, Ministry of the Interior, to the Ministry of Foreign Affairs, Division for International Law, 16 December 1996. On file with the author.

This famously led to the incorporation of the controversial article 124 into the Rome Statute[78] as a precondition for France's assent to the Statute.

In Germany, Kaul remarkably succeeded in assuaging these concerns for national interest within the Ministry of Defence in a different way. On the one hand, Kaul managed to rally the entire Ministry of Foreign Affairs behind his support for an independent ICC with a rather original manoeuvre. In 1997, Kaul penned a journal article that argued emphatically in favour of an ICC Prosecutor with *proprio motu* powers and invited the Minister of Foreign Affairs, Klaus Kinkel, to publish this article in his name in a renowned German law journal. Kinkel took up the offer.[79] With this policy statement now openly connected to Kinkel's name, the more sceptical voices within the Ministry of Foreign Affairs, some of whom had initially opposed Kaul's strong stance in favour of an independent ICC, became quieter. Professor Christian Tomuschat, who advised the German Ministry of Foreign Affairs at the time, suggests that the very outspoken advocacy and rhetorical idealism of Kaul and other German delegates in New York also made it increasingly difficult for more realist policymakers in Germany to later give up this position without the risk of considerable embarrassment.[80]

At the same time, Kaul explained 'over and over again'[81] to the two sceptical Ministries of Defence and the Interior that German soldiers would, in effect, be fully protected from the risk of extradition to The Hague by the principle of complementarity. This principle – which means that the ICC has jurisdiction only where States are not 'willing and able' to prosecute crimes themselves – had been agreed upon internationally at a very early stage and Germany had always advocated it as a basis for the ICC.[82] This

[78] Article 124 stipulates that 'a State, on becoming a party to this Statute, may declare that, for a period of seven years after the entry into force of this Statute for the State concerned, it does not accept the jurisdiction of the Court . . .' Germany's disapproval was underlined by Klaus Kinkel, 'Der Internationale Strafgerichtshof – ein Meilenstein in der Entwicklung des Völkerrechts' (1998) *Neue Juristische Wochenschrift* 2651.

[79] Klaus Kinkel, 'Für einen funktionsfähigen Weltstrafgerichtshof' (1997) 50 *Neue Juristische Wochenschrift* 2861.

[80] Tomuschat interview. On the other hand, Wilkitzki and Behrens have suggested that realists within the government simply did not believe for a long time that the creation of the ICC in the near future was a realistic prospect at all – so why waste breath on opposing it? According to participants of PrepCom, the difficult situation in New York even left many there pessimistic as to whether such an ICC would come into existence anytime soon, compare Benedetti and Washburn, 'Drafting the International Criminal Court Treaty' (n 40) 2; William A Schabas, *An Introduction to the International Criminal Court* (Cambridge, Cambridge University Press, 2007) 14f.

[81] Kaul interview.

[82] 'Let me just say we consider the principle of complementarity important', Germany had stated to the UN in 1995, for instance, further elaborating: 'Prosecution and punishment must in essence remain a responsibility of the state. Only in cases where such national trial procedures may not be available or may be ineffective should the international criminal court play a role.' Compare *Position of Germany 1995* (policy paper), cited in Grote, 'Völkerrechtliche Praxis der Bundesrepublik Deutschland im Jahre 1995' (n 21) 1123.

position was reiterated in Kinkel's 1997 journal article.[83] The Ministry of Defence in 1997 was not so easily calmed however. It expressed doubts as to whether this legal shield would really be effective in protecting German nationals under all circumstances[84] and the Ministry of Defence was able to point to recent arguments made by Kaul's own delegates at PrepCom, which actually showed a tendency to weaken the protective strength of the principle of complementarity. Germany's delegates in New York had argued in August 1997 that the determination whether or not a State is 'able and willing', ie whether it is compliant with its obligations to prosecute, should be assessed by the ICC rather than by the home State of an accused.[85]

Germany's delegates at PrepCom even proposed that the ICC should be equipped with an extensive margin of appreciation when assessing a State's compliance, thus leaving the States less chance to seek refuge behind complementarity. Mere 'considerable doubts as to the sincerity of national proceedings' should suffice to trigger the right of the ICC to intervene, Germany's delegation in New York proposed.[86] Germany's negotiators at PrepCom were actually successful in their bid to weaken the protective power of the principle of complementarity against the opposition of the United Kingdom:[87] under the Rome Statute, the authority to decide whether a situation warrants the ICC's jurisdiction or not rests with the ICC itself, not with the State. On the other hand, 'this success was bought with concessions', as one German negotiator noted in his report to the Ministry of Justice.[88] The ICC has to find that a State is 'unwilling or unable genuinely to carry out the investigation or prosecution'[89] on the basis of specified criteria, creating a much higher legal threshold for the ICC's jurisdiction than the German delegation's idea of mere 'considerable doubts'.

It is not hard to imagine how difficult it was for those same German negotiators to sell to the German Ministry of Defence the argument that German nationals would effectively be shielded from the judges at The Hague at all times. Nonetheless, at least the high legal threshold for the ICC's complementarity jurisdiction – which had ironically been agreed upon at PrepCom against the will of the German negotiators – evidently assuaged the concerns of the Ministry of Defence in Bonn.

[83] Kinkel, 'Für einen funktionsfähigen Weltstrafgerichtshof' (n 79), 2861.

[84] Kaul interview.

[85] Christopher K Hall, 'The First Two Sessions of the UN Preparatory Committee on the Establishment of an International Criminal Court' (1997) 91 *American Journal of International Law* 181.

[86] Hans-Jörg Behrens, 'Negotiation Report for the Ministry of Justice', 28 August 1997. On file with the author.

[87] ibid.

[88] ibid.

[89] This later became the wording of art 17 (1) (a) Rome Statute.

The Ministry of Defence continued to insist only that Kaul's team make absolutely sure that all offences for which the ICC has material jurisdiction would be covered by German domestic law, so that the shielding function of the principle of complementarity could take maximum effect. This insistence by the Ministry of Defence was a driving force behind the creation of the German Code of International Crimes, the *Völkerstrafgesetzbuch* (hereinafter: VStGB).[90]

The German Code of International Crimes (*Völkerstrafgesetzbuch*)

'By conforming their legislation to the ICC Statute, States are better positioned to take advantage of the principle of complementarity', notes Theodor Meron.[91] For Germany, this function is served by the VStGB.[92] By reflecting all of the ICC's material provisions on crimes in German domestic law, this code makes German courts legally capable of prosecuting any and all crimes for which the ICC could otherwise claim jurisdiction.[93]

The VStGB's significance in protecting national interests was reiterated in parliament when the bill was passed in April 2002. The former Minister of Justice, Edzard Schmidt-Jortzig of the Liberal Party (in office 1996–1998), pointed out to the members of parliament:

> Germany is not obliged by the Rome Statute to incorporate the Statute's core crimes into its domestic criminal law. If it decides against penalising these core crimes domestically though, Germany would have to surrender suspects to the ICC, even if these are nationals. Thus, by making sure with the help of the VStGB that prosecution on a domestic level is accounted for, Germany prevents having to surrender its nationals to the ICC. In fact, this alone already represents a good enough reason to support this bill.[94]

Schmidt-Jortzig's successor as Minister of Justice, Herta Däubler-Gmelin of the Social Democrats (in office from 1998 to 2002), added during the

[90] Behrens, Brink, Kaul, Kreß, Wilkitzki interviews.

[91] Theodor Meron, *The Humanization of International Law* (Leiden, Boston, Martinus Nijhoff, 2006) 149. See also Claus Kreß, *Vom Nutzen eines deutschen Völkerstrafgesetzbuchs* (Baden-Baden, Nomos, 2000); also Jutta Hartmann, 'Das deutsche Völkerstrafgesetzbuch' in Hans-Heiner Kühne, André Eichhofer and Kühne-Esser-Gerding (eds), *Völkerstrafrecht: 12 Beiträge zum internationalen Strafrecht und Völkerstrafrecht* (Osnabrück, Jonscher, 2007).

[92] Code of Crimes against International Law, Bundesgesetzblatt I 2002, 2254. English version available at www.iuscomp.org/gla/statutes/VoeStGB.pdf.

[93] To leave no room for doubt, the VStGB not only adds the definitions of the international core crimes to the long list of statutory offences in domestic law. Rather, it constitutes a separate body of domestic law besides 'regular' domestic criminal law, with its own set of general principles for individual responsibility and defences, which are also mirrored from the Rome Statute.

[94] *Bundestags-Plenarprotokoll* 14/233, 25 April 2002, 23270.

same parliamentary session that the principle of complementarity allows States Parties to 'maintain their own responsibility for prosecuting crimes against international law insofar as they are able to do this', and that Germany was 'able and willing', as everyone could now see.[95]

Conservative Positions on War Crimes

The second argument to soothe the German Ministry of Defence was that the Rome Statute would not create any new legal obligations for German soldiers. In other words, Kaul's diplomatic delegation promised German realists that the ICC's law on war crimes would not exceed unequivocal *lege lata* and that all innovations advocated by NGOs, which could create new obligations, would be rebutted at Rome. This was particularly important to Germany since Germany had only incorporated the Geneva protocol into its domestic criminal law to a limited extent.[96]

Germany's restrictive position on war crimes issues first became practical at the end of PrepCom. In the debate on the codification of war crimes, two proposals stood out in contrast. The United States, on the one hand, suggested limiting the ICC's substantive jurisdiction to the undisputed core of customary *lege lata*. The International Committee of the Red Cross (ICRC), on the other hand, whose proposal was tabled by New Zealand and Switzerland, argued to penalise a much broader set of acts, even acts the illegality of which was still disputed in some cases.[97] The PrepCom Chair turned to Germany at this point with the request to draft a suggestion for compromise. The German delegation had previously shown itself to be an able and expedient drafter. Yet the compromise draft on war crimes, which Germany produced, proved to be hardly any less restrictive than the US position, which is why a compromise had to be drafted by a different delegation in the end.[98]

The similarity between the German and the US positions was no coincidence. In order to campaign for Germany's restrictive position on war crimes, Germany had hosted a two-day workshop for NATO members in Bonn between two PrepCom meetings. At that meeting in Bonn, all NATO

[95] *Bundestags-Plenarprotokoll* 14/233, 25 April 2002, 23271.

[96] Andreas Zimmermann, 'Implementing the Statute of the International Criminal Court: The German Example' in Lal C Vohrah (ed), *Man's Inhumanity to Man: Essays on International Law in Honour of Antonio Cassese* (The Hague, Kluwer Law International, 2003) 985. In Germany's PrepCom delegation, Zimmermann was the delegate responsible for negotiations on war crimes.

[97] ibid 986.

[98] Christopher K Hall, 'The Fifth Session of the UN Preparatory Committee on the Establishment of an International Criminal Court' (1998) 92 *American Journal of International Law* 332, 334.

members had agreed on a restrictive catalogue of crimes.[99] In the end, the outcome at Rome remained rather similar to this Bonn paper, with only minor concessions to the ICRC. The list of war crimes now in the Rome Statute is more restrictive than the Geneva Convention's Additional Protocol I of 1977 and its list of grave breaches. Although Andreas Zimmermann notes that this restrictive approach of the Rome Statute was 'mainly due to the resistance of the United States',[100] it is arguably also fair to say that Germany was not so far away from the US position on this topic.

6. MORE IMPORTANTLY HOWEVER, THEY HAD A LOT TO GAIN

Whereas the principle of complementarity and a restrictive position on war crimes ensured that Germany did not have much to lose from the creation of the ICC as an independent institution, the shift towards making the system of international criminal justice independent of the UN Security Council would even promise Germany a relative gain in influence.

The Advantage of 'One Country, One Vote'

It has been explored in chapter one how the main channels of influence over prosecutorial policy are through the hand-picking of prosecutors and, subsequently, through the dependency of the prosecutors on re-election. At the ICC, the channels of influence are assuredly less wide than at the UN ad hoc tribunals. Under the ICC's Rome Statute, the ICC Prosecutor is elected by secret ballot by the Assembly of States Parties (ASP) for a period of nine years. He or she is not eligible for re-election[101] and although the ASP can theoretically remove the ICC Prosecutor before the end of his or her term provided that a majority of the ASP sees a case of 'serious misconduct',[102] this possibility will most likely remain a theoretical one.[103] This election mode applies to the ICC Prosecutor the high standards developed for securing the independence of judges.[104] What remains, however, is the hand-picking, both in the case of judges and of the ICC Prosecutor. With the UN Security Council removed from this

[99] Andreas Zimmermann, 'Neues deutsches Selbstbewusstsein: Paradigmenwechsel in der Völkerrechtspolitik?' (2002) 9 *Internationale Politik* 35.
[100] Zimmermann, 'Implementing the Statute' (n 96) 986.
[101] Art 42 Rome Statute.
[102] Art 46 (1) Rome Statute.
[103] Danner, 'Enhancing the Legitimacy and Accountability' (n 1) 524.
[104] Compare Meron, *The Humanization of International Law* (n 91) 167–69.

position of power, who can now exercise influence through hand-picking at the ICC?

This role is now taken up by the ASP. It is from here that influence can be exerted through key nominations. As a body of States, the ASP, like the UN Security Council, assembles governments (not civil society), yet the power between these national governments is obviously distributed quite differently. Instead of five States wielding the most power, all ASP members have equal voting rights here and decisions are made by the principle of 'one country, one vote'. This obviously levels the playing field when compared with the UN Security Council. The principle of 'one country, one vote' means a relative gain in power for all States that previously looked enviously at the power of the P5, which is why William Schabas even argues that 'the Rome Statute was an attempt to effect indirectly what could not be done directly, namely reform of the United Nations and amendment of the Charter'. [105]

Like many authors, Schabas assumes that this 'unprecedented challenge to the Security Council accounts for the antagonism of the United States', which, being a member of the P5, obviously had a lot to lose.[106] The logical flip side to this argument however – the relative advantage of 'one country, one vote' particularly for small and middle-sized States and for politically homogenous groups of States – is also noteworthy.

For instance, Germany stands firmly among a group of 27 member States of the European Union. Altogether this group represents only roughly twice as many inhabitants as the United States, it gains 27 times the United States' voting power under a 'one country, one vote' system.[107] Under such a system, Europe can easily outplay the United States, Russia, China and India, even if these four combine their efforts (which they did at Rome). Whenever the 27 member States of the European Union can agree on a common position – in which Germany, as the largest EU member State, will usually have considerable influence – a system of 'one country, one vote' thus plays greatly to their political advantage.

An illustration of this redistribution of power is given in an anecdote told by Kaul. A great effort had initially been made at the Rome Conference by the 'like-minded' group to win the support of India. Yet when the Head of India's delegation approached Kaul in the middle of the Conference with furious charges that Germany was apparently ignoring the vital interests of India, Kaul instructed his delegation to cease all attempts at reaching out to India. Kaul instructed his delegation to redirect Germany's resources towards talks with the numerous small States instead.

[105] Schabas, 'United States Hostility' (n 14) 720.

[106] ibid.

[107] As illustrated above in chapter one, section six, this is hardly more democratic than the previous situation.

'Ultimately, we have the principle of "one country, one vote" here, and the fact that India has one billion inhabitants will not play quite the prominent role in the end which India might think', Kaul said.[108] India's one billion inhabitants, of course, form no less than one sixth of the world's population. But Kaul knew that under a 'one country, one vote' regime, this huge constituency is ultimately reduced to one vote out of 120.

Germany's Newfound Influence on Nominations

What does this new distribution of power mean in practice? At the UN ad hoc tribunals, Germany had been one of the countless States to largely stand aside and watch whenever the P5 deliberated on whom to handpick as prosecutor.[109] (There is no indication in the public domain that Germany was ever actually displeased with these selections, yet Germany would undoubtedly have had little leverage to stop objectionable candidates either.) At the ICC, however, the ASP's regime of 'one country, one vote' changes this dramatically.

When Luis Moreno Ocampo of Argentina was selected and elected by acclamation at the ASP to become the first ICC Prosecutor in 2003, the two P5 members who were present at the ASP, France and the United Kingdom, were not in a position of any particular influence. Rather, within the wide electorate of ASP members, only the informal power structure of the like-minded group had remained intact. This meant an advantage for key like-minded members such as Germany. Participants in the selection of Ocampo – who was chosen out of a group of reportedly six or seven candidates from Africa, Latin America, Australia and Canada as well as Carla Del Ponte[110] – were very discrete and have remained discrete ever since. However, in light of the first set of nominations, it seems fair to say that the former like-minded group, and particularly its five or six core members, did not yield much of their hard-earned influence in this phase. This brought a new position of political influence, inter alia, for Germany.

Almost all of the group's core protagonists received prominent posts at the ICC. Philippe Kirsch of Canada, formerly the group's coordinator at PrepCom and later the Chairman of the Committee of the Whole at Rome, was elected judge and President of the ICC. Hans-Peter Kaul was elected judge, re-elected in 2006 and promoted to Second Vice President of the

[108] Kaul interview.

[109] See above chapter four, section I.

[110] Benjamin N Schiff, *Building the International Criminal Court* (Cambridge, Cambridge University Press, 2008) 108; Carla Del Ponte, *Madame Prosecutor* (New York, Other Press, 2009) 230.

ICC in 2009. Both Kaul[111] and Kirsch[112] had been long-time diplomats in their respective countries.[113] Argentina, which in the group's division of labour at Rome, had been primarily assigned to negotiating the role of the ICC Prosecutor, now saw an Argentine in that most prominent position at the ICC and Ocampo then made the former Head of Argentina's delegation at the Rome Conference, Silvia Fernández de Gurmendi, his first Chef de Cabinet in 2003.[114] In 2010, Fernández de Gurmendi was, as was her former like-minded colleagues Kaul and Kirsch, elected an ICC judge.

After the Rome Conference, the like-minded group's Hague bureau was renamed the 'Friends of the ICC' and Germany took over the chairmanship of that group in the crucial first years after 1998 when the first set of nominations was being discussed. German insiders agree that Germany, at this stage, came into a position where important candidates could not be elected against its opposition,[115] not least because Germany was now the single most important financial contributor to the ICC (a position which it continued to hold until Japan joined in 2007). The contrast between this new-found influence on nominations and Germany's previous position on the sidelines of ICTY and ICTR nominations is striking.

7. INDEPENDENCE AND THE CRIME OF AGGRESSION

Finally, one particular debate on substantive criminal law – which has perhaps posed the most difficult task for legal drafters in international criminal law – gives another illustration of the politics at play during the creation of the ICC. Germany played a prominent role in this particular

[111] During the internal German deliberations about whom to nominate for the position, the Ministry of Foreign Affairs had put forward Kaul, but the Ministry of Justice had favoured its own Peter Wilkitzki for the position. Wilkitzki had already been Germany's (unsuccessful) candidate for ICTY judge in 1998 (see above chapter four, section III). The Ministry of Foreign Affairs blocked Wilkitzki. To find a compromise with the Ministry of Foreign Affairs, the Ministry of Justice ultimately suggested a third candidate, Professor Albin Eser, an experienced judge and the then Director of the Max Planck Institute for Foreign and International Criminal Law in Freiburg. In the end, Kaul was put forward as the German nominee.

[112] Given his non-judicial background, Kirsch was faced in 2006 with criticism within the ranks of ICC judges, as a large part of the judges preferred to elect a colleague with more forensic experience for President. Schiff, *Building the International Criminal Court* (n 110) 127.

[113] The lack of forensic experience by many judges at international tribunals was also criticised sharply by Wolfgang Schomburg, the German ICTY judge from 2001 to 2008, at the International Commission of Jurists' conference 'Der Internationale Strafgerichtshof in der Praxis', on 13 March 2009 in Berlin.

[114] ibid 113.

[115] After it became clear that one of Ocampo's two Deputy Prosecutors should be an African and one should be a European, Germany considered nominating a second of its nationals to a high-profile position at the ICC. A high-ranking officer of the Ministry of Justice was considered a suitable candidate. However, the majority of European States preferred Serge Brammertz of Belgium for the position of Deputy Prosecutor.

debate. Germany's position regarding a prerogative of the UN Security Council in determining whether a State's use of force constitutes a case of criminal aggression shows an interesting U-turn in policy and hence exemplifies Germany's overall change of paradigm vis-à-vis the role of the UN Security Council in international criminal justice particularly clearly.

Whereas three 'core crimes' (genocide, crimes against humanity and war crimes) were already part of the statutes of the UN ad hoc tribunals in the early 1990s, the issue of whether a permanent international criminal court should be made capable of charging political leaders with the additional fourth 'core crime', the crime of aggression, had been a matter of particular controversy since the 1990s and has remained a debated issue until today. To German policymakers, the crime of aggression became a point of particular priority in the 1990s: the 'Nuremberg-type procedure' for Saddam Hussein, which Germany actively advocated in 1991 and 1992,[116] would, in theory, have gravitated entirely around a charge of Iraqi aggression against Kuwait.[117] Moreover, whereas the UN Security Council deliberately left the crime of aggression out of the Statutes of the UN ad hoc tribunals in order to avoid some of the controversies of Nuremberg,[118] Germany praised the ILC in 1994 for including the (yet undefined) crime of aggression in its Draft Statute for the ICC.[119] Also, it was Germany which sought to revive what was then a largely dormant debate on aggression with an 'intensive lobbying effort' at a 1997 PrepCom meeting in New York.[120]

Germany Campaigns for a Narrow Definition of the Crime

The problems with defining the substantive crime of aggression – that is, drawing the line between legitimate and illegitimate use of force in an abstract manner to suit all possible cases – are intricate and the debates

[116] See above chapter four, section four.

[117] Claus Kreß would later criticise the 2004 Iraqi Special Tribunal for missing a second chance to charge Saddam Hussein with the 1990 aggression: Claus Kreß, 'The Iraqi Special Tribunal and the Crime of Aggression' (2004) 2 *Journal of International Criminal Justice*.

[118] See also Richard Goldstone's recent argument that a prosecution of the crime of aggression would have entrenched the ICTY in unfathomable political crossfire and dilemmas, hence this crime should not be included in the scope of the ICC just yet: Richard Goldstone, 'Prosecuting Aggression', *New York Times*, 26 May 2010.

[119] Position of Germany 1995, quoted in Grote, 'Völkerrechtliche Praxis der Bundesrepublik Deutschland im Jahre 1995' (n 21) 1122–24. See above section two.

[120] Christopher K Hall, 'The Third and Fourth Sessions of the UN Preparatory Committee on the Establishment of an International Criminal Court' (1998) 92 *American Journal of International Law* 129. For NGO praise for Germany, see also the *International Criminal Court Monitor* No 4, May 1997, cited by Kaul, 'Auf dem Weg zum Weltstrafgerichtshof' (n 64) 181; also Hans-Peter Kaul, 'From Nuremberg to Kampala – Reflections on the Crime of Aggression', address at the Robert H Jackson Center on 30 August 2010, available at www.icc-cpi.int, 4.

voluminous.[121] While Nazi Germany's role in World War II was viewed rather unanimously as that of an aggressor in retrospect, all attempts to define aggression comprehensively with a view to the future failed in the years following Nuremberg. The Charter of the United Nations, which forbids the use of force albeit for self-defence or with a mandate by the UN Security Council, is of little help to this debate since it is exactly the distinction between aggression and self-defence which is, almost without fail, contentious in practice. And with State participants in the debate having their own controversial security policies in mind, the debate on abstract definitions is often deeply entangled in particular interests.

In 1974, the UN General Assembly presented a very wide definition of aggression as an offer of legal guidance to the UN Security Council (Resolution 3314).[122] However, these detailed provisions – stipulating, for example, that certain economic sanctions could constitute illegal aggression, whereas 'struggles of liberation' are never to be viewed as aggressive – sufficed in the eyes of many observers only to illustrate that a court applying such a norm would inevitably become entrenched in politics. The Rome Conference ended without an agreement on aggression, yet with the inclusion of a legal place-holder in article 5 (2) of the 1998 Rome Statute which simply stated that the crime was yet to be defined, thus ensuring that the matter would remain on the agenda.[123] A legal definition of aggression as a crime under international criminal law was not adopted until 2010 at an ICC Review Conference in Kampala, Uganda.

The central trajectory of Germany's proposals for a legal definition of aggression in the years leading up to Kampala was to make the definition as narrow as possible. While international policy debates made it impossible to agree on abstract yet sufficiently precise rules regarding the contentious legal grey area (such as anticipatory self-defence, interventions to rescue nationals, the extraterritorial use of force against a non-State armed

[121] For an in-depth analysis in international law, see for instance the recent study by Olaoluwa Olusanya, *Identifying the Aggressor under International Law* (Bern, Peter Lang, 2006), particularly 51–138; also Yoram Dinstein, *War, Aggression and Self-Defence* (Cambridge, Cambridge University Press, 2005). For a comprehensive criminal law drafting history (which does not include the recent results at Kampala however), see Oscar Solera, *Defining the Crime of Aggression* (London, Cameron May, 2007).

[122] GA Resolution 3314 (XXIX), 14 December 1974, Doc A/RES/3314(XXIX). The chapeau of this definition reads: 'Aggression is the use of armed force by a State against the sovereignty, territorial integrity or political independence of another State, or in any other manner inconsistent with the Charter of the United Nations, as set out in this Definition.' The definition then begins by stating that the first use of armed force by a State 'shall constitute prima facie evidence of an act of aggression' although this may be rebutted 'in light of other relevant circumstances', and continues to list acts such as the blockade of ports or the 'substantial involvement' in sending 'armed bands, groups, irregulars or mercenaries' against another State as possible examples for aggression.

[123] Gerd Westdickenberg and Oliver Fixson, 'Das Verbrechen der Aggression im Römischen Statut des Internationalen Strafgerichtshofs' in Jochen A Frowein and others (eds), *Verhandeln für den Frieden – Negotiating for Peace: Liber Amicorum Tono Eitel* (2003) 497f.

attack and 'humanitarian interventions'), Germany's suggestion in the 1990s was, essentially, to leave this entire grey area untouched by criminal charges and to focus entirely on the pitch black area instead. Perhaps unsurprisingly, this approach was central to winning State support for the inclusion of such a crime into the purview of the ICC,[124] particularly with developed States that engage in this grey area more frequently.

The narrowing of this definition was a response to States' concerns that their controversial security policies might otherwise be branded as acts of aggression. At least since the case of Kosovo in 1999, this concern is not unknown to Germany itself. In respect of a narrow definition of the crime of aggression, Germany's political interests here were thus aligned with those of its NATO allies.

At PrepCom in 1997, Germany introduced a text proposal defining aggression as 'an armed attack directed by a State against the territorial integrity or political independence of another State when this armed attack was undertaken in manifest contravention of the Charter of the United Nations'.[125] This introduced the attribute of 'manifest' for the first time, which interestingly makes the absence of reasonable political controversy over the legitimacy of a use of armed force part of the abstract legal definition itself.[126] This excludes the grey area.

In addition, in 1997 Germany suggested introducing a special requirement of intent, which would further narrow down the crime considerably: '[W]ith the object or result of establishing a [military] occupation of, or annexing, the territory of such other State or part thereof by armed forces of the attacking State.'[127]

While Germany's latter proposal for a specific requirement of intent was rejected by a number of developing States as too restrictive[128] and was

[124] ibid 493. As Coordinator of the ASP's Special Working Group on the Crime of Aggression, Silvia Fernandez de Gurmendi, 'The Working Group on Aggression at the Preparatory Commission for the International Criminal Court' (2002) 25 *Fordham International Law Journal* 598, highlighted that finding the right threshold for aggression would be instrumental in order to reach agreement.

[125] Report of the Preparatory Committee on the Establishment of an International Criminal Court, Addendum, UN doc A/CONF.183/2/Add 1, 14 April 1998, 14.

[126] Claus Kreß, 'Time for Decision: Some Thoughts on the Immediate Future of the Crime of Aggression: A Reply to Andreas Paulus' (2009) 20 *European Journal of International Law* 1142: '. . . in order not to decide major controversies about the content of primary international rules of conduct through the back door of international criminal justice.'

[127] Report of the Preparatory Committee on the Establishment of an International Criminal Court, Addendum, UN doc A/CONF.183/2/Add 1, 14 April 1998, 14.

[128] Compare the concise negotiating history offered by Garth Schofield, 'The Empty US Chair: United States Nonparticipation in the Negotiations on the Definition of Aggression' (2007) 15 *Human Rights Brief* 21f. For arguments, compare Muhammad A Shukri, 'Will Aggressors Ever be Tried Before the ICC?' in Mauro Politi and Giuseppe Nesi (eds), *The International Criminal Court and the Crime of Aggression* (Aldershot, Ashgate, 2004) 38; also Phani Dascalopoulou-Livada, 'Aggression and the ICC: Views on Certain Ideas and their Potential for a Solution' in Mauro Politi and Giuseppe Nesi (eds), *The International Criminal Court and the Crime of Aggression* (Aldershot, Ashgate, 2004) 81.

soon dropped by the German delegation itself,[129] the idea of limiting the crime to 'manifest' violations of the UN Charter (which still promises considerable restriction) gradually allowed more and more developed States to support the project.

At the 1998 Rome Conference, Germany's proposal for a narrow definition gained more support than the other options on the table,[130] while a group of predominantly Middle Eastern States continued to speak out in favour of a broader definition.[131] In the years following Rome, Germany advocated this narrow definition in the forum of the Preparatory Commission for the ICC (a series of meetings similar to the 1996–98 PrepCom) and, after 2002, in the ASP's Special Working Group on the Crime of Aggression, where Claus Kreß of Germany served as Sub-Coordinator. Here also, the group of developing, 'non-aligned' countries was mostly in favour of a broader definition, while most NATO States favoured a narrow definition with a high threshold.[132] While German policymakers continued to oppose the broad definition of aggression suggested by the UN General Assembly's Resolution 3314 in 1974, German government officials noted internally that a number of States – particularly in the Middle East – were very protective of this 1974 approach and that western criticism would thus need to be careful and diplomatic in order not to alienate these States.[133]

Along with a number of allies, Germany campaigned for a definition that would be narrow enough to soothe realist concerns in the West. Specifically, German negotiators considered it one of their priorities to make sure that aggression charges could not be incurred merely by a State allowing its military allies to use their air space[134] – a political interest important to Germany but hardly shared by many developing countries. To underscore Germany's point that a narrow definition would be functional in ruling out the danger of politicised aggression charges in the 'grey area' against western States, Kreß, among others, made efforts to

[129] Compare Hans-Peter Kaul, 'The Crime of Aggression: Definitional Options for the Way Forward' in Mauro Politi and Giuseppe Nesi (eds), *The International Criminal Court and the Crime of Aggression* (Aldershot, Ashgate 2004) 100.

[130] Solera, *Defining the Crime of Aggression* (n 121) 358–61. See also Hans-Peter Kaul, 'From Nuremberg to Kampala – Reflections on the Crime of Aggression', address at the Robert H. Jackson Center on 30 August 2010, available at www.icc-cpi.int, 5.

[131] Compare Umberto Leanza, 'The Historical Background' in Mauro Politi and Giuseppe Nesi (eds), *The International Criminal Court and the Crime of Aggression* (Aldershot, Ashgate, 2004) 13.

[132] Claus Kreß and Leonie von Holtzendorff, 'The Kampala Compromise on the Crime of Aggression' (2010) 8 *Journal of International Criminal Justice*.

[133] Minutes of inner-governmental strategic debate regarding the codification of the crime of aggression, held at the Ministry of Foreign Affairs on 26 January 2007, and follow-up meeting on 27 May 2008. On file with the author.

[134] Minutes of inner-governmental strategic debate regarding the codification of the crime of aggression, held at the Ministry of Foreign Affairs, on 26 January 2007, 3. On file with the author.

illustrate that even the US-led 2003 invasion of Iraq (which Kreß, like many others, considered illegal under international law) would still be too grey to raise the danger of aggression charges under an adequately narrow definition of the crime of aggression.[135] The same argument was also made for the case of Kosovo.[136] It speaks to Germany's success in making this point that Claus Kreß was assigned as a Focal Point at Kampala with the task of reaching out to the United States in order to soothe remaining US concerns against the inclusion of this crime into the Rome Statue.

Ultimately, the requirement of a manifest violation of the UN Charter became part of the substantive definition of the crime of aggression adopted at the ICC Review Conference in Kampala in 2010. The definition now reads:

> For the purpose of this Statute, 'crime of aggression' means the planning, preparation, initiation or execution, by a person in a position effectively to exercise control over or to direct the political or military action of a State, of an act of aggression which, by its character, gravity and scale, constitutes a manifest violation of the Charter of the United Nations.

In the Understandings attached to this text (and negotiated with the US delegation under the coordination of Kreß), the term 'manifest' is explained to a certain degree:

> It is understood that in establishing whether an act of aggression constitutes a manifest violation of the Charter of the United Nations, the three components of character, gravity and scale must be sufficient to justify a 'manifest' determination. No one component can be significant enough to satisfy the manifest standard by itself.[137]

[135] See for example Claus Kreß, 'The German Chief Federal Prosecutor's Decision Not to Investigate the Alleged Crime of Preparing Aggression against Iraq' (2004) 2 *Journal of International Criminal Justice* 256–64; also Kreß, 'Time for Decision' (n 126) 1141f: 'There is agreement that Hitler's and Saddam Hussein's aggressive wars would have come within the definition, and I suspect that the same applies with respect to some other uses of force since 1945. It is true, though, that the requirement of a "manifest violation of the Charter of the United Nations" will make successful proceedings for a crime of aggression an exceptional event. But what is wrong with this consequence? Is international criminal law (*stricto sensu*) not an instrument for exceptionally grave assaults upon the international legal order to be applied with utmost restraint? An expansionist resort to international criminal law must lead to its trivialization. This is true for the crime of aggression as it is for all other crimes under international law.'

[136] See, eg ibid 1140f. Similarly, a strong proponent of the inclusion of the crime of aggression, Solera, *Defining the Crime of Aggression* (n 121) 445–500, tested his own (narrow) suggestion for a definition against three cases, all of them of concern to Western policymakers: NATO's intervention in Yugoslavia; the NATO-led invasion of Afghanistan; and the US-led 2003 invasion of Iraq.

[137] Resolution RC/Res.6, available at www.icc-cpi.int/iccdocs/asp_docs/Resolutions/RCRes.6-ENG.pdf.

The UN Security Council or the Court: Who Makes the Call?

The most controversial question during the debates on the inclusion of the crime of aggression into the purview of the ICC – the 'question of questions', as Claus Kreß notes[138] – was the role of the UN Security Council in determining aggression. Who should hold the prerogative in determining whether a particular use of force fits the definition of aggression: the UN Security Council or a group of judges? International legal arguments can be made in both directions. On the one hand, article 39 of the UN Charter gives the Security Council the prerogative in identifying – and sanctioning – cases of aggression. On this basis, it was argued by many that this right of the Council should be respected in the judicial forum of the ICC also. On the other hand, the Security Council is not a judicial body which binds itself to an abstract legal definition of aggression or can be hoped to apply an equal standard to all situations before it.[139] On this basis, others argued that the ICC should be allowed to determine cases of aggression entirely independently.[140] The P5 in this debate guarded their interpretative authority jealously. As Oscar Solera points out, 'it is apparent that politically speaking there could be a tendency among Security Council members to dislike having an organ that could, in certain cases, have competing views of problems similar to the ones it is called to deal with'.[141] In short, the P5, once again, had something to lose.

For a long time, West Germany had supported the prerogative of the UN Security Council in determining aggression. In 1980, Germany had emphasised that it should remain for the UN Security Council alone to pin the label of aggression onto a particular use of force.[142] In 1988 at the UN, Germany warned that 'the matter cannot possibly be left in the hands of any judge in any country'.[143] Germany's support for the UN Security Council's prerogative continued in the 1990s: although Germany's envoy to the ILC, Christian Tomuschat, expressed legal concerns against leaving aggression to be determined post-crime by the UN Security Council,[144]

[138] Claus Kreß, 'The Crime of Aggression before the First Review of the ICC Statute' (2007) 20 *Leiden Journal of International Law* 859.

[139] As was expressed by Judge Schwebel in his dissenting opinion to the ICJ's Nicaragua case, 'the Security Council may take legal considerations into account but unlike a court, is not bound to apply them.' ICJ Reports 1986, 290.

[140] A particularly clear and concise overview of the competing positions, including their respective legal foundations, is offered by de Gurmendi, 'The Working Group on Aggression' (n 124) 599–603.

[141] Solera, *Defining the Crime of Aggression* (n 121) 299.

[142] UN Doc A/C.6/35/SR 12, 7 October 1980. See also above chapter two, section V.

[143] The full wording is quoted in Clemens Lerche, 'Völkerrechtliche Praxis der Bundesrepublik Deutschland im Jahre 1988' (1990) 50 *Zeitschrift für ausländisches öffentliches Recht und Völkerrecht (Heidelberg Journal of International Law)* 365f. For a summary of the statement, see UN Doc A/C.6/43/SR 34.

[144] Compare Solera, *Defining the Crime of Aggression* (n 121) 300.

Germany supported the ILC's 1994 Draft Statute, which suggested that the ICC should be allowed to charge aggression only after such a determination by the Security Council. The decision would, thus, remain in the hands of the Security Council and not be left to individual judges. In respect of the 1994 Draft Statute, in 1995 Germany reiterated that a central role for the Security Council would be 'essential' if the crime of aggression were to be included into the ICC's purview.[145] This position assured Germany's unity with the P5. Germany's 1997 text proposal for the crime of aggression at PrepCom suggested making the adjudication of aggression by the ICC 'subject to a determination by the Security Council referred to in Article 10, paragraph 2, regarding the act of a State'.[146] To challenge the UN Security Council's prerogative on the question of aggression would have been 'unthinkable' for Germany even in 1998, notes Kaul.[147]

However, Germany's position began to shift after Rome. With Germany spearheading the call to entirely remove the UN Security Council from its position of control previously held at the UN ad hoc tribunals, it also began to argue in this direction in relation to the crime of aggression. The continued prerogative of the Security Council could, in political reality, of course be expected to lead to a de facto exemption of the P5 and their allies from aggression charges, which makes for perhaps the strongest idealist argument against such a prerogative. A concise representation of this argument was given by Kreß in 2007:

> *[A]ny* rule that would subject international judicial proceedings for an alleged crime of aggression to the veto power of each of the permanent members of the Security Council must be rejected as fundamentally flawed both in international law and international policy.[148]

Assuredly, as illustrated in the sections above, this idealist position was not unrivalled within the inner-governmental debates in Germany. For German policymakers of a more realist conviction than Kreß, the prerogative of the UN Security Council in determining cases of aggression continued to offer at least one political advantage: the veto power of the P5 would form a filter which would potentially protect Germany as well. After all, three of the P5 are Germany's close NATO allies. For this reason, the four German government ministries involved in crafting Germany's strategy for negotiations around the ICC agreed in 2007 on a compromise

[145] Position of Germany 1995, quoted in Grote, Völkerrechtliche Praxis der Bundesrepublik Deutschland im Jahre 1995 (n 21), 1122–24.

[146] Report of the Preparatory Committee on the Establishment of an International Criminal Court, Addendum, UN doc A/CONF.183/2/Add 1, 14 April 1998, 14. See also Solera, *Defining the Crime of Aggression* (n 121) 355.

[147] Verbatim at the International Commission of Jurists' conference 'Der Internationale Strafgerichtshof in der Praxis', on 13 March 2009 in Berlin.

[148] Kreß, 'The Crime of Aggression before the First Review' (n 138) 860.

strategy. In principle, they would support the idealist argument against any prerogative for the UN Security Council, as presented by Kreß. However, if Germany should fail to sufficiently narrow down the substantive definition of aggression, then the UN Security Council's function as 'filter' could be accepted by Germany as an alternative.[149]

When it became apparent – not long before the Kampala Conference – that a majority of ASP members could agree on a narrow definition of the crime of aggression that included the word 'manifest', Germany's concerns in this respect were assuaged and Germany was able to maintain its opposition to the UN Security Council's power as an additional 'filter'. On the other hand, however, a radical policy position that would deny the Security Council any and all of its Charter-based claim to a prerogative over aggression would easily have alienated the P5, jeopardising the chances for political agreement in the end. The risk at hand was that Kampala would end as just another stepping stone in a long history of intricate negotiations on the crime of aggression and that the matter would be postponed again. For this reason, in negotiations, Germany effectively supported a middle-ground between 'the monopoly claim of the five permanent Council members on the one end and the rejection of any role for the Council beyond the one already recognised in Article 16 Rome Statute at the other end of the spectrum.'[150] Gerd Westdickenberg, Kaul's successor as Head of the Ministry of Foreign Affair's International Law Department, and Oliver Fixson, his Deputy, noted a 'dilemma regarding the role of the Security Council': Germany saw the need to compromise with the P5 in order to make any progress in building consensus.[151]

In this vein, when Argentina, Brazil and Switzerland made a joint effort at the Kampala Conference in 2010 to gather small States around a proposal (dubbed the 'ABS Proposal')[152] that would have granted the UN Security Council a position as a 'filter' for aggression charges only in a first stage and would then have removed the Council from this position in several consecutive steps, Germany joined Japan in criticising the

[149] Minutes of inner-governmental strategic debate regarding the codification of the crime of aggression, held at the Ministry of Foreign Affairs, on 26 January 2007, 5. On file with the author.

[150] Kreß and von Holtzendorff, *The Kampala Compromise* (n 132).

[151] Westdickenberg and Fixson, 'Das Verbrechen der Aggression' (n 123) 525. The same pragmatic reasoning was also expressed by other delegations at Rome, compare eg Solera, *Defining the Crime of Aggression* (n 121) 363.

[152] According to this proposal, *Non paper submitted by Argentina, Brazil and Switzerland as of 6 June 2010*, the adjudication of aggression should be subject to the green light of the UN Security Council in a first phase after Kampala. But subsequently, once 7/8ths of the ASP agree, that filter should be dropped, thus leaving the Court to determine aggression independently of the Security Council. Compare the detailed analysis by Beth van Schaack, 'Negotiating at the Interface of Power & Law: The Crime of Aggression' http://works.bepress.com/beth_van_schaack/2/ (2010) 22–23. Van Schaak served on the US delegation at Kampala as the Academic Adviser.

proposal as unrealistic.[153] It was argued by Germany that the ABS Proposal, although pleasing to idealists, made compromise with the P5 impossible. As Kreß and his assistant at Kampala, Leonie von Holtzendorff, note, it came as no surprise that 'a high price had to be paid' for breaking the Security Council's long-time prerogative monopoly.[154]

The solution that was ultimately agreed upon at Kampala, with the support of Germany, was then a compromise. It preserved a little more of the special role of the UN Security Council vis-à-vis the crime of aggression than the mere chance for the Council to defer cases under article 16 of the Rome Statute. On the one hand, the stipulation that a 'determination of an act of aggression by an organ outside the Court shall be without prejudice to the Court's own findings under this Statute'[155] pleased the most vital of idealist arguments. On the other hand, while it was agreed at Kampala that a procedural green light from the UN Security Council should not be *necessary* for the ICC to pursue a charge of alleged aggression, it was also assured that such a green light would nonetheless remain desirable. It was agreed that, absent a referral by the UN Security Council – for example, if one of the P5 should exercise their veto – the ICC's jurisdiction for the crime of aggression should be limited to prosecuting nationals of States parties. In addition, even States Parties who ratify the aggression amendment may 'opt out' in such a case. This means that, whenever a P5 member exercises its veto, the scope of the ICC's jurisdiction is more limited than with respect to the other three core crimes.[156] Thus, the P5 kept a little of their special influence.

8. CONCLUSION

Once the United States, along with a small number of western allies, initiated the revival of the system of international criminal justice in the early 1990s, this system soon took off in a rather unexpected direction. What started out in the early 1990s as a new instrument to bolster the powers of the UN Security Council, rapidly turned into an independent entity, in some respects even directly rivalling the UN Security Council. While the Council had initially been in full control of the UN ad hoc tribunals (created in 1993 and 1994), its influence was considerably reduced, almost 'from gatekeeper to spectator'[157] during the creation of the ICC in 1998. This was against the strong political opposition of the five permanent

[153] Desch interview (22 September 2010, by telephone).
[154] Kreß and von Holtzendorff, *The Kampala Compromise* (n 132).
[155] See draft art 15*bis* (9) and draft art 15*ter* (4) Rome Statute.
[156] This compromise still needs to be voted into effect and ratified by 30 States parties and cannot take effect any earlier than 2017.
[157] Schabas, 'United States Hostility' (n 14) 714.

Council members, particularly the United States. Germany on the other hand was a strong proponent of this shift.

Germany was among a group of small and middle-sized States that advocated reducing the UN Security Council's influence in international criminal justice. This was based on a change of legal paradigm among German policymakers: rather than continuing to support the need for democratic control over the necessarily selective execution of international criminal law, which Germany had done until the mid-1990s, Germany now spearheaded the argument for prosecutorial independence instead. The question this chapter has sought to explore is 'why?'.

As has been shown above in chapter one, lawyers on both sides of the Atlantic agree in principle that a prosecutor who is forced to make delicate policy decisions should be held accountable to some form of democratic oversight.[158] On the other hand, in political reality, there is obviously a sound legal argument in favour of preventing such oversight where it is exercised by a political body such as the UN Security Council. As has been argued by policymakers from Germany and many other States since the mid-1990s, there is the legitimate concern that such control will produce unequal justice. The German delegation which made this case at Rome was doubtlessly driven by normative ideals. Yet can it be disentangled entirely from power politics? The inner-governmental debates which led to Germany's new position, as explored in this chapter, show that the reason why this delegation was allowed by policymakers of a more realist conviction back in Bonn to proceed with its idealist arguments has something to do with Germany's power political interests as well. The fact that those realist policymakers in Bonn did not allow the negotiators to proceed in every respect – consider the restrictions on war crimes for instance – is some evidence of this. Rather than liberal ideals simply trumping traditional power politics, this chapter argues that Germany's shift in legal policy was made possible only by a remarkable *overlap* between liberal ideals and, incidentally, German national interests.

While US power politics had a lot to lose from the shift towards making the system of international criminal justice independent of the UN Security Council, Germany in fact had little to lose and even something to gain. William Schabas is probably right in declaring, 'Had the 1994 draft of the International Law Commission remained more or less intact, it is likely that today the United States would be a keen supporter of the Court.'[159] For the five permanent members of the UN Security Council,

[158] As illustrated above in chapter one, such prudence is certainly more than a 'false legal pretence' by the United States, which Charles A Smith and Heather M Smith, 'Embedded Realpolitik? Reevaluating United States' Opposition to the International Criminal Court' in Steven C Roach (ed), *Governance, Order and the International Criminal Court: Between Realpolitik and a Cosmopolitan Court* (Oxford, Oxford University Press, 2009) 31, suggest.

[159] Schabas, 'United States Hostility' (n 14) 701.

the transformation of the institutional design of international criminal justice from a system perfectly subordinated to the Security Council to a new, independent system obviously meant a loss of influence and, unsurprisingly, it has been widely argued that the fear of this loss was a driving force behind the P5's emphatic defence of such control, even if the arguments for accountability were legal in nature. The shift towards making the ICC independent of the UN Security Council also brings about a considerable redistribution of power in the system of international criminal justice: previously, the P5 had been able to exercise exclusive control over prosecutorial policies at the UN ad hoc tribunals. And while the channels of influence at the ICC are assuredly much narrower, the 'one country, one vote' system at the ICC ASP levels the playing field in terms of political nominations considerably. Here, smaller and middle-sized States that are not permanent members of the UN Security Council gain new influence. Germany, which largely held a role as spectator at the UN ad hoc tribunals, has thus gained a position as one of several gatekeepers. This is a remarkable gain in influence. The research presented in this chapter indicates that Germany's policy shift in the mid-1990s hinged, at least in part, on the prospect of this power political gain.

6

Cosmopolitan Ideals and National Interests: Concluding Remarks

DO GERMANY'S POLITICS of international criminal justice fall squarely outside of the theoretical framework offered by realists in the study of international relations? Can Germany's transformation from a long-time sceptic of international criminal law into one of its most outspoken advocates be explained only as a shift by German policymakers towards liberal rule-of-law idealism and away from old-fashioned, self-centred power politics, thus fitting nicely into liberal or idealist theories instead? As the analysis undertaken in this book has shown, Germany's stance in the political debates on international criminal justice indeed displays a clear shift towards liberal-judicial reasoning. While the initial hostile reactions to the legal rationales of the Nuremberg trials by German policymakers and legal scholars were rather openly self-interested and often ill-founded in law, a new generation later brushed these old positions aside – and has even been contrasting them with a particularly strong embrace of the legal principles of Nuremberg since the 1990s. Numerous young, idealist legal scholars were invited by the German government to make Germany's case at the Rome Conference, which established the statute of the International Criminal Court (ICC) in 1998. However, power politics have not simply disappeared.

Based on the historical analysis undertaken in this book, it would be inaccurate to disregard the important role that power politics continued to play in the background of Germany's politics of international criminal justice throughout this entire development. Faced with the revival of international criminal justice at the end of the Cold War, power political strategists in Germany did not simply step back: rather, none of the numerous shifts in German policy explored in this book, which were usually first advocated by human rights idealists, would have been implemented without more traditional, power politically-oriented policymakers discovering some advantage from their own perspective as well.

It is only the *overlap* between idealists and power politicians which made the series of policy shifts illustrated in this book possible. In cases where such an overlap did not exist, for instance in the debates on material war crimes law, Germany's position actually remained rather conservative.

So what convinced power politicians in Germany to gradually extend support to idealists and thereby support Germany's transformation into an advocate of international criminal justice in general and of an independent ('cosmopolitan') ICC in particular? Two lines of power political reasoning can be distinguished: while the first is based on the mechanisms of international criminal justice in general, which means that this line of reasoning is not unique to Germany and that comparable case studies of other States will very likely uncover similar political mechanisms (as some already have), the second is somewhat particular to Germany in light of its history.

Germany's Narrative Interests in the World

Firstly, as shown in chapter one, a functioning system of international criminal justice is a powerful institution in terms of authoritatively narrating 'historical truth' – and German policymakers at the end of the Cold War saw opportunity in this. One might perhaps object that Germany, unlike for instance the States in the war-torn Balkans, has not held a vested interest in atrocity trials since Nuremberg, but this would miss a crucial point. Many of the conflict situations, which the new system of international criminal justice turned its attention to in the 1990s, had led the newly-reunified Germany to decide on a particular course of reaction which was in need of moral justification.

To begin with, in the case of the East German GDR regime, human rights activists assuredly had a credible, value-driven interest in 1989 in avoiding impunity for heinous State crimes. But West German power politicians, on the other hand, could also find quite robustly realist motives for agreeing with them and for enabling them to go forward with their calls for justice at a time where many neighbouring post-communist countries, by contrast, preferred to stifle such calls for justice. As illustrated in chapter three, the historiography of the newly reunified German State in the early 1990s was initially far from clear. For long-time proponents of anti-communism in West Germany's conservative governments, there was consequently just as much to lose as there was to gain here: criminal trials for functionaries of the former GDR regime would promise to add authenticity to West German conservatives' condemnation of the communist GDR as a 'second dictatorship' following the Nazi regime. In the larger 'economics of legitimacy' in Germany, this point was rather significant: the narrative of the GDR as a criminal rather than merely a politically erroneous regime helped to add legitimacy to West German conservatives' initiative to simply dissolve the entire GDR and to integrate its territory into the existing legal framework of West Germany.

The *alternative* narrative of these historical events – that is, the assertion that the dissolution of the GDR was a 'takeover' by the West – was thus rebutted to some extent.

In the early 1990s, human rights activists assuredly had a genuine, idealist interest in ending impunity in the Balkans or in Iraq, but West German power politicians, on the other hand, could again find quite robustly realist reasons to agree with them. It was explored in chapter four how Germany had sided strongly with Croatia in the early days of the wars on the Balkans. This German policy was a rather controversial first appearance on the world stage after Germany's reunification and it was far from clear at this point how history would judge Germany in this case. The ICTY, as a court that could communicate a clear message on 'historical truth', promised to play no small part in deciding this. The ICTY, which was created through an initiative mainly of the United States in response to requests from Croatia, was rightly expected by German policymakers to primarily highlight Croat suffering. To Germany, such a tribunal would thus promise a gain in legitimacy for Germany's early support of Croatia against Serbia.

Finally, to design the new, permanent international criminal court as an independent institution – in contrast to the UN ad hoc tribunals which had been under close control of the UN Security Council at all times – was assuredly an idea for which human rights idealists in the mid-1990s could name good reasons. Namely, control by the UN Security Council would create the dangerous risk of the five veto-wielding permanent members of that political body blocking any proceedings against themselves or allied States. Such privileges for five States would run contrary to the fundamental legal principle of equal justice. This idea that international criminal justice should be free from any control by individual States has since become known as the 'cosmopolitan' concept for the ICC and it is favoured emphatically by liberal theorists and countless NGOs today. On the other hand, however, power politicians in Germany, as well as in many smaller States, could again find quite robustly realist reasons to agree with them. After all, under the old concept of the UN ad hoc tribunals, these smaller States were disadvantaged in comparison with the five veto-wielding members of the UN Security Council members. Firstly, to do away with the P5's privileged position in international criminal justice meant to level the playing field internationally for everyone else. Secondly, Germany and the large group of primarily smaller States with which Germany allied in this debate could even expect that the new design of international criminal justice would play to their particular advantage. This is because, with the new model of an independent ICC, the hand-picking of judges and the prosecutor is made in an open forum of all signatory States according to the principle of 'one country, one vote'. Groups of States that are large in number are in a good position to exercise influence here – regardless of how small they are in terms of economic or military power.[1] For most of the 27 member States of Europe – with Germany in their middle – this is a good bargain. Of course, for the two permanent Security Council members in Europe, France and the United Kingdom, it obviously is not.

Germany and New Nurembergs

Commentators on Germany's more recent policies of international criminal justice seldom fail to point out the historical irony that Germany, of all countries, should today advocate the Nuremberg principles so strongly – often even against the more cautious approaches of the original creators of Nuremberg.[2] This points us to an interesting aspect of the entire legal debate about international criminal justice, at least from the special perspective of Germany.

When Germany opted to hold trials for GDR crimes after 1989, these trials, legally, were 'Nuremberg revisited', as Kai Ambos has highlighted:[3] the legal rationales originally developed in light of the Nazi's historically unparalleled atrocities were transferred here to one of the smallest communist regimes in Europe and both regimes were at the same time bracketed by some West German policymakers as Germany's 'two dictatorships'. The historical subtext of this judicial decision was not missed by anyone in the inner-German debate, as is highlighted by Horst Dreier who warned of a distortion of historical proportions in 1997.[4] Given Germany's longtime resentment against the exceptional character of the Nuremberg International Military Tribunal (IMT) and given the weight of Germany's historically singular guilt highlighted at Nuremberg, the question can be asked whether such a historical subtext went on to play a role in the following years. With the United States in 1992 calling for a 'second Nuremberg'[5] for the Balkans, how could Germany's own history *not* be relevant in shaping Germany's perspective on that US proposal? With Hans-Dietrich Genscher proposing a 'Nuremberg-type procedure' to judge Saddam Hussein in 1991,[6] how could Germany's history *not* have been on the minds of German policymakers thinking about that proposal?

[1] See chapter five, section seven.

[2] This historiographic point is highlighted by Annette Weinke, '"Von Nürnberg nach Den Haag"? Das Internationale Militärtribunal in historischer Perspektive' in Helia-Verena Daubach (ed), *Leipzig – Nürnberg – Den Haag: Neue Fragestellungen und Forschungen zum Verhältnis von Menschenrechtsverbrechen justizieller Säuberung und Völkerstrafrecht* (Düsseldorf, Justizministerium des Landes NRW, 2008) 20.

[3] Kai Ambos, 'Nuremberg revisited. Das Bundesverfassungsgericht, das Völkerstrafrecht und das Rückwirkungsverbot' (1997) 17 *Strafverteidiger*.

[4] Horst Dreier, 'Gustav Radbruch und die Mauerschützen' (1997) *JuristenZeitung* 425.

[5] Elaine Sciolino, 'U.S. Names Figures It Wants Charged With War Crimes', *New York Times*, 17 December 1992.

[6] Pierre Hazan, *Justice in a Time of War* (Station, Texas A&M University Press, 2004) 9f. See chapter four, section four.

Until the end of the Cold War, Nuremberg stood out as a unique, singular judicial event, mirroring the uniquely universal outrage at Germany's unparalleled crimes in World War II: '[E]ven if Germany had been at the very centre of discussions of international justice from 1919 to 1989, its status was mostly as its object.'[7] With the creation of the UN ad hoc tribunals in 1993 and 1994 however, this historical perspective changed. Now, Nuremberg ceased to be a unique trial which had become necessary only once in the history of mankind. Rather, Nuremberg could now be described as 'only' the first of its kind, with comparable atrocities elsewhere making comparable tribunals necessary. This creates a new perspective on Nuremberg.[8]

[7] Paul Betts, 'Germany, International Justice and the Twentieth Century' (2005) 17 *History & Memory* 75.

[8] See also Weinke, '"Von Nürnberg nach Den Haag"?' (n 2) 21.

Bibliography

Ahlbrecht, Heiko, *Geschichte der völkerrechtlichen Strafgerichtsbarkeit im 20. Jahrhundert: Unter besonderer Berücksichtigung der völkerrechtlichen Straftatbestände und der Bemühungen um einen ständigen Internationalen Strafgerichtshof* (Baden-Baden, Nomos, 1999).

Akhavan, Payam, 'Justice in The Hague, Peace in the Former Yugoslavia? A Commentary on the United Nations War Crimes Tribunal' (1998) 20 *Human Rights Quarterly* 737.

Ambos, Kai, 'Nuremberg revisited, Das Bundesverfassungsgericht, das Völkerstrafrecht und das Rückwirkungsverbot' (1997) 17 *Strafverteidiger* 39.

——, 'Comparative Summary of the National Reports' in Louise Arbour and others (eds), *The Prosecutor of a Permanent International Criminal Court: International workshop in co-operation with the Office of the Prosecutor of the International Criminal Tribunals (ICTY and ICTR), Freiburg im Breisgau, May 1998* (Freiburg im Breisgau, Edition iuscrim, 2000).

——, *Der Allgemeine Teil des Völkerstrafrechts: Ansätze einer Dogmatisierung* (Berlin, Duncker & Humblot, 2002).

Arbour, Louise, 'Progress and Challenges in International Criminal Justice' (1997) 21 *Fordham International Law Journal* 531.

—— and others (eds), *The Prosecutor of a Permanent International Criminal Court: International workshop in co-operation with the Office of the Prosecutor of the International Criminal Tribunals (ICTY and ICTR), Freiburg im Breisgau, May 1998* (Freiburg im Breisgau, Edition iuscrim, 2000).

Arendt, Hannah, *Between Past and Future: Eight Exercises in Political Thought* (New York, Penguin Books, 1993).

Arnold, Jörg, 'Die "Bewältigung" der DDR-Vergangenheit vor den Schranken des rechtsstaatlichen Strafrechts' in Institut für Kriminalwissenschaften (ed), *Vom unmöglichen Zustand des Strafrechts* (Frankfurt am Main, Lang, 1995).

Augstein, Rudolf (ed), *Historikerstreit: Die Dokumentation der Kontroverse um die Einzigartigkeit der nationalsozialistischen Judenvernichtung* (Munich, R Piper, 1987).

Bader, Karl S, 'Zum Nürnberger Urteil' (1946) 1 *Deutsche Rechts-Zeitschrift* 140.

Ball, Howard, *Prosecuting War Crimes and Genocide: The Twentieth-Century Experience* (Lawrence, University Press of Kansas, 1999).

Bass, Gary J, *Stay the Hand of Vengeance: The Politics of War Crimes Tribunals* (Princeton, Princeton University Press, 2000).

Bassiouni, M Cherif, *The Statute of the International Criminal Court: A Documentary History* (Ardsley, Transnational Publishers, 1998).

Battis, Ulrich, and others (eds), *Vergangenheitsbewältigung durch Recht: Drei Abhandlungen zu einem deutschen Problem* (Berlin, Duncker & Humblot, 1992).

Beigbeder, Yves, *Judging War Criminals: The Politics of International Justice* (New York, St. Martin's Press, 1999).

Benedetti, Fanny and Washburn, John L, 'Drafting the International Criminal Court Treaty: Two Years to Rome and an Afterword on the Rome Diplomatic Conference' (1999) 5 *Global Governance* 1.

Berber, Friedrich, *Lehrbuch des Völkerrechts* (Munich, Beck, 1960).

Bergsmo, Morten, 'The Jurisdictional Regime of the International Criminal Court (Part II, Articles 11–19)' (1998) 6 *European Journal of Crime, Criminal Law, and Criminal Justice* 345.

—— and Pejić, Jelena, 'Article 15: Prosecutor' in Triffterer, Otto (ed), *Commentary on the Rome Statute of the International Criminal Court: Observers' Notes, Article by Article* (Baden-Baden, CH Beck, 1999).

Betts, Paul, 'Germany, International Justice and the Twentieth Century' (2005) 17 *History & Memory* 45.

Bloxham, Donald, *Genocide on Trial: War Crimes Trials and the Formation of Holocaust History and Memory* (Oxford, Oxford University Press, 2003).

von Bogdandy, Armin, 'Globalization and Europe, How to Square Democracy, Globalization, and International Law' (2004) 15 *European Journal of International Law* 885.

Bohlander, Michael, 'The International Criminal Judiciary, Problems of Judicial Selection, Independence and Ethics' in Bohlander, Michael (ed), *International Criminal Justice: A Critical Analysis of Institutions and Procedures* (London, Cameron May, 2007).

—— (ed), *International Criminal Justice: A Critical Analysis of Institutions and Procedures* (London, Cameron May, 2007).

Brennecke, Gerhard, *Die Nürnberger Geschichtsentstellung: Quellen zur Vorgeschichte und Geschichte des 2. Weltkriegs aus den Akten der deutschen Verteidigung* (Tübingen, Verlag der Deutschen Hochschullehrer-Zeitung, 1970).

Buchner, Silke, *Die Rechtswidrigkeit der Taten von "Mauerschützen" im Lichte von Art. 103 II GG unter besonderer Berücksichtigung des Völkerrechts: Ein Beitrag zum Problem der Verfolgung von staatlich legitimiertem Unrecht nach Beseitigung des Unrechtssystems* (Frankfurt am Main, Lang, 1996).

Buchwald, Axel, *Der Fall Tadić vor dem Internationalen Jugoslawientribunal im Lichte der Entscheidung der Berufungskammer vom 2. Oktober 1995* (Berlin, Berliner Wissenschafts-Verlag, 2005).

Bull, Hedley, *The Anarchical Society: A Study of Order in World Politics* (Houndmills, Palgrave, 2007).

Burkhardt, Nina, '"Die Stiefel ausgezogen. . .", Täterbilder und die Sicht auf Deutschland in belgischen und niederländischen Radio- und Presseberichten über den Nürnberger Hauptprozess' in Daubach, Helia-Verena (ed), *Leipzig – Nürnberg – Den Haag: Neue Fragestellungen und Forschungen zum Verhältnis von Menschenrechtsverbrechen justizieller Säuberung und Völkerstrafrecht* (Düsseldorf, Justizministerium des Landes NRW, 2008).

Cassese, Antonio, *International Criminal Law* (Oxford, Oxford University Press, 2008).

Côté, Luc, 'Reflections on the Exercise of Prosecutorial Discretion in International Criminal Law' (2005) 3 *Journal of International Criminal Justice* 162.

Cryer, Robert, *Prosecuting International Crimes: Selectivity and the International Criminal Law Regime* (Cambridge, Cambridge University Press, 2005).

Dahm, Georg, 'Das Ermessen des Richters im nationalsozialistischen Strafrecht' (1934) *Deutsches Strafrecht.*

——, *Zur Problematik des Völkerstrafrechts* (Göttingen, Vandenhoeck & Ruprecht, 1956).

Dannecker, Gerhard and Stoffers, Kristian F, 'Rechtsstaatliche Grenzen für die strafrechtliche Aufarbeitung der Todesschüsse an der innerdeutschen Grenze' (1996) 51 *JuristenZeitung* 490.

Danner, Allison M, 'Constructing a Hierarchy of Crimes in International Criminal Law Sentencing' (2001) 87 *Virginia Law Review* 415.

——, 'Enhancing the Legitimacy and Accountability of Prosecutorial Discretion at the International Criminal Court' (2003) 97 *American Journal of International Law* 510.

Dascalopoulou-Livada, Phani, 'Aggression and the ICC: Views on Certain Ideas and their Potential for a Solution' in Politi, Mauro and Nesi, Giuseppe (eds), *The International Criminal Court and the Crime of Aggression* (Aldershot, Ashgate, 2004).

Daubach, Helia-Verena (ed), *Leipzig – Nürnberg – Den Haag: Neue Fragestellungen und Forschungen zum Verhältnis von Menschenrechtsverbrechen justizieller Säuberung und Völkerstrafrecht* (Düsseldorf, Justizministerium des Landes NRW, 2008).

Däubler-Gmelin, Herta, 'Internationaler Strafgerichtshof: Erfolge und Defizite, Zum zehnten Jahrestag des Römischen Statuts' (2008) 53 *Blätter für deutsche und internationale Politik* 78.

DeGuzman, Margaret, 'Gravity and the Legitimacy of the International Criminal Court' (2008) 32 *Fordham International Law Journal* 1400.

Deitelhoff, Nicole and Burkard, Eva, Europa vor Gericht: *Die EU-Außenpolitik und der internationale Strafgerichtshof* (Frankfurt am Main, Hessische Stiftung Friedens-und Konfliktforschung, 2005).

Del Ponte, Carla, 'Prosecuting the Individuals Bearing the Highest Level of Responsibility' (2004) *Journal of International Criminal Justice* 516.

——, *Madame Prosecutor: Confrontations with Humanity's Worst Criminals and the Culture of Impunity* (New York, Other Press, 2009).

Dencker, Friedrich, 'Strafrechtliche Aufarbeitung des DDR-Unrechts und Rechtskultur' in Hansen, Hendrik (ed), *Aufarbeitung totalitärer Erfahrungen und politische Kultur: Die Bedeutung der Aufarbeitung des SED-Unrechts für das Rechts- und Werteverständnis im wiedervereinigten Deutschland. Politisches Denken. Jahrbuch 2009* (Berlin, Duncker & Humblot, 2009).

Deutscher Juristentag (ed), *Verhandlungen des sechzigsten Deutschen Juristentages: Band II/1 – Sitzungsberichte* (Munich, self-published, 1994).

Dinstein, Yoram, *War, Aggression and Self-Defence* (Cambridge, Cambridge University Press, 2005).

Dreier, Horst, 'Gustav Radbruch und die Mauerschützen' (1997) *JuristenZeitung* 421.

Drumbl, Mark A, *Atrocity, Punishment, and International Law* (Cambridge, Cambridge University Press, 2007).

——, 'The Expressive Value of Prosecuting and Punishing Terrorists, Hamdan, the Geneva Conventions, and International Law' (2007) 75 *George Washington Law Review* 1165.

——, 'Policy Through Complementarity: The Atrocity Trial as Justice' in Stahn, Carsten and El Zeidy, Mohamed (eds), *The International Criminal Court and*

Complementarity: From Theory to Practice (Cambridge, Cambridge University Press, 2010).
——, 'Policy Through Complementarity, The Atrocity Trial as Justice' in: Stahn, Carsten and El Zeidy, Mohamed (eds), *The International Criminal Court and Complementarity: From Theory to Practice* (Cambridge, Cambridge University Press, 2011).
Dupuy, Pierre-Marie and others (eds), *Common Values in International Law, Essays in Honour of Christian Tomuschat* (Kehl, NP Engel Verlag, 2006).
Eisfeld, Rainer (ed), *Gegen Barbarei: Essays Robert M. W. Kempner zu Ehren* (Frankfurt am Main, Athenäum, 1989).
El Zeidy, Mohamed, 'The Gravity Threshold under the Statute of the International Criminal Court' (2008) 19 *Criminal Law Forum* 35.
Eser, Albin and Arnold, Jörg (eds), *Criminal Law in Reaction to State Crime: Comparative Insights into Transitional Processes, Volume 1* (Freiburg im Breisgau, Max-Planck-Institut für Ausländisches und Internationales Strafrecht, 2000).
—— (eds), *Criminal Law in Reaction to State Crime: Comparative Insights into Transitional Processes, Volume 2* (Freiburg im Breisgau, Max-Planck-Institut für Ausländisches und Internationales Strafrecht, 2000).
Faulenbach, Bernd, Meckel, Markus and Weber, Hermann, *Die Partei hatte immer recht: Aufarbeitung von Geschichte und Folgen der SED-Diktatur* (Essen, Klartext-Verlag, 1994).
Fehl, Caroline, 'Explaining the International Criminal Court, A Practice Test for Rationalist and Constructivist Approaches' in Roach, Steven C (ed), *Governance, Order and the International Criminal Court: Between Realpolitik and a Cosmopolitan Court* (Oxford, University Press, 2009).
Fernández de Gurmendi, Silvia A, 'The Role of the International Prosecutor' in Roy S Lee (ed), *The International Criminal Court: The Making of the Rome Statute; Issues, Negotiations, Results* (The Hague, Kluwer Law International, 1999).
Franceschet, Antonio, 'Four Cosmopolitan Projects, The International Criminal Court in Context' in Roach, Steven C (ed), *Governance, Order and the International Criminal Court: Between Realpolitik and a Cosmopolitan Court* (Oxford, Oxford University Press, 2009).
Frei, Norbert, *Vergangenheitspolitik: Die Anfänge der Bundesrepublik und die NS-Vergangenheit* (Munich, Deutscher Taschenbuch-Verlag, 1999).
——, 'Der Nürnberger Prozess und die Deutschen' in Wette, Wolfram and Überschär, Gerd R (eds), *Kriegsverbrechen im 20. Jahrhundert* (Darmstadt, Wissenschaftliche Buchgesellschaft, 2001).
——, *Adenauer's Germany and the Nazi Past: The Politics of Amnesty and Integration* (New York, Columbia University Press, 2002).
——, van Laak, Dirk and Stolleis, Michael (eds), *Geschichte vor Gericht: Historiker, Richter und die Suche nach Gerechtigkeit* (Munich, Beck, 2000).
Frowein, Jochen A and others (eds), *Verhandeln für den Frieden – Negotiating for Peace: Liber Amicorum Tono Eitel* (Berlin, Springer, 2003).
Gausmann, Frank, 'Vergangensheitsbewältigung durch Recht? Kritische Anmerkungen zur Anklagestrategie in den Nürnberger Industriellenprozessen' in Daubach, Helia-Verena (ed), *Leipzig – Nürnberg – Den Haag: Neue Fragestellungen und Forschungen zum Verhältnis von Menschenrechtsverbrechen justizieller Säuberung und Völkerstrafrecht* (Düsseldorf, Justizministerium des Landes NRW, 2008).

Gay, Peter, *Freud, Juden und andere Deutsche: Herren und Opfer in der modernen Kultur* (Hamburg, Hoffmann und Campe, 1986).

Gerhardt, Volker (ed), *Politisches Denken: Jahrbuch 2009* (Berlin, Duncker & Humblot, 2009).

Glasius, Marlies, *The International Criminal Court: A Global Civil Society Achievement* (London, Routledge, 2006).

Glennon, Michael J, 'The Blank-Prose Crime of Aggression' (2010) 35 *Yale Journal of International Law* 71.

Goldstone, Richard J and Fritz, Nicole, '"In the Interests of Justice" and Independent Referral, The ICC Prosecutor's Unprecedented Powers' (2004) 13 *Leiden Journal of International Law* 655.

Graveson, RH, 'Der Grundsatz nulla poena sine lege und das Kontrollratsgesetz Nr. 10' (1947) *Monatsschrift für Deutsches Recht* 278.

Greenawalt, Alexander, 'Justice without Politics? Prosecutorial Discretion and the International Criminal Court' (2006) 39 *NYU Journal of International Law and Politics* 583.

Greiner, Bernd, *Die Morgenthau-Legende: Zur Geschichte eines umstrittenen Plans* (Hamburg, Hamburger Edition, 1995).

Grewe, Wilhelm, 'Rückblick auf Nürnberg' in Hailbronner, Kay (ed), *Staat und Völkerrechtsordnung: Festschrift für Karl Doehring* (Berlin, Springer, 1989).

—— and Küster, Otto, *Nürnberg als Rechtsfrage: Eine Diskussion* (Stuttgart, Klett, 1947).

Grote, Rainer, 'Völkerrechtliche Praxis der Bundesrepublik Deutschland im Jahre 1995' (1997) *Zeitschrift für ausländisches öffentliches Recht und Völkerrecht* (*Heidelberg Journal of International Law*) 923.

Fernández de Gurmendi, Silvia, 'The Working Group on Aggression at the Preparatory Commission for the International Criminal Court' (2002) 25 *Fordham International Law Journal* 589.

Haass, Dieter, *"Nulla poena sine lege" im nationalen und internationalen Recht* (Heidelberg, Diss., 1995).

Habermas, Jürgen, 'Eine Art Schadensabwicklung, Die apologetischen Tendenzen in der deutschen Zeitgeschichtsschreibung' in Augstein, Rudolf (ed), *Historikerstreit: Die Dokumentation der Kontroverse um die Einzigartigkeit der nationalsozialistischen Judenvernichtung 2nd* (Munich, R Piper, 1987).

——, *Der gespaltene Westen* (Frankfurt am Main, Suhrkamp, 2004).

——, *The Divided West* (Cambridge, Polity, 2006).

Hailbronner, Kay (ed), *Staat und Völkerrechtsordnung: Festschrift für Karl Doehring* (Berlin, Springer, 1989).

Hall, Christopher K, 'The First Two Sessions of the UN Preparatory Committee on the Establishment of an International Criminal Court' (1997) 91 *American Journal of International Law* 177.

——, 'The Fifth Session of the UN Preparatory Committee on the Establishment of an International Criminal Court' (1998) 92 *American Journal of International Law* 331.

——, 'The Third and Fourth Sessions of the UN Preparatory Committee on the Establishment of an International Criminal Court' (1998) 92 *American Journal of International Law* 124.

Hankel, Gerd (ed), *Die Macht und das Recht: Beiträge zum Völkerrecht und*

Völkerstrafrecht am Beginn des 21. Jahrhunderts (Hamburg, Hamburger Edition, 2008).

Hansen, Hendrik (ed), *Aufarbeitung totalitärer Erfahrungen und politische Kultur: Die Bedeutung der Aufarbeitung des SED-Unrechts für das Rechts- und Werteverständnis im wiedervereinigten Deutschland, Politisches Denken. Jahrbuch 2009* (Berlin, Duncker & Humblot, 2009).

Hartmann, Jutta, 'Das deutsche Völkerstrafgesetzbuch' in Kühne, Hans-Heiner, Esser, Robert, Gerding, Marc (eds), *Völkerstrafrecht: 12 Beiträge zum internationalen Strafrecht und Völkerstrafrecht* (Osnabrück, Jonscher, 2007).

Hazan, Pierre, *Justice in a Time of War: The True Story behind the International Criminal Tribunal for the Former Yugoslavia* (Station, Texas A&M University Press, 2004).

Heer, Hannes, and Naumann, Klaus, *Vernichtungskrieg: Verbrechen der Wehrmacht 1941-1944* (Hamburg, Hamburger Edition, 1995).

Heine, Günter, 'Täterschaft und Teilnahme in staatlichen Machtapparaten, NS- und DDR-Unrecht im Vergleich der Rechtsprechung' (2000) 55 *JuristenZeitung* 920.

Heller, Kevin J, 'Situational Gravity under the Rome Statute' in Stahn, Carsten and van den Herik, Larissa (eds), *Future Perspectives in International Criminal Justice* (Leiden, TMC Asser, 2010).

Higgins, Rosalyn, *Problems and Process: International Law and How We Use It* (Oxford, Clarendon, 1995).

Hillenkamp, Thomas, 'Offene und verdeckte Amnestie – über Wege strafrechtlicher Vergangenheitsbewältigung' (1996) *JuristenZeitung* 179.

Hodenberg, Hodo, 'Zur Anwendung des Kontrollratsgesetzes Nr.10 durch die deutschen Gerichte' (1947) *Süddeutsche Juristenzeitung* 113.

Horn, Norbert, and Coing, Helmut (eds), *Europäisches Rechtsdenken in Geschichte und Gegenwart: Festschrift für Helmut Coing zum 70. Geburtstag* (Munich, Beck, 1982).

Human Rights Watch, *Courting History: The Landmark International Criminal Court's First Years* (New York, Human Rights Watch, 2008).

Huntington, Samuel P, *The Soldier and the State: The Theory and Politics of Civil-Military Relations* (Cambridge, Belknap, 2002).

ICTY (ed), *The Path to The Hague: Selected Documents on the Origins of the ICTY* (The Hague, United Nations, 2001).

Ignatieff, Michael, *Virtual War: Kosovo and Beyond* (London, Vintage, 2001).

Ingrao, Charles W, and Emmert, Thomas A, *Confronting the Yugoslav Controversies: A Scholars' Initiative* (West Lafayette, Purdue University Press, 2009).

Institut für Kriminalwissenschaften (ed), *Vom unmöglichen Zustand des Strafrechts* (Frankfurt am Main, Lang, 1995).

Jäger, Herbert, 'Menschheitsverbrechen und die Grenzen des Kriminalkonzeptes, Theoretische Aspekte der Einsetzung eines UN-Kriegsverbrechertribunals' (1993) *Kritische Vierteljahresschrift für Gesetzgebung und Rechtswissenschaft* 259.

Jahrreiss, Hermann (ed), *Um Recht und Gerechtigkeit: Festgabe für Erich Kaufmann zu seinem 70. Geburtstage* (Stuttgart, Kohlhammer, 1950).

——, 'Vergangenheitsbewältigung durch Strafrecht?, Zur Leistungsfähigkeit des Strafrechts nach einem politischen Umbruch' in Battis, Ulrich and others (eds), *Vergangenheitsbewältigung durch Recht: Drei Abhandlungen zu einem deutschen Problem* (Berlin, Duncker & Humblot, 1992).

Jakobs, Günther, 'Untaten des Staates – Unrecht im Staat, Strafe für die Tötungen an der Grenze der ehemaligen DDR?' (1994) *Goldtammer's Archiv für Strafrecht* 1.

Jalloh, Charles, 'Regionalizing International Criminal Law? Prospects and Challenges for Africa and the International Criminal Court' (2009) 9 *International Criminal Law Review* 445.

——, *Die Verantwortlichkeit der Staatsorgane nach Völkerstrafrecht: Eine Studie zu den Nürnberger Prozessen* (Bonn, Röhrscheid, 1952).

Jescheck, Hans-Heinrich, 'Schlussworte' in Sieber, Ulrich and Albrecht, Hans-Jörg (eds), *Strafrecht und Kriminologie unter einem Dach: Kolloquium zum 90. Geburtstag von Professor Dr. Dr. h.c. mult. Hans-Heinrich Jescheck* (Berlin, Duncker & Humblot, 2006).

Jung, Susanne, *Die Rechtsprobleme der Nürnberger Prozesse: Dargestellt am Verfahren gegen Friedrich Flick* (Tübingen, Mohr, 1992).

Just-Dahlmann, Barbara and Just, Helmut, *Die Gehilfen: NS-Verbrechen und die Justiz nach 1945* (Frankfurt am Main, Athenäum, 1988).

Kant, Immanuel, *Perpetual Peace: A Philosophical Essay; 1795* (Whitefish, Kessinger, 2007).

Kaul, Hans-Peter, 'Auf dem Weg zum Weltstrafgerichtshof, Verhandlungsstand und Perspektiven' (1997) 45 *Vereinte Nationen* 177.

——, 'The Crime of Aggression: Definitional Options for the Way Forward' in Mauro Politi and Giuseppe Nesi (eds), *The International Criminal Court and the Crime of Aggression* (Ashgate, Aldershot, 2004).

Kenntner, Markus, 'Der deutsche Sonderweg zum Rückwirkungsverbot: Plädoyer für die Aufgabe eines überholten Verweigerungsdogmas' (1997) *Neue Juristische Wochenschrift* 2298.

Keohane, Robert O, *International Institutions and State Power: Essays in International Relations Theory* (Boulder, Westview Press, 1989).

Kinkel, Klaus, 'Ansprache auf dem deutschen Richtertag im September 1991' (1992) *Deutsche Richterzeitung* 4.

——, 'Wiedervereinigung und Strafrecht' (1992) *JuristenZeitung* 485.

——, 'Für einen funktionsfähigen Weltstrafgerichtshof' (1997) 50 *Neue Juristische Wochenschrift* 2860.

——, 'Der Internationale Strafgerichtshof – ein Meilenstein in der Entwicklung des Völkerrechts' (1998) *Neue Juristische Wochenschrift* 2650.

Klein, Anne, 'Mentalität, Massenmord, Moral: Rechts- und Geschichtsverständnis der bundesrepublikanischen Nachkriegsgesellschaft' in Neubacher, Frank and Klein, Anne (eds), *Vom Recht der Macht zur Macht des Rechts?: Interdisziplinäre Beiträge zur Zukunft internationaler Strafgerichte* (Berlin, Duncker & Humblot, 2006).

Kochavi, Arieh J, *Prelude to Nuremberg: Allied War Crimes Policy and the Question of Punishment* (Chapel Hill, University of North Carolina Press, 1998).

Kranzbühler, Otto, 'Nürnberg als Rechtsproblem' in Jahrreiss, Hermann (ed), *Um Recht und Gerechtigkeit: Festgabe für Erich Kaufmann zu seinem 70. Geburtstage* (Stuttgart, Kohlhammer, 1950).

Kraus, Herbert, *Gerichtstag in Nürnberg: Abdruck eines am 22. Oktober 1947 in der Aula der Universität Göttingen gehaltenen Vortrags* (Hamburg, Gesetz-und-Recht-Verlag, 1947).

Kreß, Claus, *Vom Nutzen eines deutschen Völkerstrafgesetzbuchs* (Baden-Baden, Nomos, 2000).

——, 'The German Chief Federal Prosecutor's Decision Not to Investigate the Alleged Crime of Preparing Aggression against Iraq' (2004) 2 *Journal of International Criminal Justice* 245.

——, 'The Iraqi Special Tribunal and the Crime of Aggression' (2004) 2 *Journal of International Criminal Justice* 347.

——, 'Germany and International Criminal Law: Continuity of Change?' in Reginbogin, Herbert R and Safferling, Christoph J M (eds), *The Nuremberg Trials: International Criminal Law since 1945: 60th Anniversary International Conference* (Munich, KG Saur, 2006).

——, 'Versailles – Nuremberg – The Hague: Germany and International Criminal Law' (2006) 40 *The International Lawyer* 15.

——, 'Versailles – Nürnberg – Den Haag: Deutschland und das Völkerstrafrecht' (2006) 61 *JuristenZeitung* 981.

——, 'The Crime of Aggression before the First Review of the ICC Statute' (2007) 20 *Leiden Journal of International Law* 851.

——, 'Time for Decision: Some Thoughts on the Immediate Future of the Crime of Aggression: A Reply to Andreas Paulus' (2009) 20 *European Journal of International Law* 1129.

—— and von Holtzendorff, Leonie, 'The Kampala Compromise on the Crime of Aggression' (2010) 8 *Journal of International Criminal Justice* 1179.

Kühne, Hans-Heiner, Esser, Robert and Gerding, Marc (eds), *Völkerstrafrecht: 12 Beiträge zum internationalen Strafrecht und Völkerstrafrecht* (Osnabrück, Jonscher, 2007).

Lampe, Ernst-Joachim (ed), *Deutsche Wiedervereinigung: Die Rechtseinheit, Volume 2: Die Verfolgung von Regierungskriminalität nach der Wiedervereinigung* (Cologne, Arbeitskreis Strafrecht, 1993).

Langenfeld, Christine, 'Völkerrechtliche Praxis der Bundesrepublik Deutschland im Jahre 1992' (1994) 54 *Zeitschrift für ausländisches öffentliches Recht und Völkerrecht* (Heidelberg Journal of International Law) 814.

Leanza, Umberto, 'The Historical Background' in Politi, Mauro and Nesi, Giuseppe (eds), *The International Criminal Court and the Crime of Aggression* (Ashgate, Aldershot, 2004).

Lee, Roy S (ed), *The International Criminal Court: The Making of the Rome Statute; Issues, Negotiations, Results* (The Hague, Kluwer Law International, 1999).

Legro, Jeffrey W and Moravcsik, Andrew, 'Is Anybody Still a Realist?' (1999) 24 *International Security* 5.

Leide, Henry, *NS-Verbrecher und Staatssicherheit: Die geheime Vergangenheitspolitik der DDR* (Göttingen, Vandenhoeck & Ruprecht, 2008).

Lerche, Clemens, 'Völkerrechtliche Praxis der Bundesrepublik Deutschland im Jahre 1988' (1990) 50 *Zeitschrift für ausländisches öffentliches Recht und Völkerrecht* (Heidelberg Journal of International Law) 309.

Lumsdaine, David H, *Moral Vision in International Politics: The Foreign Aid Regime, 1949-1989* (Princeton, Princeton University Press, 1993).

MacGoldrick, Dominic, Rowe, Peter, and Donelly, Eric (eds), *The Permanent International Criminal Court: Legal and Policy Issues* (Oxford, Hart Publishing, 2004).

Mackenzie, Ruth and others, *Selecting International Judges: Principle, Process, and Politics* (Oxford, Oxford University Press, 2010).

Maier, Charles S, 'A Surfeit of Memory? Reflections on History, Melancholy and Denial' (1993) 5 *History and Memory* 136.

Marauhn, Thilo, 'Völkerrechtliche Praxis der Bundesrepublik Deutschland im Jahre 1991' (1993) 53 *Zeitschrift für ausländisches öffentliches Recht und Völkerrecht (Heidelberg Journal of International Law)* 908.

Marxen, Klaus and Werle, Gerhard, *Die strafrechtliche Aufarbeitung von DDR-Unrecht: Eine Bilanz* (Berlin, de Gruyter, 1999).

Maser, Werner, *Nürnberg: Tribunal der Sieger* (Düsseldorf, Econ-Verlag, 1977).

McCormack, Timothy LH, 'Selective Reaction to Atrocity: War Crimes and the Development of International Criminal Law' (1996) 60 *Albany Law Review* 681.

—— and Simpson, Gerry J (eds), *The Law of War Crimes: National and International Approaches* (The Hague, Kluwer Law International, 1997).

Mearsheimer, John J, 'The false Promise of International Institutions' (1994) 19 *International Security* 5.

Mégret, Frédéric, 'The Politics of International Criminal Justice' (2002) 13 *European Journal of International Law* 1261.

Meron, Theodor, *War Crimes Law Comes of Age: Essays* (Oxford, Oxford University Press, 1998).

——, *The Humanization of International Law* (Leiden, Martinus Nijhoff, 2006).

Mezger, Edmund, 'Die materielle Rechtswidrigkeit im kommenden Strafrecht' (1936) 55 *Zeitschrift für die gesamte Strafrechtswissenschaft* 1.

——, *Kriminalpolitik und ihre kriminologischen Grundlagen* (Stuttgart, Enke, 1944).

Müller, Ingo, *Furchtbare Juristen: Die unbewältigte Vergangenheit unserer Justiz* (Munich, Droemer Knaur, 1989).

——, 'Nürnberg und die deutschen Juristen' in Eisfeld, Rainer (ed), *Gegen Barbarei: Essays Robert MW Kempner zu Ehren* (Frankfurt am Main, Athenäum, 1989).

Naumann, Klaus, 'Die "saubere" Wehrmacht: Gesellschaftsgeschichte einer Legende' (1998) 7 *Mittelweg* 36 8.

Neubacher, Frank, *Kriminologische Grundlagen einer internationalen Strafgerichtsbarkeit: Politische Ideen- und Dogmengeschichte, kriminalwissenschaftliche Legitimation, strafrechtliche Perspektiven* (Tübingen, Mohr Siebeck, 2005).

——, 'Strafzwecke und Völkerstrafrecht' (2006) 59 *Neue Juristische Wochenschrift* 966.

—— Klein, Anne (eds), *Vom Recht der Macht zur Macht des Rechts?: Interdisziplinäre Beiträge zur Zukunft internationaler Strafgerichte* (Berlin, Duncker & Humblot, 2006).

Olusanya, Olaoluwa, *Identifying the Aggressor under International Law: A Principles Approach* (Bern, Peter Lang, 2006).

Osten, Philipp, *Der Tokioter Kriegsverbrecherprozess und die japanische Rechtswissenschaft* (Berlin, Berliner Wissenschafts-Verlag, 2003).

Pace, William R and Thieroff, Mark S, 'Participation of Non-Governmental Organizations' in Lee, Roy S (ed), *The International Criminal Court: The Making of the Rome Statute; Issues, Negotiations, Results* (The Hague, Kluwer Law International, 1999).

Peskin, Victor, *International Justice in Rwanda and the Balkans: Virtual Trials and the Struggle for State Cooperation* (Cambridge, Cambridge University Press, 2008).

Peter, Jürgen, *Der Historikerstreit und die Suche nach einer nationalen Identität der achtziger Jahre* (Frankfurt am Main, Peter Lang, 1995).

Politi, Mauro and Nesi, Giuseppe (eds), *The International Criminal Court and the Crime of Aggression* (Aldershot, Ashgate, 2004).
Prunier, Gérard, *The Rwanda Crisis: History of a Genocide* (New York, Columbia University Press, 1995).
Radbruch, Gustav, 'Gesetzliches Unrecht und übergesetzliches Recht' (1946) *Süddeutsche Juristenzeitung* 105.
Ralph, Jason G, *Defending the Society of States: Why America Opposes the International Criminal Court and its Vision of World Society* (Oxford, Oxford University Press 2007).
Ramsey, MD, 'International Materials and Domestic Rights: Reflections on Atkins and Lawrence' (2004) 98 *The American Journal of International Law* 69.
Reginbogin, Herbert R and Safferling, Christoph JM (eds), *The Nuremberg Trials: International Criminal Law since 1945: 60th Anniversary International Conference* (Munich, KG Saur, 2006).
Reus-Smit, Christian, 'The Politics of International Law' in Reus-Smit, Christian (ed), *The Politics of International Law* (Cambridge, Cambridge University Press, 2009).
—— (ed), *The Politics of International Law* (Cambridge, Cambridge University Press, 2009).
Roach, Steven C, *Politicizing the International Criminal Court: The Convergence of Politics, Ethics, and Law* (Lanham, Rowman & Littlefield, 2006).
—— (ed), *Governance, Order and the International Criminal Court: Between Realpolitik and a Cosmopolitan Court* (Oxford, Oxford University Press, 2009).
Robertson, Geoffrey, *Crimes against Humanity: The Struggle for Global Justice* (London, Allen Lane, 1999).
Rossig, Kai and Ross, Antje, 'Alternativen zur strafrechtlichen Ahndung des DDR-Systemunrechts' in Eser, Albin and Arnold, Jörg (eds), *Criminal Law in Reaction to State Crime: Comparative Insights into Transitional Processes. Volume 2* (Freiburg im Breisgau, Max-Planck-Institut für Ausländisches und Internationales Strafrecht, 2000).
Rückerl, Adalbert, *NS-Verbrechen vor Gericht: Versuch einer Vergangenheitsbewältigung* (Heidelberg, Müller Juristischer Verlag, 1984).
Salter, Michael, *Nazi War Crimes, US Intelligence and Selective Prosecution at Nuremberg: Controversies Regarding the Role of the Office of Strategic Services* (New York, Routledge-Cavendish, 2007).
van Schaack, Beth, 'Negotiating at the Interface of Power & Law: The Crime of Aggression' http://works.bepress.com/beth_van_schaack/2/ 2010, 1.
Schabas, William A, 'United States Hostility to the International Criminal Court, It's All About the Security Council' (2004) 15 *European Journal of International Law* 701.
——, *An Introduction to the International Criminal Court* (Cambridge, Cambridge University Press, 2007).
——, 'Prosecutorial Discretion v. Judicial Activism at the International Criminal Court' (2008) 6 *Journal of International Criminal Justice* 731.
Scharf, Michael P, *Balkan Justice: The Story behind the First International War Crimes Trial since Nuremberg* (Durham, Carolina Academic Press, 1997).
Schäuble, Wolfgang, *Der Vertrag: Wie ich über die deutsche Einheit verhandelte* (Stuttgart, Deutsche Verlags-Anstalt, 1991).

Schiff, Benjamin N, *Building the International Criminal Court* (Cambridge, Cambridge University Press, 2008).
Schlink, Bernhard, 'Rechtsstaat und revolutionäre Gerechtigkeit' (1994) 10 *Neue Justiz* 433.
Schofield, Garth, 'The Empty US Chair: United States Nonparticipation in the Negotiations on the Definition of Aggression' (2007) 15 *Human Rights Brief* 20.
Schonfeld, Walter T, *Nazi Madness: Highlighted at Nuremberg* (London, Minerva, 2000).
Schulte, Jan E, 'Nationale Erfahrungen – Internationale Folgen: Die Verfolgung von "Nazi War Criminals" und die Unterstützung des Internationalen Strafgerichtshofs durch Kanada' in Daubach, Helia-Verena (ed), *Leipzig – Nürnberg – Den Haag: Neue Fragestellungen und Forschungen zum Verhältnis von Menschenrechtsverbrechen justizieller Säuberung und Völkerstrafrecht* (Düsseldorf, Justizministerium des Landes NRW, 2008).
Schweling, Otto and Schwinge, Erich, *Die deutsche Militärjustiz in der Zeit des Nationalsozialismus* (Marburg, Elwert, 1978).
Shepherd, Ben, 'The Clean Wehrmacht, the War of Extermination, and Beyond' (2009) 52 *The Historical Journal* 455.
Shukri, Muhammad A, 'Will Aggressors Ever be Tried Before the ICC?' in Politi, Mauro and Nesi, Giuseppe (eds), *The International Criminal Court and the Crime of Aggression* (Ashgate, Aldershot, 2004).
Sieber, Ulrich and Albrecht, Hans-Jörg (eds), *Strafrecht und Kriminologie unter einem Dach: Kolloquium zum 90. Geburtstag von Professor Dr. Dr. h.c. mult. Hans-Heinrich Jescheck* (Berlin, Duncker & Humblot, 2006).
Simpson, Gerry J, 'War Crimes: A Critical Introduction' in McCormack, Timothy L H and Simpson, Gerry J (eds), *The Law of War Crimes: National and International Approaches* (The Hague, Kluwer Law International, Boston 1997).
——, 'Politics, Sovereignty, Remembrance' in MacGoldrick, Dominic, Rowe, Peter and Donelly, Eric (eds), *The Permanent International Criminal Court: Legal and Policy Issues* (Oxford, Hart Publishing, 2004).
Sloane, Robert D, 'The Expressive Capacity of International Punishment: The Limits of the National Law Analogy and the Potential of International Criminal Law' (2007) 43 *Stanford Journal of International Law* 39.
Smith, Bradley F, *The American Road to Nuremberg: The Documentary Record, 1944–1945* (Stanford, Hoover Institution Press, 1982).
Smith, Charles A and Smith, Heather M, 'Embedded Realpolitik?, Reevaluating United States' Opposition to the International Criminal Court' in Roach, Steven C (ed), *Governance, Order and the International Criminal Court: Between Realpolitik and a Cosmopolitan Court* (Oxford, Oxford University Press, 2009).
Solera, Oscar, *Defining the Crime of Aggression* (London, Cameron May, 2007).
Stahn, Carsten and El Zeidy, Mohamed (eds), *The International Criminal Court and Complementarity: From Theory to Practice* (Cambridge, Cambridge University Press, 2011).
Stahn, Carsten and van den Herik, Larissa (eds), *Future Perspectives in International Criminal Justice* (The Hague, Kluwer, 2009).
Stoll, Peter-Tobias, 'Völkerrechtliche Praxis der Bundesrepublik Deutschland im Jahre 1994' (1996) 56 *Zeitschrift für ausländisches öffentliches Recht und Völkerrecht (Heidelberg Journal of International Law)* 998.

Stolleis, Michael, 'Rechtsordnung und Justizpolitik 1945–1949' in Horn, Norbert and Coing, Helmut (eds), *Europäisches Rechtsdenken in Geschichte und Gegenwart: Festschrift für Helmut Coing zum 70. Geburtstag* (Munich, Beck, 1982).

——, 'Der Historiker als Richter – der Richter als Historiker' in Frei, Norbert, van Laak, Dirk and Stolleis, Michael (eds), *Geschichte vor Gericht: Historiker, Richter und die Suche nach Gerechtigkeit* (Munich, Beck, 2000).

Struett, Michael J, 'The Politics of Discursive Legitimacy, Understanding the Dynamics and Implications of Prosecutorial Discretion at the International Criminal Court' in Roach, Steven C (ed), *Governance, Order and the International Criminal Court: Between Realpolitik and a Cosmopolitan Court* (Oxford, Oxford University Press, 2009).

Stuby, Gerhard, 'Nürnberg 1945/46: Von der Harmlosigkeit des Gedenkens' (2006) *Blätter für deutsche und internationale Politik* 90.

Stürmer, Michael, 'Geschichte in geschichtslosem Land' in Augstein, Rudolf (ed), *Historikerstreit: Die Dokumentation der Kontroverse um die Einzigartigkeit der nationalsozialistischen Judenvernichtung* (Munich, R Piper, 1987).

Sühl, Klaus, *Vergangenheitsbewältigung 1945 und 1989: Ein unmöglicher Vergleich?* (Berlin, Volk und Welt, 1994).

Suikkari, Satu, 'Debate in the United Nations on the International Law Commission's Draft Statute for an International Criminal Court' (1995) 64 *Nordic Journal of International Law* 205.

Taylor, Telford, *The Anatomy of the Nuremberg Trials: A Personal Memoir* (Boston, Back Bay Books, 1992).

Tomuschat, Christian, 'Sanktionen durch internationale Strafgerichtshöfe' in Deutscher Juristentag (ed), *Verhandlungen des sechzigsten Deutschen Juristentages: Band II/1 – Sitzungsberichte* (Munich, self-published, 1994).

Triffterer, Otto, *Dogmatische Untersuchungen zur Entwicklung des materiellen Völkerstrafrechts seit Nürnberg* (Freiburg im Breisgau, Diss., 1966).

——, 'Völkerstrafrecht im Wandel?' in Vogler, Theo (ed), *Festschrift für Hans-Heinrich Jescheck zum 70. Geburtstag* (Berlin, de Gruyter, 1985).

——, 'Was kann das Völkerstrafrecht zur Bewältigung der Regierungskriminalität in der DDR beitragen?' in Lampe, Ernst-Joachim (ed), *Deutsche Wiedervereinigung: Die Rechtseinheit. Volume 2: Die Verfolgung von Regierungskriminalität nach der Wiedervereinigung* (Cologne, Arbeitskreis Strafrecht, 1993).

Triffterer, Otto, 'Hans-Heinrich Jeschecks Einfluss auf die Entwicklung des Völkerstrafrechts und auf dessen Durchsetzung' (2004) 116 *Zeitschrift für die gesamte Strafrechtswissenschaft* 959.

—— (ed), *Commentary on the Rome Statute of the International Criminal Court: Observers' Notes, Article by Article* (Baden-Baden, CH Beck, 1999).

Tymkiw, Michael, 'Debunking the Myth of the Saubere Wehrmacht' (2007) 23 *Word & Image* 485.

Vasquez, John A, *The Power of Power Politics* (Cambridge, Cambridge University Press, 1998).

Vogler, Theo (ed), *Festschrift für Hans-Heinrich Jescheck zum 70. Geburtstag* (Berlin, de Gruyter, 1985).

Vohrah, Lal C (ed), *Man's Inhumanity to Man: Essays on International Law in Honour of Antonio Cassese* (The Hague, Kluwer Law International, 2003).

Walter, Christian, 'Bericht über die Völkerrechtliche Praxis der Bundesrepublik Deutschland im Jahre 1993' (1995) 55 *Zeitschrift für ausländisches öffentliches Recht und Völkerrecht* (*Heidelberg Journal of International Law*) 1095.

Walter, Michael, 'Zur Reichweite des Konzeptes Kriminalität, Einige Überlegungen zur "Makrokriminalität" Herbert Jägers' (1993) 25 *Kriminologisches Journal* 117.

Wedgwood, Ruth, 'The International Criminal Court: An American View' (1999) 10 *European Journal of International Law* 93.

Weinke, Annette, '"Von Nürnberg nach Den Haag"? Das Internationale Militärtribunal in historischer Perspektive' in Daubach, Helia-Verena (ed), *Leipzig – Nürnberg – Den Haag: Neue Fragestellungen und Forschungen zum Verhältnis von Menschenrechtsverbrechen justizieller Säuberung und Völkerstrafrecht* (Düsseldorf, Justizministerium des Landes NRW, 2008).

Werle, Gerhard, 'Menschenrechtsschutz durch Völkerstrafrecht' (1997) 109 *Zeitschrift für die gesamte Strafrechtswissenschaft* 808.

——, 'Von der Ablehnung zur Mitgestaltung: Deutschland und das Völkerstrafrecht' in Dupuy, Pierre-Marie and others (eds), *Common Values in International Law. Essays in Honour of Christian Tomuschat* (Kehl, NP Engel, 2006).

——, 'Die Entwicklung des Völkerstrafrechts aus deutscher Perspektive' in Hankel, Gerd (ed), *Die Macht und das Recht: Beiträge zum Völkerrecht und Völkerstrafrecht am Beginn des 21. Jahrhunderts* (Hamburg, Hamburger Edition, 2008).

—— and Wandres, *Thomas, Auschwitz vor Gericht: Völkermord und bundesdeutsche Strafjustiz. Mit einer Dokumentation des Auschwitz-Urteils* (Munich, CH Beck, 1995).

Westdickenberg, Gerd and Fixson, Oliver, 'Das Verbrechen der Aggression im Römischen Statut des Internationalen Strafgerichtshofs' in Frowein, Jochen A and others (eds), *Verhandeln für den Frieden – Negotiating for Peace: Liber Amicorum Tono Eitel* (Berlin, Springer, 2003).

Wette, Wolfram and Überschär, Gerd R (eds), *Kriegsverbrechen im 20. Jahrhundert* (Darmstadt, Wissenschaftliche Buchgesellschaft, 2001).

Wilkitzki, Peter, 'The Contribution of the Federal Republic of Germany and the German Länder to the Work of the ICTY' in Vohrah, Lal C (ed), *Man's Inhumanity to Man: Essays on International Law in Honour of Antonio Cassese* (The Hague, Kluwer Law International, 2003).

——, 'Glückwünsche des Bundesministeriums der Justiz' in Sieber, Ulrich and Albrecht, Hans-Jörg (eds), *Strafrecht und Kriminologie unter einem Dach: Kolloquium zum 90. Geburtstag von Professor Dr. Dr. h.c. mult. Hans-Heinrich Jescheck* (Berlin, Duncker & Humblot, 2006).

Wippermann, Wolfgang, *Dämonisierung durch Vergleich: DDR und Drittes Reich* (Berlin, Rotbuch, 2009).

Wrobel, Hans, *Verurteilt zur Demokratie: Justiz und Justizpolitik in Deutschland 1945-1949* (Heidelberg, Decker & Müller, 1989).

Zimmermann, Andreas, 'Neues deutsches Selbstbewusstsein: Paradigmenwechsel in der Völkerrechtspolitik?' (2002) 9 *Internationale Politik* 33.

——, 'Implementing the Statute of the International Criminal Court: The German Example' in Vohrah, Lal C (ed), *Man's Inhumanity to Man: Essays on International Law in Honour of Antonio Cassese* (The Hague, Kluwer Law International, 2003).

Zimmermann, Stefan, 'Die strafrechtliche "Bewältigung" der deutschen Diktaturen' (1996) *Juristische Schulung* 865.

Index

www.ingramcontent.com/pod-product-compliance
Ingram Content Group UK Ltd.
Pitfield, Milton Keynes, MK11 3LW, UK
UKHW020832290926
15470UKWH00009B/1864/J

9 781849 463133